Publications of the
Institute of Germanic Studies
Volume 35

PATHS AND LABYRINTHS

PATHS
AND
LABYRINTHS

Nine Papers read at the Franz Kafka
Symposium held at the Institute of
Germanic Studies on 20 and 21 October
1983

edited by

J. P. Stern and J. J. White

INSTITUTE OF GERMANIC STUDIES
UNIVERSITY OF LONDON
1985

British Library Cataloguing in Publication Data

Paths and labyrinths: nine papers from a Kafka symposium. —
(Publications of the Institute of Germanic Studies, ISSN 0076-0811;
v. 35) I. Kafka, Franz — Criticism and interpretation I. Stern, J. P.
II. White, J. J. III.
Series 833'. 912 PT2621.A26Z/
ISBN 0–85457–124–8

ISBN 0 85457 124 8
ISSN 0076–0811

© The Institute of Germanic Studies

Printed by W. S. Maney & Son Ltd., Leeds, England

Contents

The Contributors

Helmut Heißenbüttel, Borsfleth

J. L. Hibberd, MA, BLitt, PhD, University of Bristol

Professor Dr Gerhard Neumann, Universität Freiburg/Br.

J. M. Rignall, BA, DPhil, University of Warwick

Ritchie Robertson, MA, DPhil, Lincoln College, Oxford

Professor J. P. Stern, MA, PhD, LittD, University College London and Institute of Germanic Studies

Anthony Storr, MB, BChir, MA, Green College, Oxford

Edward Timms, MA, PhD, Gonville and Caius College, Cambridge

J. J. White, MA, PhD, King's College London

Acknowledgements

Kafka '83 — thus the title of the Institute's commemorative symposium — could not have been held without generous assistance from several quarters. These included the London branch of the German Academic Exchange Service, the Goethe-Institut London, and the Austrian Institute in London.

Special thanks are due to the fourteen contributors who came, some of them from afar, to read their papers; and also to the many members of the audience who took part in the discussions that enlivened the two days of the Symposium, most memorably those who shared their recollections of Kafka's Prague.

The staff of the Institute of Germanic Studies, including its Deputy Director Dr J. L. Flood, its Secretary Miss Karin Hellmer, its Librarian William Abbey, were all unstinting in their endeavours to cope with an unusually large audience and a very full programme.

To them all, as well as to all those who made this volume possible, including the Managers of the Bithell Bequest Fund, much gratitude is due.

All the papers printed here appear for the first time, except Helmut Heißenbüttel's, which was published in the December 1983 number of the periodical *Sprache im technischen Zeitalter*; an earlier version of J. P. Stern's paper was written for a *Festschrift* to celebrate René Wellek's eightieth birthday, which had not appeared when this volume went to press.

The Editors would like to add a particular word of thanks to Dr Karin von Abrams who supplied English translations of passages quoted in this book.

J.P.S.
J.J.W.

Abbreviations

The following editions of Kafka's works are referred to in an abbreviated form, as indicated, throughout *Paths and Labyrinths*:

Gesammelte Werke (in Einzelausgaben), hg. von Max Brod, Lizenzausgabe von Schocken Books New York (Frankfurt/M., 1950 ff.):

E   *Erzählungen* (1952).

A   *Amerika* (1953).

P   *Der Prozeß* (1950).

S   *Das Schloß* (1951).

B   *Beschreibung eines Kampfes. Novellen, Skizzen, Aphorismen aus dem Nachlaß* (1954).

H   *Hochzeitsvorbereitungen auf dem Lande und andere Prosa aus dem Nachlaß* (1953).

T   *Tagebücher 1910–1923* (1951).

Br   *Briefe 1902–1924* (1958).

BrM *Briefe an Milena* (1952).

BrF *Brief an Felice und andere Korrespondenz aus der Verlobungszeit* (1967).

BrO *Briefe an Ottla und die Familie* (1974).

SE   *Sämtliche Erzählungen*, hg. von Paul Raabe (Frankfurt/M., 1970).

Schriften. Tagebücher. Briefe, Kritische Ausgabe, hg. von. Jürgen Born, Gerhard Neumann, Malcolm Pasley und Jost Schillemeit:

KKA V I/II *Der Verschollene*, hg. von J. Schillemeit, 2 vols (Frankfurt/M., 1983).

KKA S I/II *Das Schloß*, hg. von Malcolm Pasley, 2 vols (Frankfurt/M., 1982).

All the above abbreviations are followed by page numbers in arabic.

Abbreviations for periodical titles are in accordance with those used in *The Year's Work in Modern Language Studies*.

Introduction

Writing. He wrote. His writing. Once again a whole night long he could not write a word . . . Did ever a writer use that verb with such anguish at the prospect of failure, with such hopes of redemption, justification? Beyond the modicum of self-confidence his writing provided, what else of value did his day contain? In the absence of other assurances, could *writing* — 'mein Schreiben' — ever yield an adequate assurance of *being*? If solitude was the necessary condition of Franz Kafka's creativeness and the impediment to every human relationship, what sense of community could he possibly convey? In all that he wrote, an air of unsparing, self-destructive truthfulness prevails: did self and truth, then, exclude each other?

Questions such as these provide the background to the nine papers assembled here from the symposium held on the occasion of the centenary of Kafka's birth. In Anthony Storr's view, writing is fashioned by Kafka into a link with a childhood of the utmost emotional deprivation: 'The self which he felt had been crushed in childhood, and which he feared would be crushed again by anyone who came too close to him, triumphantly asserts itself on the page.' Yet though Storr's main concern is biographical, the assertion of the self he describes is the thread that leads us through the labyrinths of *The Trial* and *The Castle*. Ritchie Roberton's essay raises the issue of community. For him, writing represents Kafka's intermittent attempts at coming to terms with his own Judaism and the Zionism which he recognized as a solution to 'the Jewish problem' in his time — a 'problem' the very formulation of which was instinct with the ideology of anti-Semitism. The historical dimension is emphasized again in Gerhard Neumann's observations on the changing concept of family. Here Goethe's *Wilhelm Meister* (1795) and Kafka's first novel, *America* (*Der Verschollene*, written 1912–14) are placed respectively at the beginning and at the end of an era in the course of which a number of social options are challenged. The family is one of them, biography — the narrativity of a life — is another. Once undermined, this 'Erzählbarkeit' ceases to provide the self with a continuous identity until, turning to parody, anecdote and 'diffusion', it ends in the loss of an identifiable self. To which one might add that the aggressive — and futile — temper of self-assertion which informs the central characters of those two later novels represents the writer's response to that early portrayal of over-determination by the world outside.

The ambiguities and indeterminacies of Kafka's stories are the source of their exceptionally wide interpretability, yet this effect is achieved by a style that has the appearance of ordinariness. As if in conscious opposition to Rainer Maria Rilke, his fellow-citizen and exact contemporary, Kafka keeps as close as possible to the prosy structures of his native idiom. This closeness to ordinary language is the foil against which Edward Timms singles out Kafka's device of thematizing a few of the images from which the metaphors and idioms of contemporary (and Prague) German were fashioned. In these areas of Kafka's text, writing is made out of transformations of the commonplace. At its most characteristic, Kafka's creativeness yields discrete scenes and mises-en-scène of single perceptions; here lies his affinity with Robert Walser, probably the only contemporary with whom he may be usefully compared. The difficulties Kafka encountered in the composition of his full-length novels have made most recent critics consider him primarily as a writer of stories and various kinds of short prose. Yet there are compensations, wholes which turn out to be greater than their parts. Thus John White examines the relationship between the stories Kafka wrote and the books written by those stories once their author has taken care to place them in a significant order. The poet Helmut Heißenbüttel, too, concentrates on Kafka's short prose, on his parables, fragments and reflections. He sees them above all as instruments for thinking, as means of subverting the commonplace. The philosophical insights arrived at in this way bear the stigma of paradox and of an irony now gentle, now radically destructive of positive meaning.

In John Rignall's account of *Beim Bau der chinesischen Mauer* (*The Great Wall of China*), all that goes under the name of 'Geschichte(n)' is exposed to those qualities of paradox and gentle irony: in history as —inconclusive — deeds; in history as — the unreliable — record of the past; and in stories as the — deceptive — record of fictional/fictitious continuities. All this suggests 'the use of rhetorical devices and a highly figurative language', designed to convey not the narrator's but the protagonists' 'sense of certainty and conviction which is without ultimate foundation'. Are all tropes, the writer's wherewithal, to be branded as lies? And yet (Rignall writes at the end of his account) a later fragment of Kafka's 'Die Abweisung' ('The Refusal'), does intimate a sense of certainty not obviously overtaken by irony, a piece of writing that stops short of exposing itself as an assertion 'without ultimate foundation'. We live (it seems to be saying) by written records, documents that do, after all, contain a truth of sorts. A truth that survives merely because further enquiry is foreclosed, a limited truth? It is not likely that the irony of *that* could have escaped the indefatigable searcher for the truth unalloyed.

Do Kafka's writings anticipate the fictions of the *nouveau roman* with their narrative perspective of 'total subjectivity', their studied inconclusiveness, their refusal to yield symbolical or allegorical meanings? John Hibberd's essay on Robbe-Grillet's reading of Kafka presents a case for the usefulness and limited validity of the parallel. 'La réalité absolue des choses que décrit Kafka', Robbe-Grillet claims, is to one side of the 'reality' of the world of experience, is an object without significant links with our consciousness, an object without meaning. If this were 'really' true, one wonders how, almost sixty years after Kafka's death, one of his readers — a Polish civil rights worker — would write:

In this strange prison, which for reasons unknown is called a Centre of Internment, the atmosphere that prevails is the same as in Kafka. Each man is waiting for his trial without knowing of what crimes he will be accused on the basis of investigations conducted by unknown investigators on an authority that remains unknown, and which have reached he knows not what stage. (Adam Michnik in a letter reprinted in *Der Spiegel*, 26 July 1982)

Surely the truth (not, for once, a limited truth) is quite simply that words like 'reality', 'realism' and 'antirealism' have ceased to be useful; that what is now needed is a new theory, if not of fiction and literature, at least of the way Kafka writes; and (the last piece in this collection suggests) Kafka's last story contains just that. Yet since that last story, and his work as a whole, are, after all, a part of the edifice of literature, the theory which that story offers should serve as an illumination of the edifice as a whole. Or is this, yet again, no more than a limited truth? At all events, Kafka's passionate search, that is, his passionate concern with *writing*, goes on to the end; but by that time — the time of the end — it *has* become synonymous with *being*.

We, however, should be aware that we can only conjecture about the writing, for all we have is the written thing, the text. Editorial efforts — tracing an image from diary to letter, from letter to aphorism, from aphorism or fragment to story or novel; or again retracing Kafka's care, often splendidly unsuccessful, to amend his manuscripts according to the norms of 'correct' German — are now helping us to unloosen the fixity of the printed text. At their best these efforts are guided by the hope that the text might become more like the writing and the unwritten experiences that went into the writing. Will they bring us closer to the enigmas? The present collection offers neither one nor several 'definitive' overall interpretations. It leaves it to the reader to decide which of its contributions are paths and which are labyrinths. The interest Kafka's work continues to evoke in circumstances he hardly envisaged, the fascination it continues to exert on readers whose ways and views of life are very different (though not wholly different) from the ways and views of the world in which he wrote — all this suggests that interpretations which are fussy with claims to totality or definitiveness are likely to end up by being more misleading than the scrutinies of individual themes and stories and the searching out of discrete meanings — the limited truths that have been attempted in these pages.

J.P.S.

August 1984

Anthony Storr
KAFKA'S SENSE OF IDENTITY

I must begin by saying that I approach the study of Kafka from the point of view of a psychiatrist rather than from that of a literary scholar. Because Kafka was both a great writer and also scrupulously honest, he is able, in a unique way, to illumine an area of psychological experience which, though not infrequently encountered in certain kinds of psychiatric patient, is remote from that of the ordinary person.

I have called this paper 'Kafka's Sense of Identity'. What do I mean by 'identity'? In *A Critical Dictionary of Psychoanalysis*, Charles Rycroft defines identity as 'The sense of one's continuous being as an entity distinguishable from all others'.[1] Erik Erikson, the psychiatrist who has written most extensively on the subject, refers to 'a subjective sense of invigorating sameness and continuity'. (I note in passing that a photographic reproduction of Michelangelo's *David* adorns the dust-jacket of the English edition of Erikson's book *Identity*. I shall return to why that particular image is associated with the notion of identity at a later point.) Erikson goes on to quote from a letter written by William James to his wife: 'A man's character is discernible in the mental or moral attitude in which, when it came upon him, he felt himself most deeply and intensely active and alive. At such moments there is a voice inside which speaks and says: "*This* is the real me"'.[2]

Jung is surely referring to the same phenomenon when he writes: 'Personality is the supreme realization of the innate idiosyncrasy of a living being. It is an act of high courage flung in the face of life, the absolute affirmation of all that constitutes the individual, the most successful adaptation to the universal conditions of existence, coupled with the greatest possible freedom for self-determination.'[3]

Although William James uses the word 'character' and Jung uses the word 'personality', they and Erik Erikson are referring to the same experience: that of being positively, fully oneself, without equivocation or pretence, and they are affirming that this experience is fulfilling and life-enhancing.

Contrast these statements with the words which Kafka puts into the mouth of the suppliant in one of the two versions of *Gespräch mit dem Beter* (*Conversation with the Suppliant*) in his early story *Beschreibung eines Kampfes* (*Description of a Struggle*).

I

'Es hat niemals eine Zeit gegeben, in der ich durch mich selbst von meinem Leben überzeugt war. Ich erfasse nämlich die Dinge um mich nur in so hinfälligen Vorstellungen, daß ich immer glaube, die Dinge hätten einmal gelebt, jetzt aber seien sie versinkend' ('There's never been a time in which I have been convinced from within myself that I am alive. You see, I have only such a fugitive awareness of things around me that I always feel they were once real and are now fleeting away'; E 15). So little is the young suppliant convinced of the validity of his own existence that he has to draw attention to himself in church by his eccentric behaviour. In one version of the story he says: 'es [ist] der Zweck meines Lebens . . ., von den Leuten angeschaut zu werden' ('it is the aim of my life to get people to look at me'; E 13). In the other version, he refers to his need to let himself be nailed down for a brief hour by those eyes ('von diesen Blicken mich für eine kleine Stunde festhämmern zu lassen'; B 31–32), as if being stared at convinced him, for the moment, of the reality of his own existence.

Although Kafka was writing fiction, I think that we can be sure that these passages refer to his own experience, and I agree with Ronald Hayman, who, in his recent biography of Kafka, writes that the characters in this story are 'transparent self-projections'.[4]

It may, at first sight, seem paradoxical that a writer who is so unlike any other, who is so uniquely himself as Kafka, should entertain doubts about his own identity. When he was actually writing, and when he read and re-read what he had written, I think his doubts about himself diminished or disappeared. But, once away from his writing desk, when in the company of others, those doubts constantly recurred. Many of those who knew Kafka were clearly deeply fond of him, and some, like Gustav Janouch, made him the object of hero-worship. With those he knew, Kafka could be at times a lively and humorous companion. But, one must recall, Kafka himself said that even with Max Brod, his closest friend, he had never been able to hold a prolonged conversation in which he really revealed himself.

With strangers, he was always ill-at-ease. In a letter to Felice Bauer dated June 1913, Kafka writes: 'Bin ich aber in einer fremden Wohnung, unter mehreren fremden Leuten oder solchen, die ich als fremd fühle, dann liegt mir das ganze Zimmer auf der Brust und ich kann mich nicht rühren, und dann scheint förmlich mein Wesen den Leuten ins Blut zu gehn und alles wird trostlos' ('But if I am in an unfamiliar place, among a number of strange people, or people whom I feel to be strangers, then the whole room presses on my chest and I am unable to move, my whole personality seems virtually to get under their skins, and everything becomes hopeless'; BrF 402).

Kafka is not the only writer to describe such feelings. In a letter to Richard Woodhouse written in October 1818, John Keats writes: 'A Poet is the most unpoetical of any thing in existence; because he has no identity'. He goes on: 'When I am in a room with People if ever I am free from speculating on creations of my own brain, then not myself goes home to myself: but the identity of every one in the room begins to press upon me that I am in a very little time annihilated — not only among Men; it would be the same in a Nursery of children'.[5]

For most people, interaction is a recurrent and necessary affirmation of identity. Indeed, without any kind of interaction with others, the term 'identity' has no meaning. For identity depends upon contrast, and contrast demands that there should be at least one other person with whom the one can be contrasted. Just as the size of an object cannot be determined without reference to other objects, so the qualities of a person cannot be described without comparison with the qualities of other persons. One cannot be 'kind' or 'clever' or 'ironical' or 'self-effacing' in a vacuum. Because of the nature of thought and language, our descriptive statements are bound to imply an opposite.

Since identity implies difference, it follows that the affirmation of identity requires a modicum of self-esteem. If a person is to hold his own in the company of others, he must have some sense of being himself worthwhile. We all know people who have no such sense of their own worth; who never put forward opinions of their own, but who always anxiously agree with the opinions of others. We rightly refer to such people as 'nonentities' because their true identities are not made manifest. These are the people who seem constantly to be apologizing for their own existence, as if they felt that they had no right to be alive. Often, these people are intermittently or permanently depressed. From time to time they may assert themselves in explosive outbursts of aggression against those to whom they too closely strive to conform; but after such outbursts are over, they revert to their habitual over-adaptation to the other.

There are others who have even greater difficulty in affirming, or even in preserving, identity. Instead of welcoming interaction with others as a life-enhancing opportunity for self-affirmation, they treat people as a threat; as potential enemies who might, at any time, attack and destroy them. R. D. Laing describes how, in the course of an analytic group session, an argument occurred between two patients. 'Suddenly, one of the protagonists broke off the argument to say, "I can't go on. You are arguing to have the pleasure of triumphing over me. At best you win an argument. At worst you lose an argument. *I am arguing in order to preserve my existence.*"'

Laing comments: 'A firm sense of one's own autonomous identity is required in order that one may be related as one human being to another. Otherwise, any and every relationship threatens the individual with loss of identity.'[6]

On what does a firm sense of one's autonomous identity depend? First, there is the question of the individual's relation with his own body. It seems probable that, to start with, the human infant has little idea of where he begins and ends. Having, for nine months, been incorporated within someone else, it takes time for him to discover that his own limbs belong to him, and that his skin is an envelope which constitutes a boundary between him and the rest of the world. He probably makes these discoveries by coming up against objects in the external world; the side of his cot, his mother's body, and so on. It is easy to understand why Freud referred to the pristine ego as a *bodily* ego.[7] The sense of 'I'ness, of identity, is for most people rooted in the body, although of course it comes to include much else in the course of time. This, no doubt, is why the publishers chose to put Michelangelo's *David* on the dust-jacket of Erikson's book *Identity*. The *David* is a paean of praise to the beauty of the male body, and one cannot imagine David's identity as not being rooted in his physical existence. However, not everyone feels like this. Some people feel that the body is a kind of appendage to their true self; almost an object in the external world with which they are connected, but with which they do not identify. Some such people actively dislike or despise their bodies.

This was certainly true of Kafka. We know, from his letter to his father, that he regarded his own body with distaste, and that he compared it unfavourably with that of his father.

Ich erinnere mich zum Beispiel daran, wie wir uns öfters zusammen in einer Kabine auszogen. Ich mager, schwach, schmal, Du stark, groß, breit. Schon in der Kabine kam ich mir jämmerlich vor, und zwar nicht nur vor Dir, sondern vor der ganzen Welt, denn Du warst für mich das Maß aller Dinge. (H 168)

For instance, I remember how we often undressed together in the same bathing-hut. There I was, skinny, weakly, slight, you strong, tall, broad. Even inside the hut I felt myself a miserable specimen, and what's more, not only in your eyes, but in the eyes of the whole world, for you were for me the measure of all things.

It is not until 15 August 1911, when he was twenty-eight years old, that Kafka is able to record in his diary: 'Die Zeit, die jetzt verlaufen ist und in der ich kein Wort geschrieben habe, ist für mich deshalb so wichtig gewesen, weil ich auf den Schwimmschulen in Prag, Königssaal und Czernoschitz aufgehört habe, für meinen Körper mich zu schämen' ('The time which has just gone by and in which I haven't written a word has been so important for me because I have stopped being ashamed of my body in the swimming pools in Prague, Königssaal and Czerno-schitz'; T 59). However, later in the same year he reverts to his former attitude: 'Sicher ist, daß ein Haupthindernis meines Fortschritts mein körperlicher Zustand bildet. Mit einem solchen Körper läßt sich nichts erreichen. Ich werde mich an sein fortwährendes Versagen gewöhnen müssen' ('It is certain that a major obstacle to my progress is my physical condition. Nothing can be accomplished with such a body. I shall have to get used to its perpetual failing'; T 171).

Kafka is writing about his body as if it were an object in the external world quite separate from himself. It is of course true that all human beings are capable of temporary detachment of this kind, and this is particularly true of intellectuals. Indeed, conceptual thought demands this degree of abstraction. However, even dedicated scholars generally find that, after a spell of concentrated work, they abandon their books and return to the life of the senses, to identification with the body. Kafka and others like him seem habitually more alienated than this. This alienation, in Kafka's case, was not related to his later ill-health. Although Kafka died of laryngeal and pulmonary tuberculosis in 1924, his first haemoptysis did not occur until August 1917. We cannot be sure when the disease took sufficient hold to interfere with his general health and vitality, but it certainly did not do so in his early years. Although, throughout his life, Kafka was concerned about his physical health and suffered from all manner of psychosomatic symptoms, he was able to swim, to row, and to go for long tramps in the country when he was in his twenties. His feeling of physical inferiority dated from childhood, and was emotionally determined, not based upon reality. A well-known photograph of Kafka, taken when he was about five, shows him as a skinny, frightened waif. Although a later portrait, taken at the age of eleven, shows a handsome boy who might justifiably have been proud of his looks, it is evidently the earlier image which impressed itself upon his mind, and which persisted, unmodified by later developments. There is a good example which demonstrates that Kafka was familiar with the experience of being dissociated from his body in his early fragment of a novel *Hochzeitsvorbereitungen auf dem Lande (Wedding Preparations in the Country)*. Raban is hesitating about whether or not to travel to the country to meet his fiancée:

Und überdies kann ich es nicht machen, wie ich es immer als Kind bei gefährlichen Geschäften machte? Ich brauche nicht einmal selbst aufs Land fahren, das ist nicht nötig. Ich schicke meinen angekleideten Körper. Wankt er zur Tür meines Zimmers hinaus, so zeigt das Wanken nicht Furcht, sondern seine Nichtigkeit. Es ist auch nicht Aufregung, wenn er über die Treppe stolpert, wenn er schluchzend aufs Land fährt und weinend dort sein

Nachtmahl ißt. Denn ich, ich liege inzwischen in meinem Bett, glatt zugedeckt mit gelbbrauner Decke, ausgesetzt der Luft, die durch das wenig geöffnete Zimmer weht. (H 11–12)

And besides, can't I do it the way I always used to as a child in matters that were dangerous? I don't even need to go to the country myself, it isn't necessary. I'll send my clothed body. If it staggers out of the door of my room, the staggering will not indicate fear, but its nothingness. Nor is it a sign of excitement if it stumbles on the stairs, if it travels into the country, sobbing as it goes, and there eats its supper in tears. For I myself am meanwhile lying in my bed, smoothly covered over with the yellow-brown blanket, exposed to the breeze that is wafted through that seldom-aired room.

The dissociation between his body and what Raban feels as himself could scarcely be more complete. Later, Raban interestingly anticipates *Die Verwandlung* (*Metamorphosis*) by phantasying that, as he lies in bed, he assumes the shape of a big beetle.

We all start life as helpless infants, totally dependent upon, and at the mercy of, those who are supposed to care for us. Some people, of whom Kafka was one, never grow out of this stage of helplessness. Those who are alienated from the body cannot feel the potentialities of the body. Their inner picture of themselves as powerless persists even though they become grown men and women who could, if they had a realistic notion of their own powers, stand up for themselves.

Melanie Klein postulated that the human infant, because of its early helplessness, reacts to frustration as if it were persecution and fears its own destruction by the powerful persons on whom it depends. According to her account, the infant, and especially the neglected infant, harbours within itself intensely destructive impulses which it tends to attribute to (project upon) those who care for it. In later life, any kind of suffering is liable to resuscitate these early feelings and is therefore conceived as an attack upon the self. This account, improbable as it may seem at first sight, is certainly borne out by Kafka's self-scrutiny. In a letter to Max Brod he wrote:

Wenn mich z.B. — es ist nur ein reines Beispiel — wenn mich mein Magen schmerzt, so ist es eigentlich nicht mehr mein Magen, sondern etwas, was sich von einem fremden Menschen, der Lust bekommt, mich zu prügeln, wesentlich nicht unterscheidet. So aber ist es mit allem, ich bestehe nur aus Spitzen, die in mich hinein gehn, will ich mich da wehren und Kraft aufwenden, heißt das nur die Spitzen besser hineindrücken. (B 254)

If for example — this is purely an example — if my stomach hurts, it is no longer really my stomach but something that is basically indistinguishable from a stranger who has taken it into his head to club me. But that is so with everything. I am nothing but a mass of spikes going through me; if I try to defend myself and use force, the spikes only press in the deeper.

It is by no means certain, and in any case unprovable, that all infants suffer the persecutory fears that Melanie Klein postulates. Even if they do so, the majority of infants pass through this 'paranoid-schizoid' stage to one in which they can trust others, and in which the expectation of loving care outweighs the anxieties consequent upon being helpless. A minority, like Kafka, do not. How far this is dependent upon the quality of care actually given to the infant, and how far it is the consequence of inherited differences in constitution, is impossible to say; but it is certainly the case that the circumstances of Kafka's infancy were somewhat unfavourable. We know that, very soon after Kafka's birth, his mother was summoned back to work in his father's shop, and that the nurse to whom he was first entrusted was replaced by another within a year or two. We know that, from his own account, Kafka never felt that he saw enough of his mother, and that he never became reconciled to her absence. In his diary for 24 October 1911 Kafka recalls that, when he was ill as a child, his mother would come back from the business to look after him, and that this was comforting. He wishes that he was ill enough to have to go to bed in order to recapture that experience. Even by the standards of the day, Kafka saw uncommonly little of his parents during infancy. In addition, his childhood was unsettled by five moves of home: one before he was two years old, another seven months later, and a third when he was about four years old, in 1877. Two further moves occurred, in 1888 and 1889. Another disturbing factor was the deaths of both his younger brothers. One, born in 1885, when Kafka was two, died less than two years later, of measles. A second brother, born in 1887, survived for only six months. These factors alone are certainly not enough to account for Kafka's persistent ontological insecurity, but may have contributed something toward it. What appears certain is that Kafka carried with him into adult life the sense of being at the mercy of other people and events; of being a victim, rather than of being someone who could act upon the world by exercising his own volition. This seems to me to be a theme which runs through nearly everything that he wrote, perhaps reaching its acme in *Der Prozeß* (*The Trial*).

Once I knew a man who graphically illustrated similar feelings. He drew a picture of a circle surrounded by arrows, all of which pointed inward toward the centre. He himself was the circle; the arrows represented the hostile impingement of the actual world upon him, against which he felt himself to be defenceless.

Another man, whose lack of early maternal care could be proven, remained terrified of any situation in which he was helpless in the hands of others. The notion of having to submit to a surgical operation, for example, so frightened him that he said he would prefer to die rather than to submit to such an ordeal.

We live in a world in which thousands of people find themselves, in reality, in the hands of malignant persecutors. It has often been suggested that Kafka was prescient in anticipating the horrors of the concentration camps, in which Milena and three of his sisters died. I do not believe this. What Kafka was able to do, in a way equalled by no-one else, was to articulate fears which lurk in the recesses of the mind in all of us, but which, in the ordinary course of events, only become manifest in those whom we label 'psychiatric patients'.

Together with the fear of being injured or annihilated goes the fear of being ignored, or treated as being of no account. Swift, writing of Gulliver in the hands of the giants of Brobdingnag, records: 'That which gave me the most Uneasiness among those Maids of Honour, when my Nurse carried me to visit them, was to see them use me without any Manner of Ceremony like a Creature who has no sort of Consequence'.[8]

To gain a sense of one's own validity as a person, one has to be treated as actually being there, as counting for something. In his *Brief an den Vater* (*Letter to his Father*), Kafka writes of this 'sense of nothingness that often dominates me' ('dieses mich oft beherrschende Gefühl der Nichtigkeit'; H 167) which, he says, comes largely from his father's influence. He recalls with particular horror an occasion on which, when he was whimpering for water at night, his father picked him up and left him outside on the balcony:

Noch nach Jahren litt ich unter der quälenden Vorstellung, daß der riesige Mann, mein Vater, die letzte Instanz, fast ohne Grund kommen und mich in der Nacht aus dem Bett auf die Pawlatsche tragen konnte und daß ich also ein solches Nichts für ihn war. (H 167)

Even years afterwards I suffered from the tormenting fancy that the huge man, my father, the ultimate authority, would come almost for no reason at all and take me out of bed in the night and carry me out on to the *pavlatche* [balcony], and that therefore I was a mere nothing for him.

For Kafka, this particular incident seems to have been of immense significance. It may be compared with the experience of the seven-year-old Proust, who never forgot that, because she was entertaining a guest at dinner, his mother once failed to give him her usual good-night kiss. George Painter, author of the standard biography of Proust, refers to this incident as the most important event in Proust's life, because 'it told him that love is doomed and happiness does not exist'.[9]

The importance of both incidents is, of course, not their actual occurrence, but what they epitomize in the lives of these great writers. Proust's *Weltanschauung* is dominated by the impossibility of love, Kafka's by the sense of helplessness.

To be treated as if one hardly existed, as if one counted for nothing, is to live in a world in which, since power is in the hands of others, there is no way of predicting what is going to happen. Although the human infant is entirely dependent upon those who care for him, he is equipped with means for indicating his needs. If those needs are met in a way that is rational and considerate, he will grow up to conceive of the world as likely to be rational and considerate. Thus, if he is fed when he is hungry, allowed to sleep when he is tired, played with when he is lively, and cleaned when he is wet and dirty, there will appear to be a firm connection between what goes on in the external world and what he himself is feeling. But suppose that the infant's feelings are not considered; that he is fed when adults happen to think of it; that he is kept awake when he wishes to sleep, and put down to sleep when he wishes to be played with; that he is picked up and moved around at the whim of adults, without reference to his protests. For such a child the world will seem incomprehensible and unpredictable. Because what actually happens is unrelated to his feelings, it will appear to him that the world is ruled by capricious giants whom he cannot influence. Moreover, one can see that such a dislocation between the inner and outer worlds of the child must lead to an intensified preoccupation with phantasy and a sense of despair. If one can neither understand the world nor gain any satisfaction for one's needs from it, one is bound to be driven in upon oneself.

The capriciousness and unpredictability of authority is a central theme in both *Der Prozeß* and *Das Schloß*. Even the giants make a brief appearance when, in *Der Prozeß*, Josef K. listens to the manufacturer and the deputy manager discussing the former's business scheme. 'Als dann die beiden sich an den Schreibtisch lehnten und der Fabrikant sich daran machte, nun den Direktor-Stellvertreter für sich zu erobern, war es K., als werde über seinem Kopf von zwei Männern, deren Größe er sich übertrieben vorstellte, über ihm selbst verhandelt' ('Then, as the two of them leaned against his desk, and the manufacturer set out to win the newcomer's approval for his scheme, it seemed to K. as if two giants of enormous size were bargaining above his head for himself'; P 157). This is surely a child's-eye view. Cannot most of us recall our parents, or other adults, discussing what should be done with us, perhaps to which school we should be sent, as if we had no say in the matter, as if we hardly existed?

I do not believe or suggest that Kafka's treatment by his father entirely accounted for the way in which he viewed authority, nor did Kafka himself think so. But his *Brief an den Vater* does illustrate the fact that injudicious handling can damage sensitive natures. Hermann Kafka seems to have been a dogmatic, hearty bully who could tolerate no disagreement with his views, and who was subject to fits of rage which terrified his son. In addition he was inconsistent. He insisted on good table manners but was constantly infringing his own injunctions. Even if he himself had no firm opinion about a particular subject, he would confidently assert that anyone who did so was wrong. Hermann Kafka sounds as if he belonged to that not inconsiderable number of persons who can only maintain their own self-esteem by putting others down. It is an effective technique for undermining the sensitive and those who cannot stand up for themselves. Kafka wrote:

Du konntest zum Beispiel auf die Tschechen schimpfen, dann auf die Deutschen, dann auf die Juden, und zwar nicht nur in Auswahl, sondern in jeder Hinsicht, und schließlich blieb niemand mehr übrig außer Dir. Du bekamst für mich das Rätselhafte, das alle Tyrannen haben, deren Recht auf ihrer Person, nicht auf dem Denken begründet ist. (H 169).

You were capable, for instance, of running down the Czechs, and then the Germans, and then the Jews, and what is more, not only selectively, but in every respect, and finally there was no-one left but yourself. For me you took on the enigmatic quality that all tyrants have whose rights are based on their person and not on their ideas.

In a later passage Kafka writes:

Dadurch wurde die Welt für mich in drei Teile geteilt, in einen, wo ich, der Sklave, lebte, unter Gesetzen, die nur für mich erfunden waren und denen ich überdies, ich wußte nicht warum, niemals völlig entsprechen konnte, dann in eine zweite Welt, die unendlich von meiner entfernt war, in der Du lebtest, beschäftigt mit der Regierung, mit dem Ausgeben der Befehle und mit dem Ärger wegen deren Nichtbefolgung, und schließlich in eine dritte Welt, wo die übrigen Leute glücklich und frei von Befehlen und Gehorchen lebten. Ich war immerfort in Schande, entweder befolgte ich Deine Befehle, das war Schande, denn sie galten ja nur für mich; oder ich war trotzig, das war auch Schande, denn wie durfte ich Dir gegenüber trotzig sein, oder ich konnte nicht folgen, weil ich zum Beispiel nicht Deine Kraft, nicht Deinen Appetit, nicht Deine Geschicklichkeit hatte, trotzdem Du es als etwas Selbstverständliches von mir verlangtest; das war allerdings die größte Schande. (H 173)

Hence the world was for me divided into three parts: one in which I, the slave, lived under the laws that had been invented only for me and which I could, I did not know why, never completely comply with: then a second world, which was infinitely remote from mine, in which you lived, concerned with government, with the issuing of orders and with annoyance about their not being obeyed: and finally a third world where everyone else lived happily and free from orders and from having to obey. I was continually in disgrace, either I obeyed your orders, and that was a disgrace, for they applied after all only to me, or I was defiant, and that too was a disgrace, for how could I presume to defy you, or I could not obey because for instance I had not your strength, your appetite or your skill, in spite of which you expected it of me as a matter of course; this was of course the greatest disgrace of all.

A triple bind, therefore, in which the child, whatever he did, was always in the wrong. It is not surprising that Kafka writes to his father: 'Ich hatte vor Dir das Selbstvertrauen verloren, dafür ein grenzenloses Schuldbewußtsein eingetauscht' ('I had lost my self-confidence where you were concerned, and in its place had acquired a boundless sense of guilt'; H 196).

Kafka's complaint to his father that he, the slave, lived under laws which existed for him alone, is expressed in the parable *Vor dem Gesetz* (*Before the Law*), told by the priest to K. in the penultimate chapter of *Der Prozeß*. It will be recalled that a countryman seeks access to the Law through a door which is always open, but which is guarded by a door-keeper who will not allow the countryman in. After many years of importunate waiting, the countryman is near his end. He complains: '"Alle streben doch nach dem Gesetz . . . wie kommt es, daß in den vielen Jahren niemand außer mir Einlaß verlangt hat?" Der Türhüter . . . brüllt . . . ihn an: "Hier konnte niemand sonst Einlaß erhalten, denn dieser Eingang war nur für dich bestimmt. Ich gehe jetzt und schließe ihn"' ('"Everyone strives to reach the law . . . so how does it happen that for all these many years no one but myself has ever begged for admittance?" The doorkeeper . . . roars in his ear: "No one else could ever be admitted here, since this gate was made only for you. Now I am going to shut it"'; P 257).

Just as 'The Law' is for ever inaccessible, so 'The Laws' can never be known. In one of his short fragments, 'Zur Frage der Gesetze' (The Problem of our Laws'), Kafka writes: 'Unsere Gesetze sind nicht allgemein bekannt, sie sind Geheimnis der kleinen Adelsgruppe, welche uns beherrscht' ('Our laws are not generally known; they are kept secret by the small group of nobles who rule us'; B 91). He goes on to speculate that it is possible that no body of Law really exists; that 'Was der Adel tut, ist Gesetz' ('the Law is whatever the nobles do'; B 92). The parallel with Kafka's view of his father as a tyrant whose domination was based upon his person and not on reason is inescapable.

Der Prozeß also illustrates what Kafka called his 'boundless sense of guilt' ('grenzenloses Schuldbewußtsein'). In the novel, K. is arrested without having done anything wrong. His guilt is taken for granted. As one of the warders who arrests him tells him, the high authorities who order his arrest are well informed about the reasons. 'Unsere Behörde . . . sucht doch nicht etwa die Schuld in der Bevölkerung, sondern wird, wie es im Gesetz heißt, von der Schuld angezogen und muß uns Wächter ausschicken. Das ist Gesetz. Wo gäbe es da einen Irrtum?' ('The authorities . . . never go hunting for crime in the populace, but, as the Law decrees, are drawn towards the guilty and must then send out us warders. That is the Law. How could there be a mistake in that?'; P 15).

K.'s crime is never specified, in spite of the fact that he is finally executed by stabbing. It does not need to be spelled out. In one passage, K. says: 'Es kommt auf viele Feinheiten an, in denen sich das Gericht verliert. Zum Schluß aber zieht es von irgendwoher, wo ursprünglich gar nichts gewesen ist, eine große Schuld hervor' ('It is a matter of countless subtleties in which the Court is lost sight of. And in the end, out of nothing at all, an enormous fabric of guilt will be conjured up'; P 179). It is, I think, evident that K.'s sense of guilt is existential. No crime need be named, since he feels that it is a crime for him to be alive at all. It is a feeling which children who think of themselves as always in the wrong not infrequently develop. If guilt is boundless, if nothing the child does is ever right, and if he has no way of finding out what would be right, he cannot develop any confidence in himself as an authentic person with a separate identity. Earlier, I quoted R. D. Laing's example of a patient who had to withdraw from an argument because he felt that his very existence was threatened. If one has always felt oneself to be in the wrong, and then tries to assert one's separate existence by gently putting forward an opinion of one's own, anyone who rides roughshod over that opinion is a threat to that separate existence. It is not surprising that people whose childhood experience was like that of Kafka tend to withdraw into an ivory tower of isolation where interaction with others cannot threaten them.

That K.'s crime is his very existence is confirmed in the passage in which Kafka describes the impossibility of K. ever being able to complete a plea which could be presented to the Court in support of his case:

Man mußte keinen sehr ängstlichen Charakter haben und konnte doch leicht zu dem Glauben kommen, daß es unmöglich war, die Eingabe jemals fertigzustellen. Nicht aus Faulheit oder Hinterlist, die den Advokaten allein an der Fertigstellung hindern konnten, sondern weil in Unkenntnis der vorhandenen Anklage und gar ihrer möglichen Erweiterungen das ganze Leben in den kleinsten Handlungen und Ereignissen in die Erinnerung zurückgebracht, dargestellt und von allen Seiten überprüft werden mußte. (P 154–55)

One did not need to have a timid and fearful nature to be easily persuaded that the completion of this plea was a sheer impossibility. Not because of laziness or constructive malice, which could only affect the advocate, but because to meet an unknown accusation, not to mention other possible charges arising out of it, the whole of one's life would have to be passed in review, down to the smallest actions and accidents, clearly formulated and examined from every angle.

This is one passage in which Kafka really does seem to anticipate the techniques of interrogation employed by both the Russian and Chinese interrogators when they wish to obtain confessions. When a person is arrested, a warrant may be produced and read, but the prisoner's supposed crimes are never specified. After a period of total isolation, the interrogation begins. The interrogator assumes that the prisoner is undoubtedly guilty and acts as though all his crimes are known to the authorities. The prisoner is told that there is no hope for him unless he makes a full confession. The whole of his past life is reviewed, and, in many instances, the prisoner is required to write a detailed autobiography which may have to be corrected over and over again. Most people have some feelings of guilt connected with past episodes in their lives, and religious people, especially, often have a deep sense of sin. It is not difficult for Communist interrogators to make use of this, and to link real or imagined transgressions with so-called 'crimes against the people' which the prisoner becomes ready to confess.

In Kafka's world, just as in a Communist state, there is no real possibility of acquittal. In *Der Prozeß*, the painter Titorelli, whose aid K. seeks because he has access to the Judges whose portraits he paints, tells him the position. Even if K. is acquitted and allowed to walk out of the Court a free man, he is only

. . . scheinbar frei oder, besser ausgedrückt, zeitweilig frei. Die untersten Richter nämlich, zu denen meine Bekannten gehören, haben nicht das Recht, endgültig freizusprechen, dieses Recht hat nur das oberste, für Sie, für mich und für uns alle ganz unerreichbare Gericht. Wie es dort aussieht, wissen wir nicht und wollen wir, nebenbei gesagt, auch nicht wissen. (P 190)

. . . ostensibly free, or more exactly, provisionally free. For the Judges of the lowest grade, to whom my acquaintances belong, haven't the power to grant a final acquittal, that power is reserved for the highest Court of all, which is quite inaccessible to you, to me, and to all of us. What the prospects are up there we do not know, and, I may say, do not even want to know.

So the charge which may be temporarily lifted from K.'s shoulders may be laid upon him again at any time.

I suppose that, for most people, the sexual act is an important means of self-affirmation. Although it can be argued that sexual intercourse is impersonal, since it is designed by nature for the propagation of the species, the majority of people do not experience it in this way. Nor does the fact that many people feel a temporary loss of identity in merging with the beloved contradict their prior or simultaneous experience that, in sexual intercourse, they are expressing the essence of their physical and spiritual nature. But this way of affirming his identity as a man was barred to Kafka, at least initially. Kafka's first sexual experience was with a shop-girl, soon after his twentieth birthday. In a letter he wrote to Milena seventeen years later, he recalled that

. . . das Mädchen im Hotel in aller Unschuld eine winzige Abscheulichkeit gemacht hat (nicht der Rede wert), eine kleine Schmutzigkeit gesagt hat, (nicht der Rede wert), aber die Erinnerung blieb, ich wußte im gleichen Augenblick, daß ich das nie vergessen werde und gleichzeitig wußte ich oder glaubte es zu wissen, daß dieses Abscheuliche und Schmutzige, äußerlich gewiß nicht notwendig, innerlich aber sehr notwendig mit dem Ganzen zusammenhänge und daß mich gerade dieses Abscheuliche und Schmutzige (dessen kleines Zeichen nur ihre kleine Handlung, ihr kleines Wort gewesen war) mit so wahnsinniger Gewalt in dieses Hotel gezogen hatte, dem ich sonst ausgewichen wäre mit meiner letzten Kraft. (M 181–82)

. . . at the hotel the girl in all innocence made a tiny repulsive gesture (not worth mentioning), had uttered a trifling obscenity (not worth mentioning), but the memory remained — I knew at that moment that I would never forget it and simultaneously I knew or thought I knew that this repulsiveness and smut, though outwardly not necessarily, was inwardly, however, very necessarily connected with the whole thing, and that just this repulsiveness and obscenity (whose little symptom had only been her tiny gesture, her trifling word) had drawn me with such terrible power into this hotel which otherwise I would have avoided with all my remaining strength.

Max Brod records that 'in later years he steered clear of dalliance, looked at the erotic side of life only from the most serious angle, and never told a dirty story or even stood for one being told in his presence. That is to say, he never protested against one; it simply would not have occurred to anyone to tell one in his presence'.[10]

Although in the last year of his life Kafka was able to move in with Dora Dymant and, one hopes, became able to enjoy some of the rewards of physical closeness, he refers to the step of actually living with her as 'a reckless move which can only be compared to some great historical event, like Napoleon's Russian campaign'.[11]

As everyone familiar with Kafka's life knows, Kafka did from time to time have actual sexual involvements and, according to Max Brod, fathered a son of whose existence he remained ignorant. But, right up to, and including, his relationship with Milena, he thought of sex and himself as 'dirty'. Marthe Robert, in her recently translated book, *Franz Kafka's Loneliness*, interprets Kafka's vacillation about women in standard Oedipal terms. She supposes that Kafka was unable to venture on marriage because, for him, all women were mothers, and sexual intercourse was therefore incestuous. This is a superficial interpretation which shows no appreciation of the terrible dilemma which Kafka, and others like him, actually face. Before his terminal relationship with Dora Dymant, Kafka's two most important relationships with women were with Felice Bauer and with Milena Jesenská. Kafka managed to contrive that these relationships remained almost entirely epistolary. During the five years of his relationship with Felice, the couple met no more than nine or ten times, often for no more than an hour or two. The same pattern was repeated though for a shorter time, with Milena. Kafka perfectly exemplifies the schizoid dilemma: a desperate need for love nullified by an equally desperate fear of actual proximity.

In his letters to Felice, Kafka constantly abuses himself; says that he would be impossible to live with; that he is quite unable to manage life; that he is a hopeless person. This pattern of confessional self-abasement is repeated in the letters to Milena, to whom he also sent his diaries. There are people who feel themselves compelled to behave particularly badly with, and toward, those they love. They seem to be seeking something which they feel they never had: an unconditional love which accepts the very worst in themselves without rejection. Kafka, in these distressing letters, is seeking a total acceptance which demands nothing in return; the kind of love which a mother may be expected to offer her new-born baby who, although squalling, incontinent and totally unaware of anyone else's needs, is nevertheless entitled to a loving acceptance of a kind which it will never again experience. This kind of total demand is made by psychiatric patients in analysis who have been deprived or neglected in early childhood, and especially by those who have had to learn, too early in life, that love is a reward for compliance rather than a gift which is freely given. Kafka is looking for a relationship in which he is not required to adapt to the other person, since, all his life, he has tended to lose his sense of identity by never asserting himself and by striving to comply with the demands of the other.

After Felice has accepted his proposal of marriage in June 1913, Kafka writes letters in which he demands to know everything about her life, down to the smallest detail: what she is wearing, how she spends her time, what her room is like, whom she sees, what she eats. These obsessive enquiries can be interpreted in more than one way. To know exactly what the beloved is doing, every moment of the day, is reassuring. Even if she is too far away for actual control to be exercised, as was true of Felice, she is, in imagination, pinned down, potentially accessible at any moment. One can guess that, had they ever lived together, Kafka would have infuriated her by demanding to know, as anxious, insecure spouses often do, when she was going out, when she would be back, and so on. And such enquiries would not have been pathological jealousy, though this may be a part of the picture, but rather the intense anxiety of the small child whose very existence depends upon his mother's actual presence.

Another way of looking at Kafka's anxious enquiries is to realize that, by knowing every detail about the life of the girl to whom he was writing, he would be able to give reality to a person who, because he saw her so seldom, remained largely a figure of his imagination. This is a technique employed by some novelists, who lend their characters verisimilitude by inventing for them all manner of details of dress, habits, and surroundings, so that they end by knowing exactly how a particular character would behave in any situation demanded by the plot of the novel. By not becoming actually, physically involved with the women he loved, Kafka was better able to make them into denizens of his inner, imaginative world, the only world in which he felt he could cope with them.

At the same time, Kafka's anxiety makes almost impossible demands. He used to carry Felice's letters around with him, saying that they gave him continuous support and made him feel better and more competent. If she fails to reply at once, he is absolutely desolate:

Ist, Felice, im letzten Vierteljahr ein Tag gewesen, an dem Du keine Nachricht von mir bekommen hättest. Sieh mal, einen solchen Tag gab es nicht? Mich aber läßt Du heute, Dienstag, ganz ohne Nachrichten, vom Sonntag 4 Uhr ab weiß ich nichts von Dir, das sind morgen bis zur Postzustellung nicht weniger als 66 Stunden, die für mich mit allen guten und bösen Möglichkeiten abwechselnd sich anfüllen. (BrF 205)

Has there ever been, Felice, in the last three months, a single day on which you have not had news from me? You see, there hasn't been such a day. But today, Tuesday, you leave me entirely without news; since four o'clock on Sunday I know nothing about you; until tomorrow's delivery that will be no less than sixty-six hours, filled in my mind with every alternating good and bad contingency.

This absolute, total dependency, this aching, unassuageable need is combined with a fearful anxiety about what would happen if she were actually there:

Einmal schriebst Du, Du wolltest bei mir sitzen, während ich schreibe; denke nur, da könnte ich nicht schreiben (ich kann auch sonst nicht viel) aber da könnte ich gar nicht schreiben. Schreiben heißt ja sich öffnen bis zum Übermaß; die äußerste Offenherzigkeit und Hingabe, in der sich ein Mensch im menschlichen Verkehr schon zu verlieren glaubt und vor der er also, solange er bei Sinnen ist, immer zurückscheuen wird — denn leben will jeder, solange er lebt — diese Offenherzigkeit und Hingabe genügt zum Schreiben bei weitem nicht. Was von dieser Oberfläche ins Schreiben hinübergenommen wird — wenn es nicht anders geht und die tiefern Quellen schweigen — ist nichts und fällt im den Augenblick zusammen, in dem ein wahreres Gefühl diesen obern Boden zum Schwanken bringt. Deshalb kann man nicht genug allein sein, wenn man schreibt, die Nacht ist noch zu wenig Nacht. (BrF 250)

You once said that you would like to sit beside me while I write. Listen, in that case I could not write (I can't do much anyway), but in that case, I could not write at all. For writing means revealing oneself in excess; that utmost of self-revelation and surrender, in which a human being, when involved with others, would feel he was losing himself, and from which, therefore, he will always shrink as long as he is in his right mind — for everyone wants to live as long as he is alive — even the degree of self-revelation and surrender is not enough for writing. Writing that springs from the surface of existence — when there is no other way and the deeper wells have dried up — is nothing and collapses the moment a truer emotion makes that surface shake. This is why one can never be alone enough when one writes, why there can never be enough silence around one when one is writing, why even night is not night enough.

Kafka's anxiety is twofold. On the one hand, probably rightly, he feels that his need is so great that no-one could possibly meet it; or, if any woman were to attempt to meet it, he fears that she would be drained and ultimately destroyed in the process. On the other hand, if she were to be with him, his independence, his identity, and therefore his capacity to write would be annihilated.

Kafka's anxiety in the presence of other people made him diffident to the point of self-effacement. Once, when visiting Max Brod, he woke up the latter's father. 'Instead of apologizing, he said, in an indescribably gentle way, raising a hand as if to calm him and walking softly on tiptoe through the room, "Please look on me as a dream"' (Brod, *Franz Kafka*, pp. 73–74).

It is characteristic of such a man that he should prefer Nature cures to conventional medicine, and, for long periods, be vegetarian. In an aquarium he was heard addressing the fish: 'Now at last I can look at you in peace, I don't eat you any more' (ibid., p. 74). He drank no alcohol, tea, or coffee, and never smoked. It is also characteristic that he should plan an idealist 'Guild of Workmen without Possessions' in which members were not to be allowed money or valuables, but only the minimum of clothing and books and materials necessary for work. Everything else in this Utopia was to belong to the poor.

Self-effacement and self-denial of this kind is the very opposite stance from the joyous affirmation of one's own identity to which I referred earlier. Kafka's anxiety not only made him reluctant to compete, but also made him almost too acutely aware of what the other person was feeling. Over-adaptation to the other means loss of the self as a separate entity. Only in the silent watches of the night, when Kafka was entirely alone, could he get in touch with his innermost depths and be really and truly himself.

In his penultimate letter to Felice, written after he knew that he had tuberculosis, he demonstrates that his wish to please is not really based on concern for what others are feeling, but upon his own wish to be accepted and to gain love. It is a remarkable piece of insight:

Wenn ich mich auf mein Endziel hin prüfe, so ergibt sich, daß ich nicht
eigentlich danach strebe, ein guter Mensch zu werden und einem höchsten
Gericht zu entsprechen, sondern, sehr gegensätzlich, die ganze Menschen-
und Tiergemeinschaft zu überblicken, ihre grundlegenden Vorlieben,
Wünsche, sittlichen Ideale zu erkennen, sie auf einfache Vorschriften
zurückzuführen, und mich in dieser Richtung möglichst bald dahin zu
entwickeln, daß ich durchaus allen wohlgefällig würde, und zwar (hier
kommt der Sprung) so wohlgefällig, daß ich, ohne die allgemeine Liebe zu
verlieren, schließlich, als der einzige Sünder, der nicht gebraten wird, die
mir innewohnenden Gemeinheiten offen, vor aller Augen, ausführen
dürfte. Zusammengefaßt kommt es mir also nur auf das Menschengericht
an und dieses will ich überdies betrügen, allerdings ohne Betrug. (BrF 755–
56)

When I examine my ultimate aim, it shows that I do not actually strive to be
good, to answer to a supreme tribunal. Very much the opposite. I strive to
know the entire human and animal community, to recognize their
fundamental preferences, desires, and moral ideas, to reduce them to simple
rules, and as quickly as possible to adopt these rules so as to be pleasing to
everyone. Indeed (here comes the inconsistency), to become so pleasing that
in the end I might openly act out my inherent baseness before the eyes of the
world without forfeiting its love — the only sinner not to be roasted. In
short, my only concern is the human tribunal, and I would like to deceive
even this, and what's more without actual deception.

Everyone who tries to suppress all aggression and self-assertion pays a
price for doing so. 'Naturam expellas furca, tamen usque recurret.' It is
no surprise that Kafka, the gentle ascetic, is haunted by horrific sado-
masochistic phantasies:

. . . daß ich ausgestreckt auf dem Boden liege, wie ein Braten zerschnitten
bin und ein solches Fleischstück langsam mit der Hand einem Hund in die
Ecke zuschiebe (Br 114–15)

. . . that I lie stretched out on the floor, sliced up like a roast, and with my
hand am slowly pushing a slice of the meat towards a dog in the corner.

Torture, violence, flagellation are recurrent themes in both Kafka's
diaries and his fiction. But beyond and beneath the suffering, there is
also a glimmer of hope. On 13 March 1915, he writes in his diary:

Manchmal das Gefühl fast zerreißenden Unglücklichseins und gleichzeitig
die Überzeugung der Notwendigkeit dessen und eines durch jedes Anziehen
des Unglücks erarbeiteten Zieles. (T 466)

Occasionally the feeling of an unhappiness which almost dismembers me,
and at the same time the conviction of its necessity and of the existence of a
goal to which one makes one's way by undergoing every kind of
unhappiness.

In that most terrifying of all his stories, *In der Strafkolonie* (*In the Penal Settlement*), we can get an idea of what that goal really is. When the officer in charge is explaining how the apparatus of torture and execution really works, he points out that it is so designed that the victim under the harrow does not die until twelve hours have passed. However, after the needles have been inscribing their message of judgement into the victim's flesh for about six hours, a change comes over him:

Wie still wird dann der Mann um die sechste Stunde! Verstand geht dem Blödesten auf. Um die Augen beginnt es. Von hier aus verbreitet es sich. Ein Anblick, der einen verführen könnte, sich mit unter die Egge zu legen. Es geschieht ja weiter nichts, der Mann fängt bloß an, die Schrift zu entziffern, er spitzt den Mund, als horchte er. Sie haben gesehen, es ist nicht leicht, die Schrift mit den Augen zu entziffern; unser Mann entziffert sie aber mit seinen Wunden. (E 212–13)

But how quiet the man grows at the sixth hour. Enlightenment comes to the most dull-witted. It begins around the eyes. From there it radiates. A moment that might tempt one to get under the harrow with him. Nothing more happens after that, the man only begins to understand the inscription, he purses his mouth as if he were listening. You have seen how difficult it is to decipher the script with one's eyes; but our man deciphers it with his wounds.

The most striking sentence in this extract is surely that in which the officer refers to his temptation to get under the harrow with the victim. Perhaps, if a man suffers enough, as he nears death, he will finally attain enlightenment: at last understand what law it is that he has transgressed, and come to terms with the guilt which is so deeply inscribed that it is an inescapable part of his physical being. When, near the end of the story, the officer does replace the condemned man, the machine goes wrong. The officer is deprived of enlightenment because he is killed prematurely and has not therefore suffered for long enough.

How is it that long endurance of suffering can bring enlightenment? Only, perhaps, when we do not try to avoid it.

Wordsworth, in his ode 'Intimations of Immortality from Recollections of Early Childhood', regrets the passing of the child's pristine vision of the world:

> Heaven lies about us in our infancy!
> Shades of the prison-house begin to close
> Upon the growing Boy.

But Wordsworth also recognizes that creativity has its origin in early childhood and that it is vital to preserve what links we can with what is past:

> But for the first affections
> Those shadowy recollections
> Which, be they what they may,
> Are yet the fountain light of all our day,
> Are yet a master light of all our seeing;[12]

From what Kafka wrote, in his diaries, in his letters, and in his fiction, we may surmise that it was Hell rather than Heaven which lay about him in his infancy, and the hounds of Hell continued to pursue him. But Kafka realized that, for him, as for Wordsworth, the link with his childhood must be preserved. Most of us paper over our miseries with a variety of defensive devices. We put on masks; we pretend that what is important does not matter; we betray ourselves and therefore we betray others; we twist and turn, pose and pretend, drink, fornicate and try to forget. This why we so often end up stereotyped and sterile.

Kafka, until nearly the end of his life, was tempted by suicide. Like Georg Bendemann in *Das Urteil* (*The Judgement*), he was drawn to obey his father's injunction that he had no right to exist. But Kafka, the man with no identity, for ever ironic, gentle, self-effacing, was, in his inner world, courageous, uncompromising, ruthlessly honest. If his fate was to live under the harrow, that was where he had to be, and he was not going to wriggle out from it. As a writer, he not only did not flinch, but discovered his real identity. In a letter to Felice written in August 1913, he complains of the inaccuracies of a graphologist to whom she has evidently shown his writing. The graphologist has attributed 'artistic interests' to him. Kafka writes: 'Nicht einmal das "künsterliche Interesse" ist wahr, es ist sogar die falscheste Aussage unter allen Falschheiten. Ich habe kein literarisches Interesse, sondern bestehe aus Literatur, ich bin nichts anderes und kann nichts anderes sein' ('Even "artistic interests" is not true; in fact, of all the erroneous statements, that is the most erroneous. I have no literary interest, but am made of literature, I am nothing else, and cannot be anything else'; BrF 444).

The self which he felt had been crushed in childhood, and which he feared would be crushed again by anyone who came too close to him, triumphantly asserts its uniqueness on the page; and we should not recognize and celebrate that uniqueness if Kafka had emancipated himself from suffering instead of laying hold upon it.

Kafka's fear of the external world, of involvement with others, and of the loss of his own identity, made him seek writing as a retreat. Writing was the only way which he could be entirely himself, and yet still preserve lines of communication. Schizophrenics protect themselves in similar fashion. They retreat into an inner world in which they achieve all manner of wonderful things in spite of the machinations of their enemies and their perpetual fear of being engulfed and overwhelmed.

Those who feel powerless in the external world commonly develop a compensatory inner world in which they are omnipotent; in which the hard facts of reality are denied and replaced by psychotic phantasies in which the subject is all-important and possessed of magical powers. Jung quotes a striking example of a schizophrenic who told him that the world was his picture-book: he had only to turn the pages to see a new vision. Kafka was no stranger to omnipotence of thought. In his early story *Beschreibung eines Kampfes* (*Description of a Struggle*), he writes of a traveller who flattens out a steep road, causes an enormously high mountain to rise, and who forgets to let the moon come up. Kafka also exhibited a paranoid side to his nature. In December 1917 he wrote to Max Brod about the mice who were invading his bedroom:

Das was ich gegenüber den Mäusen habe, ist platte Angst. Auszuforschen woher sie kommt, ist Sache der Psychoanalytiker, ich bin es nicht. Gewiß hängt sie wie auch die Ungezieferangst mit dem unerwarteten, ungebetenen, unvermeidbaren, gewissermaßen stummen, verbissenen, geheimabsichtlichen Erscheinen dieser Tiere zusammen, mit dem Gefühl, daß sie die Mauern ringsherum hundertfach durchgraben haben und dort lauern, daß sie sowohl durch die ihnen gehörige Nachtzeit als auch durch ihre Winzigkeit so fern uns und damit noch weniger angreifbar sind. (Br 205)

My reaction towards the mice is one of sheer terror. To analyse its source would be the task of the psychoanalyst, which I am not. Certainly, this fear, like an insect phobia, is connected with the unexpected, uninvited, inescapable, more or less silent, persistent, secret aims of these creatures, with the sense that they have riddled the surrounding walls through and through with their tunnels and are lurking within, that the night is theirs, that because of their nocturnal existence and their tininess they are so remote from us and thus outside our power.

Kafka was not psychotic; but I believe that it was his writing which prevented him from retreating into a world of psychotic phantasy. For writing is a means of communication, and therefore a means of retaining contact with others, albeit at a distance. Indeed, for people of Kafka's temperament, the gift of being able to write is an ideal way of expressing oneself, since it does not involve direct contact with others. Writing also serves another function for those plagued with horrors. Kafka told Janouch that writing *Das Urteil* had exorcized a spectre. So writing was not only a way of affirming his identity without direct involvement, but also a form of abreaction, of laying ghosts by confronting them and pinning them down in words. Kafka perfectly illustrates the fact that, for some people, writing, or some other form of imaginative activity, is a way of survival. I agree with Erich Heller who writes of Kafka: 'Of course, this is a disposition akin to madness, separated from it only by writing table, an imagination capable of holding together what appears to have an irresistible tendency to fall apart, and an intelligence of supreme integrity'.[13]

Although writing may have saved Kafka from madness, writing is not, and can never be, a total substitute for living life in the world, and Kafka, with his customary insight, realized this. I think that *Der Bau* (*The Burrow*) demonstrates this insight. Professor Thorlby, in his study of Kafka, has given a very interesting interpretation of this story. If my emphasis is different, this is not only because I am a psychiatrist rather than a literary scholar, but because Kafka contains such multitudes that different interpretations of his work can often be complementary rather than contradictory.

Der Bau is the story of an animal which attempts to find security by constructing a hugely elaborate burrow in which it can find safety from potential enemies and a retreat from the external world. The burrow has taken a very long time to construct; the network of passages is elaborate, and, not quite in its centre, chosen to serve as a refuge in case of extreme danger, is a cell called the 'Castle Keep', in which the animal assembles its store of food. It is, as a rule, beautifully still within the burrow; the air is balmy, there is hardly any noise, and the animal feels that he can sleep: 'den süßen Schlaf des Friedens, des beruhigten Verlangens, des erreichten Zieles' ('the sweet sleep of tranquillity, of satisfied desire, of achieved ambition'; B 176). But, in spite of all the complex defences, certain anxieties cannot be altogether eliminated. There is, for example, the entrance. Although this is concealed by a covering of moss, and has so far not attracted the attention of enemies, it is impossible to be confident that this will be so for ever. It is dangerous, but perhaps advisable, to look at the entrance from the outside from time to time. Moreover, the burrow is rather confined, and the food outside is better. Sometimes the animal spends quite long periods outside, concealed from enemies, gloating over the burrow which lies waiting for him with its promise of infinite bliss. When he is in the burrow, it is difficult to leave it for the outside world. When he is in the outside world, it is equally difficult to descend into the burrow. One solution might be to enlist a confidant, who could keep watch over the burrow and warn of danger. But no, there is no-one he can trust; and he could certainly never let anyone else into the burrow itself.

Kafka perfectly illustrates the dilemma in which he finds himself. He can neither be fully engaged in the external world, nor can he entirely withdraw into his inner world. In the story, the two worlds may even exchange their characteristics, so that what appeared tranquil becomes threatening, and vice versa.

At last, the animal settles for retreat. Exhausted by conflict and perpetual watchfulness, he makes his way to the safety of the Castle

Keep. He sleeps for a prolonged period, but, after a while, is awakened by a disturbing whistling noise. At first he concludes that this noise is made by the small fry, the tiny animals which do not threaten him, but which are always around and which constitute his food. But the noise grows louder and more insistent. It is, he decides, some new type of beast which he has never before encountered. Perhaps all his precautions against attack are insufficient. He tries to guess at its plans. One thing is certain; if they do encounter each other, there will be a bloody battle. He finally contents himself with the hope that the beast, although undoubtedly a threat, may never have heard of him. The story (of which the final pages are missing) ends on this note of unresolved unease.

Kafka is surely saying that security is not attainable, either in the external world, or in the enclosed world of the imagination. The fate of those who are unable to risk loving and living, and who seek to be safely protected within the burrow of their own narcissism is, inevitably to be haunted by creatures of the imagination (like Kafka's own sado-masochistic phantasies) which will not leave them in peace.

The theme of this story seems to me to be similar to that of one of Henry James's most powerful tales, 'The Beast in the Jungle'. This is the story of John Marcher, who for years has led a futile existence, because he is haunted by the conviction that he is being reserved for an unusual, perhaps terrible experience, which he pictures as a beast tracking him through the jungle. He confides his story to a sympathetic woman who becomes his Platonic companion. Only when they become old and the woman is ill does he learn the truth. He has been haunted by the beast because he has avoided commitment and has lost the woman he might have loved. The beast is a product of his own blindness, self-centredness and lack of courage; and it springs when he realizes that his own life has been rendered sterile by his efforts to protect himself.

Kafka was originally driven to affirm his identity through writing because he found involvement with others threatening; but it is clear that, through his writing, and through recognition of his talent by others, and their acceptance of the self which manifested itself in his stories, he became more confident. What would have happened to him if his life had not been prematurely brought to a close by tuberculosis? My guess is that he would finally have been able to commit himself to Dora or to some other woman, and have become more capable of living something approaching a normal life. What would have been the effect upon his writing is another matter. Kafka's writing is so bound up with the more pathological parts of his personality, that, if he had become happier, his drive to write might have been greatly diminished.

NOTES

[1] Charles Rycroft *A Critical Dictionary of Psychoanalysis* (London, 1968), p. 68.

[2] Erik Erikson, *Identity* (London, 1958), p. 19.

[3] Carl Gustav Jung, *Collected Works* (London, 1954), XVII, para. 289.

[4] Ronald Hayman, *K. A Biography of Kafka* (London, 1981), p. 47.

[5] *The Letters of John Keats*, ed. M. B. Forman (Oxford, 1935), p. 228.

[6] Ronald D. Laing, *The Divided Self* (London, 1960), p. 45.

[7] Sigmund Freud, *The Ego and the Id*, Standard Edition (London, 1961), XIX, 26.

[8] Jonathan Swift, *A Voyage to Brobdingnag*, in *Gulliver's Travels and Selected Writings in Prose and Verse*, ed. John Hayward (London, 1963), p. 115.

[9] George Painter, *Marcel Proust* (London, 1959), I, 9.

[10] Max Brod, *Franz Kafka* (New York, 1963), p. 116.

[11] Quoted by Allan Blunden in 'A Chronology of Kafka's Life', in *The World of Franz Kafka*, ed J. P. Stern (London, 1980), p. 28.

[12] William Wordsworth, *The Poems*, vol. I, ed. John O. Hayden (Harmondsworth, 1977), p. 525.

[13] Erich Heller, *Franz Kafka* (New York, 1975), p. 15.

Ritchie Robertson

'ANTIZIONISMUS, ZIONISMUS': KAFKA'S RESPONSES TO JEWISH NATIONALISM

In his diary for 23 January 1922, Kafka listed the many undertakings which he had, in the course of his life, begun and then abandoned. It is an oddly assorted list, beginning with piano lessons, continuing with hobbies like gardening and carpentry, and ending with his abortive plans to get married and to set up a home of his own. In the midst of this catalogue we find the pair 'Antizionismus, Zionismus' (T 560). Did either of these ever represent a serious commitment for Kafka? And if so, how serious and how prolonged was either his opposition to Zionism or his interest in it?

These questions have been much discussed. Kafka's close friends Max Brod and Felix Weltsch had no doubt of his Zionist sympathies, and recently Klara Carmely has argued the same case.[1] But while Brod and Weltsch can scarcely have been altogether mistaken about Kafka's views, their own intense commitment to Zionism may well have led them to simplify Kafka's attitude. To counteract their possible bias, I shall briefly summarize the evidence for Kafka's anti-Zionism and then for his Zionism, and suggest a slightly more qualified conclusion. I shall then examine the particular version of Zionist ideology that Kafka encountered and show how his own complex and thoughtful response to it is expressed in two well-known stories, *In der Strafkolonie* (*In the Penal Settlement*) and *Ein Bericht für eine Akademie* (*A Report for an Academy*).

Theodor Herzl published *Der Judenstaat* when Kafka was thirteen, but until his late twenties Kafka's attitude to Zionism was one of blank indifference. In 1899 Jewish students at Prague University had founded a Zionist society, named the Bar Kochba after the Jewish resistance leader of the second century A.D., which was to become the most important Zionist organization in Central Europe. Since Kafka's school friend Hugo Bergmann was one of its most active members, Kafka must have been dimly aware of its existence, but both he and Brod ignored it until 1909, when a writer in its journal, *Selbstwehr*, attacked the treatment of nationality problems in one of Brod's innumerable novels,

26 *Ritchie Robertson*

Ein tschechisches Dienstmädchen.[2] The resulting dispute taught Brod the principles of Zionism. At first he regarded the Bar Kochba with some reserve, feeling unable to share their dismissal of all aspects of Jewish life in the Diaspora, but by 1913 at the latest he had been completely won over to Zionism. His efforts to proselytize Kafka were worse than ineffectual, for they produced a temporary estrangement between Brod and Kafka. In a discussion in August 1913 Kafka professed to be wholly without a sense of community,[3] and in his diary four months later Kafka writes (perhaps in response to further persuasion): 'Was habe ich mit Juden gemeinsam? Ich habe kaum etwas mit mir gemeinsam' ('What do I have in common with Jews? I have scarcely anything in common with myself'; T 350). Even in 1916, when his interest in Zionism had undoubtedly developed and he was urging Felice to help in a Zionist-run home for refugee children, he told her that if put to the test he would probably prove not to be a Zionist (BrF 698), and in 1918, in a passage not cited by Carmely, he noted that he, unlike the Zionists, had no contact with Jewish religious practice — 'ich habe nicht den letzten Zipfel des davonfliegenden jüdischen Gebetmantels noch gefangen wie die Zionisten' ('I have not, like the Zionists, still grasped at the last vanishing tassle of the Jewish prayer mantle'; H 121). As Helen Milfull has noted, Kafka never refers to the Balfour Declaration, which to any Zionist would have been an epoch-making event.[4] From 1912 to the end of his life he repeatedly considered emigrating to Palestine: at one time he thought of working as a book-binder there (Br 277); later he and Dora Dymant planned to work in a restaurant in Palestine, where she would be a cook and Kafka a waiter, but she herself was not sure how far these plans were simply fanciful (Weltsch, p. 39).

On the positive side, we have to note that Kafka's professions of indifference did not prevent him from attending at least ten lectures and recitals organized by the Bar Kochba between 1910 and 1914. In a draft review of Brod's novel *Jüdinnen*, dating from March 1911, Kafka implied that Zionism was at least a possible solution to the Jewish question (T 52–54). In May 1912 he expressed great enthusiasm for another novel by Brod, *Arnold Beer* (see Br 94, T 277), which is significant because the novel, although not explicitly Zionist, does end with the protagonist acquiring a sense of Jewish identity from a visit to his grandmother, and, as Karlheinz Fingerhut has shown, Brod's novel, and particularly this climactic episode, strongly influenced *Das Urteil* (*The Judgement*).[5] But we must also note that Kafka, who was not a clubbable man, felt ill at ease at Zionist gatherings — 'Ich wie aus Holz, ein in die Mitte des Saales geschobener Kleiderhalter' ('I'm as if wooden, a clothes rack shoved into the middle of the room'; T 466) is how he describes his demeanour on such an occasion, and when he took advantage of a visit to Vienna in 1913, where he had to attend an international conference on industrial safety and hygiene, to look in on the Eleventh World Zionist Congress, he felt uncomfortable and out of place (Br 120). Where he did feel at ease was in the theatre. In the winter of 1911–12 he attended at least twenty performances by the Yiddish theatre troupe from Lemberg who performed in the sleazy Café Savoy. He got to know the actors, despite some difficulty in following their rapid Yiddish, and one of them, Jizchok Löwy, became a close friend. In the Yiddish theatre, and nowhere else, he had a sense of belonging to a national community. This emerges most clearly from his comment on a performance of Yiddish songs by Frau Klug, one of the actresses:

Bei manchen Liedern, der Ansprache 'jüdische Kinderlach', manchem Anblick dieser Frau, die auf dem Podium, weil sie Jüdin ist, uns Zuhörer, weil wir Juden sind, an sich zieht, ohne Verlangen oder Neugier nach Christen, ging mir ein Zittern über die Wangen. (T 81)

Hearing certain songs, hearing the expression 'jüdische Kinderlach', seeing some of this woman's expressions (who on stage, because she is a Jew, draws us listeners to her, because we are Jews, without any longing for or curiosity about Christians), I felt my cheeks tremble.

For Kafka at least the theatre did indeed fulfil the purpose that Schiller had claimed for it in 1784, towards the close of his lecture 'Was kann eine gute stehende Schaubühne eigentlich wirken?' ('What can a well-established theatre really accomplish?'): that of producing a consensus in the beliefs and emotions of the audience and thus creating a national spirit. His interest in the Yiddish theatre separated him further from the Zionists of the Bar Kochba. None of them attended the performances in the Café Savoy. They took almost no interest in the Yiddish-speaking Jewish communities of Eastern Europe. Being Hebraists, they wished to discard Yiddish as a shameful relic of Jewish subjection, an attitude which goes back to Moses Mendelssohn and was fully shared by Herzl.[6] They were to become much more friendly to the 'Ostjuden' (Eastern European Jews) in the next few years, first in theory, under the influence of Martin Buber, and then in practice, when large numbers of Jewish refugees from Galicia flooded into Prague and had to be cared for. During the war there developed a veritable 'Kult alles Ostjüdischen', in Gershom Scholem's phrase.[7] But Kafka's interest in the Eastern European Jews developed years before such an interest was fashionable, and not in response to the theoretical arguments of Buber or anyone else, but as a result of meeting Galician Jews, attending their theatrical performances, and hearing their poetry recited. Kafka himself tried to convey his enthusiasm for Yiddish culture to the Bar Kochba. He did succeed in persuading Bergmann and a few others to attend a performance, and in February 1912 he organized a recital of Yiddish poems by Löwy, introduced by Kafka with a talk on the Yiddish language. It was not until 1915, however, that the Bar Kochba's members took any practical interest in the Jews of Eastern Europe. We cannot therefore accept Kafka's declaration that he had no sense of community. He had a powerful sense of kinship with the Jews from Eastern Europe, but the medium in which he felt this kinship was culture — poetry and the theatre — rather than politics. From 1915 onward we find him paying more attention to the society and the religion of the 'Ostjuden', though from his remarks on Zionism in letters to Felice of 1916 it is clear that he takes no interest in the political side of Zionism; he considers Zionism 'nur der Eingang zu dem Wichtigern' ('Only the entrance to that which is more important'; BrF 675), but something which one must be either for or against — indifference he now considers impossible (BrF 697). In the spring of 1917 he began learning Hebrew and must have made good progress, for we know that he learnt to speak Hebrew fluently and that by 1923 he was able to read the Old Testament, the Talmud, and a modern Hebrew novel, all in the original (see Weltsch, p. 38, and Br 453, 456).

There can, I think, be no doubt that by 1916 Kafka had developed powerful Zionist sympathies, though his attitude to the movement was an unorthodox and individualistic one, and he took no part in political activity on behalf of the Zionist cause. However, Zionism struck him as valuable because it could make possible a Jewish national community which would preserve the values of the Eastern European Jews and repudiate those of Western Jews. He felt that the latter, including himself, were trapped uncomfortably between a sheltering Jewish community to which they could never return and a Western society which would never completely accept them. He agreed with Karl Kraus that the father-complex exhibited by so many Jewish writers (notably himself) was directed not against the father, but against the father's Jewishness. 'Weg vom Judentum . . . wollten die meisten, die deutsch zu schreiben anfingen, sie wollten es, aber mit den Hinterbeinchen klebten sie noch am Judentum des Vaters und mit den Vorderbeinchen fanden sie keinen neuen Boden' ('Most of those who began to write German wanted to escape from Judaism; they wanted to do so, yet with their hind legs they were still stuck fast in the Judaism of their fathers, and with their forelegs they found no new ground'; Br 377). Hence Kafka can remark casually, as though it were a commonplace, that since the Westernized Jew has no clear religious principles he has no right to marry.[8] After attending a social evening intended to bring Eastern and Western Jews together, Kafka noted that the former despised the Jews of Prague, and added that they were right to do so (T 465). The Galician refugees seemed to him to exhibit 'das selbstverständliche jüdische Leben' ('the self-evident Jewish life'; T 468) which the Jew living in Gentile society had forgotten how to lead. They appeared to him to form a community of the sort to which his upbringing had denied him access. The possibility that the Zionist movement could help to recreate such a community was the basis for Kafka's sympathy with Zionism.

We need now to ask in more detail what version or versions of Zionism he had encountered in the years before 1916, and how he reacted to them. The members of the Bar Kochba were middle-class Jews who, like Kafka, had been brought up in almost complete ignorance of Judaism by parents who were anxious to assimilate to Western society. One of them, Hans Kohn, recalls: 'My father went to the synagogue only on the high holidays, my mother almost never. None of the ceremonial laws were observed in our house. Yiddish [. . .] was not spoken in Prague [. . .]; the Eastern European Jews were regarded more as aliens than as "brothers".'[9] When Brod and Kafka first made contact with the Bar Kochba, its main ideological preceptor was no longer Herzl but Ahad Ha'am, the proponent of cultural Zionism. Ahad Ha'am argued that since only a small proportion of the world's Jews could possibly emigrate to Palestine, it should constitute a spiritual rather than a political centre. In the words of some of his followers, he was advocating not so much a Jewish national state as a Jewish Vatican. The Jews remaining in the Diaspora should concentrate on developing their Jewish self-awareness, which included learning Hebrew.[10] For some years, therefore, the main concern of the Bar Kochba, as proclaimed in the first issue of *Die Selbstwehr*, was with the 'Belebung der jüdischen Idee' ('animating the Jewish Idea'),[11] or what we might now call consciousness-raising. They took little interest in the Palestinian settlements until 1911, when one of their number, Viktor Kellner, emigrated there. (Kafka met him when he was revisiting Prague the following year, and heard from him a less than encouraging account of conditions in Palestine, with emphasis on the fanatical nationalism of his pupils there; T 289).

Alongside Ahad Ha'am's stress on Jewish consciousness, there were other, more political lines of thought in early Zionism. One that eventually impinged on the Bar Kochba, and hence on Kafka, originated with Max Nordau, a close frend of Herzl and author of the polemical critique of contemporary Western culture, *Entartung* (*Degeneration*). In a speech to the First Zionist Congress in Basle in 1897, Nordau took his hearers aback by denying that the traditional Jewish ghetto had been a shameful form of confinement; on the contrary, it had provided the Jews with an indispensable refuge in which they could develop their full human potential:

So lebten die Ghettojuden in sittlicher Hinsicht ein Volleben. Ihre äußere Lage war unsicher, oft schwer gefährdet, innerlich aber gelangten sie zur allseitigen Ausgestaltung ihrer Eigenart und sie hatten nichts Fragmentarisches an sich. Sie waren harmonische Menschen, denen keins der Elemente des Normaldaseins eines Gesellschaftsmenschen fehlte.[12]

Thus the Jews of the ghetto lived, in terms of their customs, a full life. Their position relative to the outside world was uncertain, often seriously endangered; internally, however, they achieved a multi-faceted realization of their uniqueness, and there was nothing fragmentary about them. They were harmonious beings, lacking none of the elements of the normal existence of any social person.

In Nordau's wake, other Zionists were able to discover in the Jewish communities of Eastern Europe something approaching the social cohesion of the medieval ghetto, and to praise it as the model for a future Jewish society. In 1912 Kafka attended a meeting of the Bar Kochba which was addressed by Nathan Birnbaum, the great champion of Yiddish. Birnbaum spoke passionately on behalf of the Eastern Jews: 'Die Ostjuden sind ganze, lebensfrohe und lebenskräftige Menschen' ('The Eastern European Jews are whole, vigorous human beings, full of the joy of life'; *Kafka-Handbuch*, I, 392). The *Sammelbuch vom Judentum*, a collection of essays issued by the Bar Kochba in 1913, contained a contribution by Adolf Böhm which restated Nordau's praise of the ghetto and stressed the interpenetration of all aspects of life by religion:

Im Ghetto war das Gemeinschaftsleben ein vollständiges, es umfaßte nicht nur Religion, sondern auch Sitte, Recht, Sprache, Familienleben, in vollständiger Einheit. . . Das 'Judentum' war keine bloße Konfession, nicht allein Individualreligion, sondern umfaßte die Gesamtheit aller durch Gesetz und Tradition geheiligten Formen des Gemeinschaftslebens in ihrer bestimmten Eigenart.[13]

The communal life in the ghetto was a complete one; it encompassed not only religion, but also custom, law, language, and family life in a complete unity . . . 'Judaism' was no mere creed, not solely the religion of individuals, but encompassed the totality of all aspects of communal life hallowed, in their particular uniqueness, by law and tradition.

But the most powerful influence on the social thinking of the Bar Kochba was Martin Buber. Buber had been a Zionist since 1898, but in 1904 he had withdrawn from active participation in Zionism in order to study the Eastern European Jews and especially the religious movement called Hasidism, which had grown up among them in the mid-eighteenth century and still had hundreds of thousands of adherents in Russia and Poland, and especially in Galicia. Their communities seemed to him to suggest a superior alternative to Western society for several reasons. Firstly, it was permeated with religion, while Western society was secular. Secondly, it was organic, while Western society seemed to Buber to consist of individuals held together merely by self-interest. Thirdly, he admired the charismatic authority exercised by a Hasidic *rebbe* (Rabbi) over his followers. In his essay, 'Mein Weg zum Chassidismus' (1924) Buber recalled the impression made on him as a child by this spectacle: 'als ich den Rebbe durch die Reihen der Harrenden schreiten sah, empfand ich: "Führer", und als ich die Chassidim mit der Thora tanzen sah, empfand ich: "Gemeinde"' ('as I saw the Rabbi stride through the rows of waiting people, I felt: "Leader", and when I saw the Hasidim dancing with the Torah, I felt: "Community"').[14] Fourthly, Hasidism, with its tradition of teaching in parables, provided a creative, myth-making force in contrast to the arid intellectualism of orthodox Rabbinism and of the West. And finally, the Eastern Jews seemed to Buber to retain a primitive vitality which had largely vanished from Western society.

It is easy to see that Buber was projecting onto the Eastern Jews the social categories, especially the contrast between organic 'Gemeinschaft' ('community') and utilitarian 'Gesellschaft' ('society'), familiar from Ferdinand Tönnies and, on a lower intellectual level, from Paul de Lagarde and other popular thinkers. The historian George Mosse has compared Buber to Lagarde, no doubt with such passages in mind as the following:

Ein Volk wird zusammengehalten durch primäre Elemente: das Blut, das Schicksal — soweit es auf der Entwicklung des Blutes beruht — und die kulturschöpfende Kraft — soweit sie durch die aus dem Blut entstandene Eigenart bedingt wird.[15]

A people is held together by primary elements: its blood, its fate—insofar as it rests on the development of that blood—and the power that creates culture—insofar as this is determined by that uniqueness arising from the blood.

Buber's favourite words include 'Blut', 'Boden', 'Volkstum', 'Gemeinschaft' and 'Wurzelhaftigkeit' ('blood', 'soil', 'national character', 'community' and 'rootedness'). He also has a penchant for words beginning with the prefix 'Ur-'. The essay 'Mein Weg zum Chassidismus' alone contains 'Urmenschliches', 'Urjüdisches', 'Uraltes' and 'Urkünftiges' ('the primevally human', 'the primevally Jewish', 'the primeval' and 'coming from primeval times'). Besides 'völkisch' ideologies, Buber was also influenced by primitivism, both from Nietzsche and from the Hebrew writer Micha Josef Berdyczewski, a Nietzschean who despised the Jewish prophets for having sapped the primitive vitality of Judaism and who considered Herod a specimen of the 'Übermensch' ('Superman').[16]

Despite all this, it would be wrong to lump Buber together with Lagarde, Langbehn and other spokesmen of cultural despair. He should be associated rather with the outstanding German intellectuals of his day who were attracted by romantic nationalism and organicism. The obvious comparison is with the Thomas Mann of *Betrachtungen eines Unpolitischen* (*Reflections of a Non-political Man*), especially since Buber, like Mann and many other German and Austrian intellectuals, enthusiastically supported the First World War. In December 1914 Buber told an audience of Berlin Zionists that by taking part in the War Jews would achieve mystical liberation, 'deepen their experience of community ('Gemeinschaftserlebnis') and out of it build their Judaism anew':[17] this is simply a Jewish variant of the 'ideas of 1914' which, as T. J. Reed has said, were 'the common coin of the majority of self-respecting intellectuals'.[18]

We should also remember that Buber's irrationalism served a very different purpose from the imperialism of a Lagarde. Buber wished to combat the widespread stereotype of the Jew as a purely rational being with no access to 'deeper' instinctive feelings of religious awe or intuitive patriotism. He wanted to show that Germans did not, as anti-Semites claimed, have a monopoly of irrationalism. The Bar Kochba shared this aim. One of their number, Robert Weltsch, led discussions on Fichte's *Reden an die deutsche Nation*, transposing Fichte's nationalism from a German to a Zionist context, and even declared in 1913 that every Jew must become a 'little Fichte'.[19]

Buber's compound of mysticism, 'völkisch' thought and primitivism therefore met with an enthusiastic response from the Bar Kochba. He addressed them three times in 1909 and 1910, and the third speech probably had Kafka in its audience. In this address, 'Die Erneuerung des Judentums', Buber described the principal traits of the Jewish character and exhorted his hearers to develop these traits and thus attain a 'positives Volksbewußtsein' ('positive communal consciousness').[20] Some of his hearers were electrified by his speech, others were left cold, and Kafka seems to have been among the latter, if this is the occasion he is referring to when he says of Buber, in a letter to Felice, 'ich habe ihn schon gehört, er macht auf mich einen öden Eindruck' ('I have already heard him speak, he makes a dreary impression on me') (BrF 252). But we must remember that his contact with Buber's ideas was indirect as well as direct, for they were a constant topic of conversation among his Zionist friends, and I think that his response to Buber's Zionism can be found in *In der Strafkolonie*, written in 1914.

This story turns on the contrast between the past and the present. The traveller from Europe, visiting a penal settlement which apparently belongs to another European power, finds it in a state of transition between an old and a new order. In the past, the colony was administered by the Old Commandant, a figure who was once soldier, judge, engineer and draughtsman, and who invented the punishment machine. Under his regime, punishments were carried out in the presence of the entire population of the colony, children included. They witnessed the twelve-hour ceremony with awe and with assurance that absolute justice was being enacted before their eyes: 'alle wußten: Jetzt geschieht Gerechtigkeit' (E 218). Now that the new Commandant has taken over, the punishment machine has only one devotee left, the officer, and since he can no longer obtain spare parts the machine is breaking down. Though the new Commandant has not prohibited the use of the machine, he and his throng of admiring ladies try to temper its severity by visiting the condemned man and feeding him with sweets (which he can't keep down, since his diet hitherto has consisted of rotten fish); but most of the new Commandant's attention is given to building extensions to the harbour.

The basic contrast is clear enough. On the one hand, the closely-knit society of the past, united by the focus of a ceremony which combined justice with religious awe; on the other, present-day society, in which religious practices are conceded a marginal place but no longer give meaning even to their adherents (the officer is not transfigured, merely mangled, by submitting himself to the machine), and in which a half-hearted and ineffectual humanitarianism accompanies an inhuman devotion to large-scale technological schemes. Kafka is setting 'Gemeinschaft' against 'Gesellschaft'. His 'Gemeinschaft', like Buber's, is dominated by religion. It is now commonplace to point out that the Old Commandant suggests Jehovah; that the message inscribed on the prisoner's body recalls the Ten Commandments by being termed a 'Gebot' ('commandment'); and that the squiggles and curlicues around it may be meant to suggest the detailed commentaries with which Talmudists had surrounded the Mosaic Law. Malcolm Pasley, who first drew attention to some of these hints, also points out how deeply Kafka is indebted to Nietzsche's critique of religion in *Zur Genealogie der Moral*. The central image comes from Nietzsche's description of the religious exploitation of suffering as 'Heils-Maschinerie' ('the machinery of salvation') and his account of cruelty as an integral part of religion, an occasion for public festivities, and an indispensable means of imprinting moral commands on the unreceptive memory of the human animal.[21] What Kafka is doing in *In der Strafkolonie*, then, is imagining what an organic community based on religion would be like. It would give meaning to an individual's life at the cost of extreme suffering. Yet despite its harshness, it might still be preferable to a society in which religious values have declined and nothing but an obsession with technology ('Hafenbauten, immer wieder Hafenbauten!' ['Harbour

construction, always more harbour construction!']; E 224) has taken
their place. But Kafka is not simply concerned with the general
antithesis of 'Gemeinschaft' and 'Gesellschaft'. The numerous allusions
to Jewish religious practices, and the setting in a sandy valley in a
'Kolonie' (the Jewish settlements in Palestine were called 'Kolonien'),
suggest that he is responding specifically to the proposals for recreating a
Jewish 'Gemeinschaft' which he had encountered in the Bar Kochba and
which stemmed mainly from the influence of Buber.

In der Strafkolonie, then, is Kafka's critical response to the social
programme of the Prague Zionists. He is at least equally critical of
modern society in the story, and this attitude is consistent with his
increasing certainty that Western society could not provide an adequate
home for the Jews. As I mentioned earlier, he felt that the 'Westjude' was
sick, an outsider, compelled to torment himself in a fruitless struggle to
adapt to his surroundings. Assimilation was not a feasible solution to the
Jewish question. The only cure for what Kafka called the 'Mangel jedes
festen jüdischen Bodens unter den Füßen' ('the lack of any firm Jewish
ground under one's feet'; Br 404) was immersion in a Jewish community. When advising Felice on her work in the Berlin home for Jewish
refugees, Kafka remarked that he would far prefer another kind of
asylum in which the Berlin Jews, Felice and himself among them, would
be looked after by ordinary Jews from Galicia (BrF 697). I have
discussed elsewhere the positive solution to the Jewish problem which
Kafka tentatively envisaged;[22] here I must concentrate on showing how
Kafka envisaged the problem itself, and my last illustration is the story
Ein Bericht für eine Akademie, written in April 1917. Criticism of the story
has largely concentrated on its more general and abstract themes, like
the concepts of 'Freiheit' ('freedom') and 'Ausweg' ('a way out') which
receive such emphasis. Many critics, most recently Gerhard Kurz, have
of course seen the ape's confinement in the cage as typifying the human
situation; Walter Sokel has placed the ape among Kafka's artist-figures
and argued that, unlike most of them, he does achieve a partially
successful compromise with his public; and Gerhard Neumann has
brilliantly analysed the story as a self-reflexive meditation on the
possibility of mimesis.[23] Very few have followed Max Brod in relating
the story to Kafka's (and his own) social context. As early as 1918 Brod
declared that the story was the most brilliant satire ever written on
Jewish assimilation. In 1952 this interpretation was independently
proposed by William C. Rubenstein, with the further suggestion that
Rotpeter's learning to drink schnaps symbolized Holy Communion and
hence his conversion to Christianity. Evelyn Torton Beck took up
Rubenstein's interpretation in her valuable book on Kafka and the
Yiddish theatre, and argued that the ape was modelled on the figure of

Berele, a converted Jew in one of the plays Kafka saw in the Café Savoy. [24] This is perhaps a not wholly plausible source, since Berele is forced into apostasy by the intolerance and brutality of the Hasidim, while Rotpeter is forcibly separated from his tribe by Hagenbeck's expedition; but I think the interpretation itself is correct, and needs to be worked out in detail. The story, moreover, was first published in *Der Jude*, a Zionist monthly edited by Buber, and one would expect it to have some relevance to its immediate context.

After his capture on the Gold Coast, the ape was first put in a cage too narrow for him to stand upright or sit down, and he squatted with his face to the packing-case which formed its fourth wall. This would seem to represent the position of the Jew in much of Europe before emancipation: confined to a ghetto and refusing to have any contact with the Gentile world outside. The ape's enforced contact with humanity is first with the captors who shoot him (implying that the Jew in Western society, in contrast to the 'Ostjuden', is lamed or disabled), then with the sailors who torment him. Similarly, many Jews in Eastern European communities had little contact with Gentiles except when they were the victims of attacks from anti-Semites. Rotpeter interprets their tricks — teaching him to smoke and drink schnaps, and occasionally burning his skin with a lighted pipe — as kindly attempts to instruct him for his own good. This betrays his ignorance of human behaviour, no doubt; but it also shows that, being dependent for his very existence on the goodwill of the sailors, he is obliged to put the most favourable interpretation on their actions. His situation allows him no independence of judgement. His very name reflects his helplessness: since he originally had no name, he had to be given one, and he finds it repulsive and inappropriate. One of the earliest stages in the emancipation of the German and Austrian Jews was legislation requiring them to assume family names instead of patronymics. Joseph II issued the first such edict in 1787. Attractive-sounding names such as Rosenthal, Goldstein or Demant had to be paid for; poor Jews were often given ridiculous or offensive names. Alfred Döblin, walking through the Warsaw ghetto in 1924, noted the following names seen above shops: 'Waiselfisch, Klopfherd, Blumenkranz, Brandwain, Farsztandig, Goldkopf, Gelbfisch, Gutbesztand'. [25] Kafka himself mentions in his travel diaries a Bohemian Jew named Puderbeutel (T 676).

When the ship reaches Hamburg, Rotpeter has to choose between the zoo and the music-hall and works feverishly to qualify himself for a theatrical career by attaining 'die Durchschnittsbildung eines Europäers' ('the average education of a European'; E 195). He becomes a celebrity. In his own opinion, he has become human. But of course the reason for his fame is that he is not human — he is an ape who has learnt to imitate a human being with remarkable faithfulness. Thanks to his efforts, he has been accepted in human society, but not as a member of human society, rather as an alien whose imitative skill makes him seem almost human. The greater his fame, the further he is from real membership of society. This, I suggest, is Kafka's portrayal of the situation of the Jew in Western society. The Jew can enter Western society only by acting the part of a Westerner. If he can act the part skilfully enough, he will be accepted, and he may imagine that his mimicry has been successful. But to the non-Jews around him it remains obvious that he is an actor, and they appreciate the act without being taken in by it. There is a Jewish figure of this type, Polledi, in Max Brod's first novel, *Schloß Nornepygge* (1908). Though he comes of a poor ghetto family, Polledi is accepted socially because he can adapt himself perfectly to any surroundings and because cultivated society welcomes him as a clown. In other words, people tolerate him as long as he amuses them. His talent for mimicry is so great that one of his most popular party tricks is to imitate Kainz and other actors — that is, to imitate imitators.[26]

For the reader, Rotpeter and Polledi must be disturbing and embarrassing figures in several obvious ways. Kafka and Brod seem to be drawing on a Jewish stereotype familiar among anti-Semites. The Jew is seen as lacking in 'depth'. He has no profound emotions, no imaginative resources, no traditional allegiances. He can slip into any disguise, simply because he himself is so shallow. What he does have is a ruthless determination to make his way in society by assimilating himself to any and every environment. Houston Stewart Chamberlain claims that the distinguishing feature of the Jew is an abnormally developed will, and cites the example of a Jewish scholar who, unable to make money in his profession, became a manufacturer of soap; when foreign competition put him out of business, he became a playwright and amassed a fortune. He owed his success not to any commercial or literary talent but to sheer force of will.[27] Wagner, in 'Das Judentum in der Musik', sketches a portrait of the educated Jew which would fit Rotpeter almost perfectly:

Der gebildete Jude hat sich die undenklichste Mühe gegeben, alle auffälligen Merkmale seiner niederen Glaubensgenossen von sich abzustreifen: in vielen Fällen hat er es selbst für zweckmäßig gehalten, durch die christliche Taufe auf die Verwischung aller Spuren seiner Abkunft hinzuwirken. Dieser Eifer hat den gebildeten Juden aber nie die erhofften Früchte gewinnen lassen wollen: er hat nur dazu geführt, ihn vollends zu vereinsamen, und ihn zum herzlosesten aller Menschen in einem Grade zu machen, daß wir selbst die frühere Sympathie für das tragische Geschick seines Stammes verlieren mußten. Für den Zusammenhang mit seinen ehemaligen Leidensgenossen, den er übermütig zerriß, blieb es ihm unmöglich, einen neuen Zusammenhang mit der Gesellschaft zu finden, zu welcher er sich aufschwang.[28]

The educated Jew has gone to the most unimaginable lengths to cast off all the conspicuous peculiarities distinguishing his lowly fellow Jews: in many cases he himself has thought it expedient to aim, through Christian baptism, at the obliteration of all traces of his origins. This zeal, however, has never permitted the educated Jew to grasp the fruits he hoped for; it has led only to his complete isolation, and to his being the most heartless of men, to such a degree that we ourselves inevitably lost our earlier sympathy for the tragic fate of his race. Having arrogantly destroyed his relationship with his previous companions in sorrow, he always found it impossible to create a new connection with that society to which he pretended.

Rotpeter has made the tremendous exertions that Wagner describes, in order to lose his ape-like characteristics. And his attitude to other apes is just as callous as the attitude to other Jews which Wagner ascribes to the assimilant. He refers with hostility to the trained 'Affentier' Peter who has recently 'krepiert' (significant choice of word!) in order to stress the gulf that supposedly separates him from Peter. He is almost as callous towards the half-trained female chimpanzee with whom he spends his nights. During the day he cannot stand the sight of her, obviously because she reminds him of what he really is. Rotpeter describes other animals as being 'trained', but speaks of himself as having studied ('ich lernte', E 194) and calls his instructors teachers rather than trainers.

To understand this aspect of Rotpeter's character, one must realize that a Jew intent on assimilation to Western society was liable to be constantly embarrassed by encountering Jews who were less assimilated than himself. This explains the over-reaction of Kafka's father when Kafka brought Jizchok Löwy back to the family flat: 'Wer sich mit Hunden zu Bett legt, steht mit Wanzen auf' ('Whoever goes to bed with dogs, gets up with fleas'; T 139, cf. H 171). Kafka senior felt that he had worked his way up from poverty so that his son should *not* be associated with people like Löwy. Kafka junior, however, came to feel that assimilation was not possible, that the 'Westjude' could only escape from anti-Semitic stereotypes by giving up the attempt at assimilation altogether and helping to create a completely Jewish society. He must have reached this conclusion by 1917 and derived from it enough detachment to make possible his bitterly satirical portrait of the 'Westjude' in *Ein Bericht*. It should be noted that Kafka was not forced to this conclusion by any anti-Semitic persecution. The only occasion on which he encountered anti-Semitism directed against him personally was when staying in a hotel in Merano in May 1920. The Munich Soviet, most of whose leaders were Jews — Gustav Landauer, Ernst Toller, Eugen Leviné — had just been brutally suppressed, and when the old ladies and retired officers in the hotel, all of them 'deutsch-christlich' in Kafka's phrase (Br 270), learnt that their fellow-guest was not only a vegetarian but Jewish, they reacted frostily from a fear that he might be tarred with the revolutionary brush.[29] Later in 1920 Kafka witnessed the anti-Semitic riots in Prague. They lasted for three days, during which a mob stormed the Jüdisches Rathaus and Hebrew parchments were burnt in the street outside the Alt-Neu Synagogue. Though Kafka was naturally horrified by this violence, it did not harm him personally. Like Herzl, who had only twice in his life had 'Hep hep' (the standard anti-Semitic catcall, inherited from the Crusaders' slogan 'Hierysolem est perdita') shouted at him,[30] Kafka became a Zionist not because he himself was persecuted but because reflection on the situation of the European Jews persuaded him that assimilation was impossible, and that attempts to assimilate could only degrade the Jew.

There is no avoiding the sheer offensiveness of the central image of *Ein Bericht* — the assimilated Jew being represented by the ape who tries to become a man. The image is meant to shock, and there is no point in trying to soften its effect. But we do need to see it in perspective, and to remember it is not only Jews who have had difficulties in assimilating to an alien society and who have felt shame at their own efforts and embarrassment at the inferior success of others. Any social or national group whose members are trying, at different speeds and with different degrees of success, to adopt the manners and customs of another group, will often experience just this shame and embarrassment. But though this is far from being a peculiarly Jewish problem, it is one that Jewish authors have written about very memorably. *Ein Bericht* belongs (as does another story dating from 1917, *Schakale und Araber*) (*Jackals and Arabs*) to a group of works by Jewish writers who use animal imagery, often degrading in its implications, to express their ambivalent feelings about the Jewish people. One example is familiar, Heine's 'Prinzessin Sabbat', which tells of a prince named Israel who has been transformed into a dog. During the week he leads an animal existence in filth and squalor; only on the Sabbath is he temporarily restored to human shape:

> Hund mit hündischen Gedanken,
> Kötert er die ganze Woche
> Durch des Lebens Kot und Kehricht,
> Gassenbuben zum Gespötte.

> Aber jeden Freitag Abend,
> In der Dämmrungstunde, plötzlich
> Weicht der Zauber, und der Hund
> Wird aufs neu' ein menschlich Wesen.

> Mensch mit menschlichen Gefühlen,
> Mit erhobnem Haupt und Herzen,
> Festlich, reinlich schier gekleidet,
> Tritt er in des Vaters Halle.[31]

Dog with the thoughts of a dog, all week he slinks cowering
through the garbage and filth of life, mocked at by street urchins.

Yet every Friday evening, in the hour of twilight, suddenly
the spell is loosed, and the dog becomes once more a human creature.

Man, with human feelings, with uplifted head and heart, festively,
almost cleanly dressed, he walks into his father's hall.

It is worth drawing attention to the contrast Heine makes between the
dog's canine thoughts and his human feelings. During the week, the Jew
has to employ his intellect in the struggle to stay alive. The determination and rationality for which H. S. Chamberlain later censured the Jews
are forced on him by his circumstances. But he does have feelings,
though it is only on the Sabbath that he can indulge them, and his
feelings make him truly human. Thus Heine is anticipating by some
sixty years the Zionists' polemic against the stereotype of the rational
Jew without emotional depth. It is also worth mentioning the bitter little
phrase 'reinlich schier gekleidet', dressed almost cleanly: Heine is
hinting that even on the Sabbath the Jew cannot be completely clean,
and thus revealing his own ambivalence towards his fellow Jews. As
S. S. Prawer has recently said, 'It is a portrait from the outside, an
unassimilated Jew partially seen by a Europeanized observer'.[32] Heine's
dog is an image almost as complex in its implications as Kafka's ape.

My second example is from a work that was inspired by 'Prinzessin
Sabbat' but will be less familiar to Germanists: the allegorical novel *Di
Kliatsche* by the classic Yiddish writer Mendele Moykher Sforim.[33] This
is a great satiric work with two targets: the misery in which the Jews in
the Russian Pale of Settlement are kept by their oppressors, and the
bookish ineffectuality of the *maskilim* (adherents of the Jewish Enlightenment) who try to improve their condition through educational
projects instead of social reform. The protagonist, Ishrulik, is a clever
boy who resolves to study and attend university and thus escape from
the servitude of his fellow-Jews. The chapter in which he makes this
resolution is headed 'Ishrulik vil veren a mentsh', i.e. 'Ishrulik wants to
become a human being', with a double-edged irony: Mendele means
that the misery of the Jews is unworthy of human beings, but Ishrulik
means that his fellow-Jews are sub-human and that he must make his
way in Gentile society if he is to enter humanity. He is a callous 'Streber'
('climber') without concern for his fellow-Jews. He is, however, as
befits an educated man, a member of the Society for the Prevention of
Cruelty to Animals, so when he comes upon some boys tormenting a
skinny, broken-down mare he feels obliged to step in. His intervention,
characteristically, is ineffectual, and he has to wait until the boys leave
off tormenting the mare of their own accord. Left alone with Ishrulik,

the mare speaks to him, citing the precedent of Balaam's ass to reduce his astonishment, and reveals that it is a Prince who has been transformed into a mare by sorcery. Since the mare has wandered through the world, acquiring the sobriquet *di eivige kliatshe*, and suffering incessant exploitation and ill-treatment at the hands of the righteous. In giving this satiric account of Jewish life in the Diaspora, Mendele is not trying to paint a flattering picture of the Jews, any more than Heine or Kafka; his word *kliatsche*, 'mare', also means any broken-down, wretched old horse; 'nag' or 'Gaul' would be possible equivalents. But he shows clearly that if the Jews are wretched, it is their Gentile persecutors who have made them so.

The tradition of the Jewish animal fable still survives. A recent and brilliant example is 'The Evolution of the Jews', a story narrated in the first person by a Yiddish-speaking giraffe, in Clive Sinclair's *Hearts of Gold* (1979). Since other stories by Sinclair allude explicitly to Kafka, the latter's animal stories may have helped to inspire 'The Evolution of the Jews'. Further back in the tradition, the satires by Heine and Mendele may have had some indirect influence on *Ein Bericht für eine Akademie*, though some of Hoffmann's tales of talking animals, especially the *Schreiben Milos, eines gebildeten Affen, an seine Freundin Pipi, in Nord-Amerika* (*Writings of Milo, an educated ape, to his friend Pipi in North America*), are probably more direct sources of inspiration. Still, Kafka certainly knew Heine's poetry, though he did not greatly care for it (BrF 640), and *Di Kliatsche* was known to him at second hand from Pinès's *Histoire de la littérature judéo-allemande*, which he read in January 1912 (T 242) and which contains a twenty-page summary of the story.[34] But whether these works helped to influence *Ein Bericht* is less important than the fact that they, along with Sinclair's later story, are analogues to Kafka's tale. These four works, by Heine, Mendele, Kafka and Sinclair, all present a more or less unflattering picture of the Jew as animal, though with obvious differences in the direction of the satire: Mendele's mare and Heine's dog represent the ghetto Jew, while Kafka's ape stands for the supposedly assimilated Jew who is the same type as Mendele's Ishrulik. All express their authors' ambivalent feelings about the Jews, and are at the same time masterpieces of satire. The attitude implied in *Ein Bericht* is finally too complex to be taken as a straightforward expression of Zionist or anti-Zionist feelings. It serves to remind us that Kafka's undoubted sympathy with Zionism went along with a critical, independent, and individual attitude to that cause.

NOTES

1 Brod, *Franz Kafkas Glauben und Lehre*, in *Über Franz Kafka* (Frankfurt/M, 1966), p. 270; Weltsch, *Religion und Humor im Leben und Werk Franz Kafkas*

(Berlin–Grunewald, 1957), p. 38; Klara P. Carmely, *Das Identitätsproblem jüdischer Autoren im deutschen Sprachraum* (Königstein, 1981), pp. 162–66.

[2] See Brod, *Streitbares Leben* (Munich, 1960), p. 353. For more information about the Bar Kochba, see Hartmut Binder, 'Franz Kafka und die Wochenschrift *Selbstwehr'*, *DVLG*, 41 (1967), 283–304, and *Kafka-Handbuch*, ed. Hartmut Binder, 2 vols (Stuttgart, 1979), I, 370 ff.

[3] Brod, *Franz Kafka: Eine Biographie*, in *Über Franz Kafka*, p. 100.

[4] Helen Milfull, 'Franz Kafka — The Jewish Context', *Yearbook of the Leo Baeck Institute*, 23 (1978), 227–38. This is a useful introduction to the topic. Far the best and most thorough study of Kafka and Judaism is Anne Oppenheimer, 'Franz Kafka's Relation to Judaism' (D.Phil. thesis, Oxford, 1977).

[5] See 'Ein Beispiel produktiver Lektüreverarbeitung (Max Brods *Arnold Beer* und *Das Urteil*)', in *Kafka-Handbuch*, II, 278 ff.

[6] For Mendelssohn's disapproval of Yiddish, see Sander L. Gilman, '"Ebrew and Jew": Moses Mendelssohn and the Sense of Jewish Identity', in *Humanität und Dialog: Lessing und Mendelssohn in neuer Sicht*, ed. Ehrhard Bahr, Edward P. Harris and Laurence G. Lyon (Detroit and Munich, 1982), pp. 67–82; for Herzl's, see 'Der Judenstaat', in Theodor Herzl, *Zionistische Schriften*, ed. Leon Kellner (Berlin, 1920), p. 80.

[7] *Von Berlin nach Jerusalem* (Frankfurt/M, 1977), p. 60.

[8] Quoted in Brod, *Über Franz Kafka*, p. 147.

[9] Kohn, *Living in a World Revolution* (New York, 1964), p. 37. Cf. Kafka, 'Brief an den Vater', especially H 197 ff., and Brod, *Streitbares Leben*, pp. 347–48.

[10] See especially his comments on the First Zionist Congress, 'Judenstaat und Judennot', in Achad Haam [*sic*], *Am Scheidewege: Gesammelte Aufsätze*, tr. Israel Friedländer and Harry Torczyner, 4 vols (Berlin, 1923), II, 45–67.

[11] Quoted in Binder, 'Franz Kafka und die Wochenschrift *Selbstwehr*', p. 283.

[12] Max Nordau, *Zionistische Schriften*, 2. vermehrte Auflage (Berlin, 1923), p. 48. See further Shlomo Avineri, *The Making of Modern Zionism* (London, 1981).

[13] Adolf Böhm, 'Wandlungen im Zionismus', *Vom Judentum: Ein Sammelbuch* (Leipzig, 1913), p. 143.

[14] Buber, *Schriften zum Chassidismus* (Munich, 1963), p. 964.

[15] 'Die Schaffenden, das Volk und die Bewegung' (1902), in Martin Buber, *Die Jüdische Bewegung*, 2 vols (Berlin, 1920), I, 68–69. See George L. Mosse, *Germans and Jews* (New York, 1970), p. 85. On the origins of this vocabulary, see Fritz Stern, *The Politics of Cultural Despair* (Berkeley, 1961).

[16] On the sources of Buber's primitivism, see Hans Kohn, *Martin Buber: Sein Werk und seine Zeit* (Cologne, 1961), pp. 21, 36.

[17] Quoted in David Biale, *Gershom Scholem: Kabbalah and Counter-History* (Cambridge, Mass., 1979), p. 59.

[18] Reed, *Thomas Mann: The Uses of Tradition* (Oxford, 1974), p. 182.

[19] See Kohn, *Buber*, p. 316; Mosse, p. 89.

[20] Buber, *Der Jude und sein Judentum* (Cologne, 1963), p. 43.

[21] See Nietzsche, *Werke*, 3 vols (Munich, 1966), II, 809; Malcolm Pasley, 'Introduction', in Franz Kafka, *Der Heizer, In der Strafkolonie, Der Bau* (Cambridge, 1966).

[22] See my 'Kafka's Zürau Aphorisms', *Oxford German Studies*, 14 (1983), 73–91.

[23] See Sokel, *Franz Kafka — Tragik und Ironie* (Munich, 1964), pp. 330–55; Neumann, '*Ein Bericht für eine Akademie*: Erwägungen zum Mimesis-Charakter Kafkascher Texte', *DVLG*, 49 (1975), 166–83; Kurz, *Traum-Schrecken* (Stuttgart, 1980), pp. 138 ff. The most recent discussion is by Lawrence O. Frye, 'Word Play: Irony's way to Freedom in Kafka's *Ein Bericht für eine Akademie*', *DVLG*, 55 (1981), 457–75.

[24] Brod's interpretation is quoted by Binder, 'Franz Kafka und die Wochenschrift Selbstwehr', pp. 301–02. See also Rubenstein, 'Franz Kafka's "A Report to an Academy"', MLQ, 13 (1952), 372–76, reprinted in Franz Kafka Today, ed. Angel Flores and Homer Swander (Madison, Wis., 1958), pp. 55–60; Beck, Kafka and the Yiddish Theatre (Madison, Wis., 1971), pp. 181 ff.

[25] Döblin, Reise in Polen (Olten, 1968), p. 74. On the compulsory adoption of surnames, see Benzion C. Kaganoff, A Dictionary of Jewish Names and their History (London, 1978), pp. 20 ff.

[26] Brod, Schloß Nornepygge (Leipzig, 1918), p. 139. See also the chapter 'Assimilation und Unsicherheit. Der Graeculus und der Clown' in Claudio Magris, Weit von wo: Verlorene Welt des Ostjudentums, tr. Jutta Prasse (Vienna, 1974), pp. 75 ff.

[27] Chamberlain, Die Grundlagen des Neunzehnten Jahrhunderts, 2 vols (Munich, 1899), I, 241, 244.

[28] 'Das Judentum in der Musik' (1850), in Richard Wagner, Sämtliche Schriften und Dichtungen, Volksausgabe, 12 vols (Leipzig, n.d.), V, 73–74.

[29] On anti-Semitism in Kafka's Prague, see Christoph Stölzl, Kafkas böses Böhmen: Zur Sozialgeschichte eines Prager Juden (Munich, 1975), and as a corrective to Stölzl's slightly one-sided presentation, Gary B. Cohen, 'Jews in German Society: Prague, 1860–1914', Central European History, 10 (1977), 28–54.

[30] See Herzl, Tagebücher 1895–1905, 3 vols (Berlin, 1922–23), I, 6.

[31] Heine, Sämtliche Werke, ed. Ernst Elster, 7 vols (Leipzig, 1893), I, 433.

[32] Prawer, Heine's Jewish Comedy (Oxford, 1983), p. 555. For the most thorough recent discussion, see Gerhard Sauder, 'Blasphemisch-religiöse Körperwelt: Heinrich Heines Hebräische Melodien', in Heinrich Heine: Artistik und Engagement, ed. Wolfgang Kuttenkeuler (Stuttgart, 1977), pp. 118–43.

[33] There is an English translation in Great Works of Jewish Fantasy, ed. and tr. Joachim Neugroschel (London, 1976). I am very grateful to Dovid Katz for giving me a copy of the Yiddish text of Di Kliatsche.

[34] M. Pinès, Histoire de la littérature judéo-allemande (Paris, 1910). This was the only account of the subject available to Kafka. Unfortunately it is full of errors, and aroused outrage when translated into Yiddish in the 1920s. For a reliable account of Mendele's life and works, see Charles Madison, Yiddish Literature: Its Scope and Major Writers (New York, 1971).

Gerhard Neumann

DER WANDERER UND DER VERSCHOLLENE:

ZUM PROBLEM DER IDENTITÄT IN GOETHES *WILHELM MEISTER* UND IN KAFKAS *AMERIKA*-ROMAN

ABSTRACT

Goethe's *Wilhelm Meister* and Kafka's *America* stand respectively at the beginning and end of a new concept of subjectivity and personal development which owes its being to the French Revolution and which finds its expression in literature. During Goethe's time the problem, central to the Bildungsroman, of the subject's capability of being narrated is placed within the new social, cultural and psychological context. Wilhelm Meister's theatrical activities, mediating between the game of art and that of life, the interplay between natural organic growth and ordered contractual socialization, the changing role of the family, the new place given to love in the social context and the legitimacy offered by the various guiding codes and models which the individual has to choose from — all these are seen to play a crucial role in Wilhelm's development during his journey through life. The stages of Goethe's struggle with this complex of interrelated issues is traced through the Wilhelm Meister novels (*Lehrjahre*, 1795), as well as in the *Conversations of German Emigrants* (1795–97) and *Elective Affinities* (1809). The four-fold factors of aesthetic role-playing, family, love, and private and socially ratified models for organizing behaviour and knowledge are explored in *Wilhelm Meister*, to the point where the Society of the Tower supersedes all other legitimizing agents. Kafka's *America* is investigated within the same framework. Karl Rossmann is shown largely to be restricted in the growth of his personality by the very things which assist Goethe's hero to fulfilment. Role-playing, the recurrence of oppressive father figures, sexual encounters and society (the Theatre of Oklahoma) all fail to help him to a new identity. Seen within the framework of the Western anagnorisis-ritual, Wilhelm is able to arrive at an answer to the question of who he is, whereas Kafka's hero eventually abandons identity and name, his very being 'swallowed up by the vastness of the American Continent'.

I

Der Gang durch die Welt als Gang zu sich selbst; das reflektierende, handelnde, beobachtende oder träumende Ich als Reisender, als

Spaziergänger, als Wanderer, als Flaneur und als Exilierter — es sind historisch begründbare Formen der Selbsterfahrung, die Selbst-*Sein* als Selbst-*Werden* zu bestimmen suchen, als Bewegung des Körpers durch die Landschaft, als Bewegung der Phantasie im Weltraum der Seele. Nirgends sind diese Wandlungen deutlicher wahrnehmbar als in jenen Texten, die den Versuch machen, ein 'Leben zu erzählen', den deutschen 'Bildungsromanen', die 'Modell' und 'Biographie' zugleich sind, gestalteten Lebenssinn im doppelten Spiel von Phantasie und Körper, von schöpferischer Einbildungskraft und Handlungszwang zu bewähren suchen.

Das Konfliktfeld von innerer und äußerer Freiheit als Raum, in dem 'Subjektivität' entspringt — dies ist die Form, mit der die Französische Revolution das neue Bewußtsein des zu sich selbst erwachenden 'Bürgers' ausstattet. Wenn demnach die Vorstellung von 'Subjektivität' mit der Französischen Revolution eine neue Struktur erhielt, so bleibt gleichzeitig bedeutsam, daß sich diese Wandlung zuerst in der Literatur bewahrheitete, differenzierte und präzise spiegelte; ferner aber, daß im Bereich der deutschen Literatur Goethes Romane wohl den Anfang dieses Prozesses bezeichnen, Kafkas *Verschollener* eine Art von aporetischer Endvision dieses Vorgangs in Szene setzt.

Einige Worte sind nötig zum sozialgeschichtlichen Hintergrund dieses Anfangs: Goethes erste Niederschriften zum *Wilhelm Meister* von 1777 stehen im Vorfeld der Französischen Revolution und lassen sich als aus diesem Vorfeld entbunden lesen. Denn sie bezeugen ein deutliches Bewußtsein jener Konfliktlage, die die neue Rede vom Ich aus sich entläßt. Diese Lage läßt sich von vier Seiten her beleuchten.

Zum einen geht es um das Problem der 'Erzählbarkeit von Leben' als selbstbewußter Geschichte eines Subjekts. Diese Frage hat ihrerseits drei Aspekte. Sie ist aus einer kritischen *sozialen* Situation geboren, dem Aufeinanderprallen divergierender politischer und ökonomischer Interessenlagen von Bourgeoisie und Adel; sie gestaltet sich zugleich als eine kritische *kulturgeschichtliche* Situation, indem sie Besitz und Bildung, Ökonomie und Kunst als bestimmende soziale Kräfte artikuliert; sie offenbart sich letztlich als eine kritische *psychische* Erfahrung, die aus den Schwierigkeiten einer Vermittlung von Augenblick und Lebensganzem, von Spontaneität der Wünsche und Ordnung der Vernunft erwächst.

Alle drei Aspekte dieser Krise verdichten sich in der in allen Disziplinen der Lebenserfahrung — der Naturwissenschaft, der Kunst, der Ökonomie[1] — aufbrechenden Frage, ob es möglich ist, Zeichenordnungen zu begründen, die Realisationsfelder von Identität in diesem neuen, bisher unerfahrenen sozialen Spannungsbereich eröffnen.

Die von Goethe versuchte Antwort auf diese Frage ist die Gestaltung von Wilhelm Meisters Lebensgeschichte als Theater-Roman. Die

Zeichenwelt des Theaters erscheint als jene Ordnung, in der Rollenspiel als repräsentatives soziales Spiel der Identifikation begriffen werden kann, die Institution des Theaters als Vermittlungsraum von Kunst-Spiel und Lebens-Spiel erscheint. Meisters Wunsch, Begründer eines deutschen National-Theaters zu werden, bezeugt diese utopische Konvergenz von privater und öffentlicher Identität in der nationalen Vorstellung der 'Repräsentation' auf das eindringlichste.

Ein zweiter Aspekt jener Konfliktlage, aus der Goethes Romankonzept sich zu entwickeln beginnt, ist das Bewußtsein von der Entstehung zweier konkurrierender Modelle menschlicher Realisation. Diese sind durch Rousseaus Erwägungen zur Ermöglichung menschlicher Identität im Gegenspiel von Natur und Kultur begründet: auf der einen Seite als Regelung der Identität aus dem Ursprung, der 'natürlichen' Zeugung (*generatio*) im Zeichen des Blutes und seiner identifikatorischen Kraft; auf der andern Seite als Ableitung der Identität aus Regeln der Kommunikation, dem auf das Kulturgesetz gegründeten 'contrat social' (*translatio*) im Zeichen der Schrift. Organisches Wachstum und Gesellschaftsvertrag, paradiesische Natur und Bund der Vernunft erscheinen so als Ordnungen, in deren Gegenspiel sich menschliche Selbsterfahrung bildet.

Ein dritter Aspekt, von dem her sich Goethes Bildungsroman und seine Problemstellung begreifen läßt, ist die Umwertung der Funktion der Familie im gesellschaftlichen Rahmen, dasjenige, was man gelegentlich einen 'Paradigmenwechsel' genannt hat: daß nämlich die Familie sich aus einer 'Produktionseinheit' (wie noch im siebzehnten Jahrhundert) in ein 'Gefühlszentrum' sozialer Erfahrung (im achtzehnten und neunzehnten Jahrhundert) umzuwandeln beginnt, aus der ökonomisch orientierten Großfamilie die bürgerliche Kleinfamilie sich entwickelt. Hieraus erwächst die so zuvor nicht gestellte Frage, ob die neue Familie mit ihrer Dreiecksstruktur den Rahmen einer Selbstfindung abzugeben vermag, die aus der Intimität eines Affektzentrums in die Öffentlichkeit ökonomischer Wert- und Zielsetzungen hinüberwechselt. Eigentlich ist es das Problem der 'Sozialisierbarkeit von Liebe', das mit dem Bewußtsein des Konflikts von Intimität und Öffentlichkeit sich zum ersten Mal stellt und gravierend für die Selbstwerdung des Subjekts sich auszuwirken beginnt, als glückende oder mißlingende Einzeichnung der Wünsche des Einzelnen in das Spiel der Gesellschaft. Ich sage bewußt 'Einzeichnung', denn es handelt sich in diesem historischen Augenblick wohl tatsächlich um ein Problem der Zeichen und ihrer Ordnungen, die auf eine Neubestimmung des Verhältnisses von Körper und Zeichen, von Bewegung durch die Welt und Bewegung durch die Phantasie drängen, und zwar in einem neu organisierten Wertfeld der Gesellschaft: als Vermittlung der 'Liebe' an Ökonomie, Ästhetik und Politik.

Die Frage, der dieses neu entstandene Subjekt nicht mehr auszuweichen vermag, lautet denn auch: Welches Spiel muß gespielt werden, damit diese Vermittlung gelingt? Goethes *Wilhelm Meister* erzählt eine Geschichte, die die Suche nach den Leseregeln dieser Zeichen, die Suche nach den Spielregeln dieses Spiels zum Gegenstand hat. Dabei kristallisieren sich zwei 'Schaltstellen' heraus, in denen die Vermittlung der 'Liebe' an ästhetische, ökonomische und politische Ordnungen der Öffentlichkeit vonstatten gehen könnte, der Schauspielerberuf auf der einen Seite, die Turmgesellschaft auf der anderen. Beide werden von Goethe als Instanzen sozialer Legitimation des Subjekts und seiner Wünsche ins Spiel gebracht; die Bühne als Ort der Inszenierung unbedingter Leidenschaft, die Stiftung der Ehe als deren Überführung in den Sozialvertrag.

Damit ist aber zugleich *der vierte Aspekt* in den Blick gerückt, der das 'Erzählen einer Lebensgeschichte' in der eben entstehenden bürgerlichen Welt zwiespältig macht. Es ist die mit der prätendierten Autonomie des Subjekts gesetzte Verunsicherung des Ordnungsrahmens, innerhalb dessen das Spiel solcher Zeichen noch garantiert werden könnte; denn in der Welt, die sich jetzt auftut, machen verschiedene einander ebenbürtige 'Ordnungs'-Konzepte sich den Rang streitig: Mythos, Kunst, Geschichte, Ökonomie, Medizin und Rechtsordnung erscheinen nicht mehr als integrierte oder gar integrierende Instanzen *eines* umfassenden Weltbildes, sondern zunehmend disfunktional.[2] Die Aufgabe, ihnen legitimierende Kraft zu geben, wird allein dem Subjekt und seiner freien Entscheidung für *eine* dieser Ordnungen zugemutet.

Alle vier genannten Aspekte der Konstitution von Subjektivität und ihrer gleichzeitigen Gefährdung spielen in Goethes Roman-Konzept eine wichtige Rolle:[3] und zwar als Elemente der Selbstverwirklichung des *männlichen* Helden — denn um diesen geht es, nicht um die Ermöglichung einer *weiblichen* Lebensgeschichte.[4]

Es ist *zunächst* das Thema des Theaters mit seinen Begleitvorstellungen von Rolle, Schauspieler und Spiel-Raum, das in Wilhelms Entscheidung für die Schauspieler-Laufbahn zentrale Bedeutung für seine Ich-Suche erhält.

Es ist *sodann* das Thema von Natur und Kultur als zwei verschiedenen Verwirklichungsfeldern menschlicher Beziehungen, das sich in Goethes Roman auf das Problem der Vaterschaft konzentriert: als Zeugung auf der einen, als Adoption auf der andern Seite, namentlich im Spiel der Verhältnisse zwischen Wilhelm und Felix vergegenwärtigt. Der Roman zeichnet in seinen verschiedenen Stufen einen Prozeß nach, der von der Organisation menschlicher Beziehungen durch Bindungen des Blutes zu solchen des Sozialvertrags fortschreitet, das erste im zweiten 'aufhebt' und so Liebe als Form sozialer Ordnung zu etablieren sucht.[5]

Es ist *ferner* das Problem der Verwandlung von Familienempfindung in soziale Zeichen, von Liebe in gesellschaftliche Verhältnisse, das sich im Roman unter dem wechselnden Aspekt von Wilhelms Beziehungen zu Frauen darstellt, seinem Weg aus der Familie (dem Blick der Großmutter in der ersten, der Mutter in der zweiten Fassung der *Lehrjahre*) über die Geliebte zur eigenen Familiengründung.

Es ist *schließlich* das Problem der Legitimation solcher Zeichen, das im Roman als Frage nach mythischen Modellen aufgeworfen wird, die nachgespielt werden und damit identifikatorischen Wert erhalten könnten: gewissermaßen 'privaten' Modellen auf der einen Seite, die aus der Familienrede erwachsen; 'öffentlichen' oder 'halböffentlichen' Modellen auf der andern Seite, die durch staatliche oder halbstaatliche ('geheime') Institutionen zur Verfügung gestellt werden. Modelle der ersten Art liefert namentlich die Bibel, in der Stimme der Frau lebendig, die dem Kind in der Familie die Figuren und Geschichten des Alten Testaments zuspricht und dieses zum Nach-Dichtenden, Nach-Spielenden macht. Die Sozialisation des kleinen Wilhelm in der Familie erfolgt durch das von der Großmutter ihm zugeeignete Puppenspiel, aus dem Blick der mütterlichen Frau, die ihm die Elemente seines Lebensspiels schenkt, geboren; verwandelt dann im selbstverantworteten Nachspielen von Tassos *Befreitem Jerusalem*, der Liebesbegegnung von Tankred und Chlorinde (Zwölfter Gesang).

Modelle der zweiten Art liefert der europäische Kulturraum im weiteren Sinne; sie betreffen die Sozialisation des Kindes außerhalb der Familie und werden durch jene pädagogischen Ordnungen repräsentiert, die Disziplin- und Gesetzcharakter haben und Figurationen der überlieferten Religionen darstellen; vertreten von der pädagogischen Provinz, den Archiven der Turmgesellschaft, der in der Schrift und ihrer Niederlegung bezeugten Welt des Mannes, jener nicht blutsverwandten 'Oheime' zumal, die Gegenfiguren zur mütterlichen Welt der Stimme sind, nicht Poesie mehr als Organ der Selbstwerdung des Kindes, sondern soziale Verantwortung, Beruf und Disziplin dem werdenden Bürger eröffnend.

Die Schwierigkeiten, die verschiedenen Einfluß-Sphären bei der Entstehung des 'modernen Subjekts' in Goethes Wilhelm Meister-Roman zu beobachten, mögen darin begründet sein, daß Goethe sich der neuen, durch die politischen Umwälzungen sichtbar und fühlbar werdenden Wandlungen in verschiedenen, stockenden und wieder auflebenden Romanansätzen näherte — nicht ohne Brüche und Widersprüche im Vorgang der Gestaltung.

Erst ein Blick auf den Gesamtkomplex der Wilhelm Meister-Romane und ihres Umfeldes macht deutlich, in wie hohem Maße diese ein Dokument der Schwierigkeiten sind, die Goethe mit der 'Darstellung der Lebensgeschichte eines modernen Subjekts' hatte, mit der Frage, wie dieses sich zwischen der Selbstdefinition durch Sexualität (repräsentiert durch 'Marianne' und ihre Nachfolgerinnen) und der Selbstdefinition durch Besitz (repräsentiert durch 'Werner' und seine Geistesverwandten in der Welt der Schauspieler) zu bewähren vermag, welche Rolle die Familie, die Gesellschaft und die vermittelnden Instanzen der Kunst und des Theaters dabei spielen.

Goethes Kampf um die Darstellung dieser Frage im Kontext sozialer Zeichen und ihrer möglichen kulturellen Legitimation spielt sich nicht nur in den drei *Meister*-Romanen ab, sondern, parallel dazu, auch in den Konzeptionen der *Unterhaltungen deutscher Ausgewanderten* und der *Wahlverwandtschaften*.

Die Stationen dieses Prozesses möchte ich wenigstens andeuten.

1777 beginnt Goethe mit der Niederschrift der *Theatralischen Sendung*; es ist der Versuch, die Eigentümlichkeit der schöpferischen Kraft des Subjekts zum Kern der Identität zu machen, die soziale Selbstzeugung des Subjekts aus der Phantasie, aus der ästhetischen Welt des Schauspielers zu entbinden. Diesen Versuch bricht Goethe, wohl aus der Einsicht in seine Aussichtslosigkeit, ab.

Ein zweiter Ansatz, die Geburt des neuen Subjekts modellhaft nachzuspielen, erfolgt, unter dem Eindruck der Französischen Revolution und in Anpassung an Schillers Kulturkonzept,[6] 1795 in den *Unterhaltungen deutscher Ausgewanderten*. Der politische Konflikt gebiert aus sich jene Krise, in der die Zeichenordnung der Liebe und die Welt der ökonomischen Zeichen aufeinanderprallen: Öffentlichkeit und Intimität als unversöhnliche, das Subjekt in seiner Identität bedrohende Wirklichkeiten.

Der in den Jahren 1794–96 niedergeschriebene Neuansatz des Romans (*Wilhelm Meisters Lehrjahre*) ist nur aus der in den *Unterhaltungen deutscher Ausgewanderten* parallel erprobten apolitischen Konstitution des Subjekts und dessen halb resignativer, halb poetischer Bewahrheitung zu begreifen: als nunmehr romanhaft konzipierte Konfrontation von ökonomischer und ästhetischer Zeichenwelt und als das letztliche Versagen des 'ästhetischen' Vermittlungsmodells, das sich in der Abwendung Wilhelms vom Schauspielerberuf bezeugt.

Ein vierter Ansatz, dem ungelösten Problem beizukommen, wird in den *Wahlverwandtschaften* von 1809 sichtbar, die ursprünglich als Novelle dem Wilhelm Meister-Komplex zugeordnet werden sollten. Est ist die am weitesten getriebene tragische Gegenprobe zu dem versöhnlichen Konzept der Wilhelm Meister-Geschichte, die nun nicht mehr von seiten der Politik, sondern von seiten der Naturwissenschaft gestellte Frage, ob es Zeichen geben könne, die zwischen Natur und Kultur vermitteln; ob Sprachzeichen noch die Kraft aufzubringen vermöchten, die Asozialität der Liebe zu heilen.

In der ersten Fassung der *Wanderjahre* von 1821[7] erfolgt dann die utopische Bewältigung des Zeichenproblems aus halböffentlicher, dem Status der Geheimgesellschaft verdankter sozial-ethischer Verantwortung, repräsentiert im Archiv der Turmgesellschaft, das die Schrift des Lebens enthält und durch sie in alle Handlungskreise sanft hineinwirkt; repräsentiert dann aber durch die ethische Welt des Arztes, in die Wilhelm sein Subjekt und dessen Wünsche entsagend einbettet.

Es ist dabei gattungsgeschichtlich wie kulturhistorisch nicht unwichtig, daß Goethe die Frage möglicher Identifikation des Subjekts von zwei Seiten her beleuchtet: als Vermittlung von *Augenblick* und *Lebensganzem*, von Moment und Folge im immer wieder umgestalteten *Roman*korpus; als minutiös herauspräparierte *Krise des Subjekts* in der *novellistischen* Gestaltung, als Augenblick der 'Geschichte' (Politik), der mit dem Augenblick der 'Liebe' in kaum versöhnbarer Weise kollidiert.[8]

Goethes ständige 'Umwälzung' des Problems eines 'erzählbaren Ich' verdeutlicht, vielleicht stärker, als er selbst dies wahrhaben wollte, die letztlich aporetische Lage der Konstitution des 'bürgerlichen Selbst' um 1800: die ebenso nötige wie unmögliche Bestimmung des 'Subjekts' durch 'Erzählung seiner Lebensgeschichte'.

Die *Wanderjahre* haben dann schließlich die divergierenden Erfahrungsmomente zu einem Kompromiß geführt: inhaltlich, indem sie die Lebensgeschichte unter den Begriff der Entsagung stellen und damit die Entfaltung des Subjekts als Einschränkung, dessen Autonomie als Selbstentäußerung definieren; formal, indem sie *Roman*gestalt (als versöhnende Darstellung von Augenblick und Lebensganzem) und *Novellen*gestalt (im Zeichen des krisenhaft sich zuspitzenden Augenblicks) auf kompliziert vermittelte Weise ineinanderarbeiten.

II

Im zweiten Teil meiner Darstellung möchte ich nun versuchen, zunächst die vier als Voraussetzung des 'Bildungsromans' entwickelten Problemkomplexe anhand von Goethes Texten zu erläutern, sodann die hierbei sichtbar gewordenen Ergebnisse auf Kafkas Roman *Der Verschollene* zu beziehen und schließlich ein kurzes, kritisches Resümee zu geben.

Als erstes einige Bemerkungen zum Thema von Rollenspiel, Theater und Schauspielerexistenz: Es ist von eminenter Bedeutung für die Konzeption des Romans, daß Wilhelm Meisters ganze Lebensgeschichte aus *einer* prägenden 'Urszene' hervorgeht, der Begabung des Kindes mit den Elementen seines künftigen Lebensspiels durch die Großmutter.[9] Diese Begabung erfolgt als 'Bescherung' innerhalb des sozialen Rituals des Weihnachtsfestes, das ja den Mythos von der Geburt des Helden alljährlich nachspielt. Wesentlich ist dabei, daß Wilhelm keine feste Geschichte zugesprochen erhält, sondern Puppen, als jene Elemente möglicher Konfigurationen, aus denen er in frei verantworteter schöpferischer Gestaltung ein Lebensspiel aufzubauen vermag. Wilhelm erhält keinen Besitz, sondern Phantasie zum Geschenk, nicht Disziplin, sondern Schöpfungskraft. Saul, Samuel, David und Jonathan erweisen sich als wechselnde Identifikations-Subjekte, aus denen soziale Wirklichkeit und deren identifikatorische Kraft sich dem Kind erschließt. Das Entscheidende hierbei bleibt, daß nicht der durch seinen Vater legitimierte Saul, sondern der sich selbst autonom beglaubigende David schließlich den Sieg davonträgt und 'ein Königreich' findet. Die *Theatralische Sendung* ist denn auch eine solche Selbstlegitimationsphantasie im eminenten Sinne. Die Stationen dieses Prozesses sind deutlich genug bezeichnet.

Am Anfang steht der aus dem Geschenk der Großmutter entbundene Wunsch Wilhelms zur Schauspielerexistenz, genährt durch Begegnung mit der Theatertruppe. Im Erwerb von realen Erfahrungen kristallisiert sich dann die Selbstdefinition des 'bürgerlichen Helden' von der 'Repräsentanz' her: aus dem Konflikt zwischen Adel und Bürgertum, dessen Oppositionen von 'Sein' und 'Haben' in der Existenz des Schauspielers vermittelt erscheinen. Ein Versuch bedingungsloser ästhetischer Selbstbegründung schließt sich an: Wilhelm unternimmt es, sich als Schreiber, Schauspieler und Regisseur seines Selbst zugleich zu begreifen und zu begründen, als Selbstschöpfer aus der identifikatorischen Kraft der Phantasie. Die Unterzeichnung des Kontrakts mit der Schauspielergesellschaft erfolgt denn auch unmittelbar nach dem Tod des Vaters: selbstgeschaffene ästhetische Existenz scheint die versagende Legitimationsinstanz der Familie zu ersetzen. Am Schluß des Fragments deutet sich eine ästhetisch definierte Utopie an: die Begründung eines Nationaltheaters, das die Identität des Subjekts und der Nation zu vermitteln vermöchte.[10]

Der zweite für die Entstehung des modernen Subjekts wesentliche Problembereich steht in Goethes Roman im Zeichen der Vaterschaft, wie sie die Familie als Gefühlszentrum bürgerlicher Identität prägt: unter dem Doppelaspekt von Zeugung und Adoption. Es ist die für die Familie als Ort der Identifikation wesentliche Frage nach der Beziehung von Vater und Sohn. Prägendes Motiv dieser Beziehung ist im Roman das immer wiederkehrende Bild vom 'kranken Königssohn': der Vater, der zugunsten des liebeskranken Sohnes auf die eigene Liebe verzichtet.[11] Dieses — wie ich meine — antiödipale Motiv bildet den Schlüssel zu Goethes Phantasie von der männlichen Identität. Es eröffnet die Welt der entsagenden Väter, die dem Sohn die Freiheit zu identifikatorischer Entfaltung in der Liebe geben; ihn damit zugleich reif machen zu *eigener* Entsagung dem eigenen Sohn gegenüber, wie sich dies in der Konfiguration von Wilhelm, Felix und Hersilie innerhalb der *Wanderjahre* abzeichnet.

Wie der schenkende Blick der mütterlichen Frau dem Sohn die freie, spielerische Verfügung über die Elemente seines Lebensganzen in der Phantasie gewährt, so widerruft der entsagende Blick des Vaters auf die Geliebte des Sohnes die blinde Kraft der patriarchalischen Gewalt — dieses Motiv des entsagenden Vaters erscheint nicht nur in der Fabel des Romans, es wird auch in verschiedenen Novellenhandlungen gespiegelt. Der den Konflikt heilende Grundgedanke ist derjenige der Verwandlung von blutbestimmten Zeugungs-Beziehungen in solche der durch Vernunft und Entsagung geregelten Adoption; der Verwandlung von Trieb in Vernunft, von Blut in Schrift, von Vaterschaft in soziale Instanzen, wie sie durch den 'Turm' und die 'pädagogische Provinz' vertreten werden.

Der dritte, das neu entstehende Subjekt prägende Vorstellungszusammenhang ist dann der einer Selbstdefinition des Menschen von der Liebe her, nicht von der Jenseitigkeit des verklärten Leibes, sondern aus der Diesseitigkeit des im geliebten Du sich erfüllenden Wunsches.[12] Diese 'eigentümliche' Form der Selbsterfahrung entwickelt sich für das männliche Kind aus dem Blick der Frau. Es ist die in der *Theatralischen Sendung* gesetzte Urszene, aus der sich Wilhelms Leben entfaltet: die Großmutter, die den Enkel selbstlos mit dem Spiel seiner eigenen Wünsche beschenkt. In den Wiederholungen dieser Urszene, den Begegnungen Wilhelms mit den Frauen seines Lebensspiels, prägt sich die gedoppelte Form eines 'Anfangs' aus, der Lebensgeschichte, die aus dem Körper *und* der Sprache entwickelt werden kann — paradigmatisch in der Begegnung Wilhelms mit Mariane vergegenwärtigt: der ihm nicht bewußten Zeugung eines Sohnes einerseits; dem Versuch, aus dieser Liebe eine Geschichte sprechend zu entwickeln, andererseits. Wilhelm erzählt Mariane seine Lebensgeschichte in der Hoffnung, daß 'kein Wort auf den Boden fällt' (VII, 27).[13] Mariane verweigert die Erzählung ihrer eigenen Lebensgeschichte und schläft ein. Diese Szene, als versuchte Entwicklung einer identifikatorischen Geschichte aus dem Blick der Frau, wiederholt sich im Roman immer wieder: in jenen Augen-Blicken, die Wilhelm mit Mignon, Hersilie, Philine, Aurelie, Natalie, der Gräfin, mit Hilarie, Therese und Makarie verbinden.

Auffallend ist, daß in diesen Begegnungen das Motiv des Blutes eine zentrale Rolle spielt — Wilhelms Verletzung bei der ersten Begegnung mit Natalie; Mignon, die das Blut seiner Wunde mit ihrem Haar stillt; Aurelies Messerschnitt in Wilhelms Hand[14] — und daß immer wieder Versuche unternommen werden, diesem Motiv des Blutes die erzählte

Lebensgeschichte entgegenzusetzen, wie dies etwa in der Erfragung von Thereses Lebensgang durch Wilhelm erfolgt. Das Motiv des Blutes, von Goethe mit auffälliger Konstanz benutzt, bezeugt die sozial noch nicht verarbeitete Bestimmung des Subjekts durch 'Liebe': seine ambivalente Situierung zwischen Leidenschaft und Sozialvertrag, zwischen Körper und Gesetz, deren Vermittlung später im Zeichen der Entsagung erfolgt.

Am Anfang dieses Weges, geboren aus der 'Gabe' der Großmutter, steht die vom Kind Wilhelm nachgespielte mythische Urszene: Tankred und die tödlich verwundete Chlorinde, als Repräsentanten feindlicher Welten in Tassos *Befreitem Jerusalem* einander gegenübergestellt, miteinander im Zeichen des Blutes und der dieses stillenden Taufe versöhnt, eine Anagnorisis aus der Entzweiung — die Geschichte des Romans entfaltet hieraus eine in Stufen sich abzeichnende Struktur der Identifikation Wilhelms.

Eine erste Stufe bildet die Begegnung mit Mariane und die unbewußte Zeugung des Sohnes Felix. Eine zweite wird in der Begegnung mit Natalie als der noch namenlose Augenblick der Zweiheit im Zeichen des Blutes deutlich. Ein drittes Mal wird diese Konstellation im Traum Wilhelms sichtbar, in dem alle Frauen seines Lebensganges noch einmal zu ihm in Beziehung treten, ein Spiel von Entsagung und Adoption inszenieren: der Vater Wilhelms, der sich mit Mariane entfernt; Natalie, die Wilhelm sanft zurückhält; Felix, der Natalie entgegenschwimmt und von ihr aufgenommen wird (VII, 494 f.); eine vierte Stufe wird durch die Begegnung mit Makarie repräsentiert (VII, 843). Im Erlebnis auf der Sternwarte lernt Wilhelm, den selbstbefangenen Blick im doppelten Sinne zu öffnen, ihn in die Seele wie in den Kosmos zu erweitern, Innen und Außen im Blick zu versöhnen, als Traum vom Stern Makaries, der unmerklich sich in dessen wirkliches Erblicken im Kosmos verwandelt.

Die 'Sozialwerdung' beider Träume schließlich — des Traums der Liebe, der Entsagung will; des Sternentraums, der Kosmos und Seele als ein und dasselbe weiß — erfolgt in jener Szene, die Felix im Schoß von Wilhelm und Natalie zeigt, als zur Lebensgemeinschaft gestillte Leidenschaft (VII, 699).

Es sind diese fünf Stationen, die die Erwerbung des Lebensspiels durch Wilhelm, die Verwandlung von Phantasie in Sozialvertrag bewahrheiten; sie bezeichnen jenen Weg, der von der Zeugung zur Adoption, vom ichbefangenen zum kosmischen Blick, vom Blut zur Schrift führt, und den die im Archiv der Turmgesellschaft bewahrte Lebensgeschichte Wilhelms dokumentarisch festhält. Es ist der Weg des Romans, der zur Situierung, der zur Entzifferung der Zeichen führt, die Zeichen der 'Liebe' und Zeichen von deren sozialer Repräsentanz zugleich sind:

Schleier, Kästchen, die Perlen Marianes, das Arztbesteck. Es ist auch der Weg, der zur Erwerbung der wahren Namen führt, die Natalie und Wilhelm schließlich finden und einander zugestehen: eine Zweiheit, die zu sozialer Vergewisserung wird, die blutige Anagnorisis des Mythos von Tankred und Chlorinde in der Schrift der 'Lebensgeschichte' still aufhebend, die das Archiv der Turmgesellschaft bewahrt.

Der vierte Aspekt schließlich, dem der Roman identifikatorische Kraft zubilligt, ist derjenige der Legitimationsinstanzen, die die gefundenen Zeichen zu 'beglaubigen' vermögen. Auch hier zeichnet der Roman einen Weg der Verwandlung 'individueller Mythen' — die man als 'private' Organisationsmodelle von Wirklichkeit begreifen mag — in umfassende, sozial begründete nach; einen Weg vom intimen Spiel zum soziale Kräfte bindenden Wissenssystem.

Die aus der Familie und ihrer Intimität entwickelte mythische Konstellation nimmt ihren Ausgang von der doppelten Selbstbegegnung des Kindes im Blick; dem männlichen Blick, der aus der Konfiguration des Bildes vom 'kranken Königssohn' entspringt, im Paradigma der 'entsagenden Väter' inszeniert als das Spiel Hamlets, als die Verwandlung des väterlichen Rache-Geistes in einen von der Turmgesellschaft entsandten Schutz-Geist; dem weiblichen Blick sodann als dem 'Erkennen' von Mann und Frau, wie es die Anagnorisis zwischen Tankred und Chlorinde blutig bezeugt, wie es die Versöhnung im Ehevertrag und seiner Archivierung sozial domestiziert.

Der kritische Punkt, wo diese private Erfahrung in soziale umschlägt, wird durch jenen Brief Wilhelms an Natalie bezeichnet, in dem solches Spiel der Wünsche in soziale Verbindlichkeit umschlägt (VII, 1011–28): dem Brief über den ertrunkenen Knaben, die kindliche Begegnung Wilhelms mit dem Mädchen, wo Männer- und Frauenrolle spielerisch aus der Eigentümlichkeit der Körpererfahrung entwickelt und in soziale Begründungszusammenhänge hinübergeleitet werden — das kindliche Spiel ungeregelter Lust, das über die Körper-Kunst des Schauspielers zur Körper-Therapie des Arztes wird, das vom 'Erleben' des subjektiven Körpers zur 'Verwaltung' des sozialen Körpers führt. Es ist der Punkt, wo die individuellen Mythen in jene beiden Institutionen eingebracht werden, die im Roman die Würde sozialer Utopien annehmen: als Archivierung der Lebensgeschichte in der Schrift der Turmgesellschaft; als Operationalisierung der Lebensgeschichte in der pädagogischen Provinz. Es ist die Überführung des Lebens*spiels*, das dem Kindzauber der Marionetten entspringt, in die sanfte Verwaltung des Lebens*ernstes*; indem die Turmgesellschaft die Vaterschaft Wilhelms legitimiert und seine Berufsentscheidung insinuiert, gelingt zugleich die utopische Bewältigung zerfallender Mythen und ihrer individuellen Unverbindlichkeit durch Bürokratie und Sozial-Technologie. Diese

gipfelt in der Verwandlung freien Rollenspiels in verbindliche Sozial-
funktion, in der Erfassung und Beglaubigung von Namen, Vaterschaft,
Beruf und Lebensgeschichte Wilhelms im Archiv.

Es ist die Ersetzung des Theaters als Legitimationsinstanz durch die
Turmgesellschaft, des Spiel-Platzes der Identifikation, wie ihn die
Rollen auf der Bühne des Theaters gewähren, durch Verwaltungsin-
stanzen, die soziale Funktionen zuschreiben. Schlüsselbegriff, der dies in
Freiheit ermöglicht, ist derjenige der 'Entsagung'.

III

Ich will nun versuchen, Kafkas Roman auf diese vier Kernkonzepte des
Identitätsproblems, wie es Goethes *Wilhelm Meister* zum ersten Mal
exponiert, zu beziehen.

1. Auch Kafkas Roman bindet die Frage der Selbstwerdung seines
Helden an die Vorstellungen des Theaters, des Rollenspiels und der
Schauspielerschaft; auch Karl Roßmann, wie Wilhelm Meister, wird
Schauspieler, freilich nicht von vornherein, sondern auf eher unvermit-
telte Weise erst am Ende des Roman-Fragments. Ein Paralipomenon,
das vermutlich nach Abbrechen des Manuskripts noch
niedergeschrieben wurde, bezeugt, daß Kafka daran dachte, den
Augenblick des Eintritts Karls in den Schauspielerberuf auch szenisch
auszugestalten:

'Herr Direktor, ein neuer Schauspieler ist gekommen' hörte man ‹deutlich›
††, denn die Tür ins Vorzimmer war vollständig geöffnet, †den Diener
melden†. 'Ich will Schauspieler erst werden' sagte [Karl] [halblaut] für sich
und stellte so die Meldung des Dieners richtig. 'Wo ist er?' sagte der
Direktor und streckte den Hals. (KKA V II 49)

Allerdings zeigt sich bei genauerer Prüfung, daß Kafka, wie Goethe, die
Geburt seines Helden zum Schauspieler an eine mythische Urszene
bindet, die Elemente des Bühnenhaften, des kindlichen Lebensspiels
und der familialen Identifikation miteinander verknüpft. Dies geschieht
in dem Augenblick, wo Karl im Haus seines Onkels — 'die ersten Tage
eines Europäers in Amerika seien ja einer Geburt vergleichbar'
(KKA V I 56) — mit dem amerikanischen Wunderschreibtisch kon-
frontiert wird, der, als ein Repräsentationsobjekt modernster Technik,
sich unter dem Blick des Helden unvermittelt in die Krippe eines Prager
Weihnachtsmarktes verwandelt, das befangene Leben im Heiligen Stall
als mythische Geburt des Helden in Szene setzt:

In seinem Zimmer stand ein amerikanischer Schreibtisch bester Sorte, wie
sich ihn sein Vater seit Jahren gewünscht und auf den verschiedensten
Versteigerungen um einen ihm erreichbaren billigen Preis zu kaufen gesucht

hatte, ohne daß es ihm bei seinen kleinen Mitteln jemals gelungen wäre. Natürlich war dieser Tisch mit jenen angeblich amerikanischen Schreibtischen, wie sie sich auf europäischen Versteigerungen herumtreiben nicht zu vergleichen. Er hatte z.B. in seinem Aufsatz hundert Fächer verschiedenster Größe und selbst der Präsident der Union hätte für jeden seiner Akten einen passenden Platz gefunden, aber außerdem war an der Seite ein Regulator und man konnte durch Drehen an der Kurbel die verschiedensten Umstellungen und Neueinrichtungen der Fächer nach Belieben und Bedarf erreichen. Dünne Seitenwändchen senkten sich langsam und bildeten den Boden neu sich erhebender oder die Decke neu aufsteigender Fächer; schon nach einer Umdrehung hatte der Aufsatz ein ganz anderes Aussehen und alles ging je nachdem man die Kurbel drehte langsam oder unsinnig rasch vor sich. Es war eine neueste Erfindung, erinnerte aber Karl sehr lebhaft an die Krippenspiele die zuhause auf dem Christmarkt den staunenden Kindern gezeigt wurden und auch Karl war oft in seine Winterkleider eingepackt davor gestanden und hatte ununterbrochen die Kurbeldrehung, die ein alter Mann ausführte, mit den Wirkungen im Krippenspiel verglichen, mit dem stockenden Vorwärtskommen der heiligen drei Könige, dem Aufglänzen des Sternes und dem befangenen Leben im heiligen Stall. Und immer war es ihm erschienen, als ob die Mutter die hinter ihm stand nicht genau genug alle Ereignisse verfolge, er hatte sie zu sich hingezogen, bis er sie an seinem Rücken fühlte, und hatte ihr solange mit lauten Ausrufen verborgenere Erscheinungen gezeigt, vielleicht ein Häschen, das vorn im Gras abwechselnd Männchen machte und sich dann wieder zum Lauf bereitete, bis die Mutter ihm den Mund zuhielt und wahrscheinlich in ihre frühere Unachtsamkeit verfiel. Der Tisch war freilich nicht dazu gemacht um an solche Dinge zu erinnern, aber in der Geschichte der Erfindungen bestand wohl ein ähnlich undeutlicher Zusammenhang wie in Karls Erinnerungen. (KKA V 1 57 f.)

Was aber bei Goethe zu freier Verfügung über die Elemente künftigen Lebensspiels führt, wird für Karl zu einer beklemmenden und sprachlosen Vision; die Mutter öffnet dem Kind nicht die schöpferische Kraft der Phantasie und des Wortes, sondern drängt es in eine kontemplative Haltung zurück und bringt es zum Verstummen: Die Mutter hält dem Kind den Mund zu. Hier wird keine Eröffnung der Kompetenz des Rollenspiels in freier Gabe gewährt, hier erfolgt im Gegenteil eine sanfte, aber entschiedene Blockierung aller Selbstentfaltung.

2. Auch das Thema der Vaterschaft wird — genau wie bei Goethe — von Kafka in seinem Romanfragment als Identifikationsrahmen des Helden in Anspruch genommen. Freilich erscheint hier nicht mehr das prägende Bild vom 'kranken Königssohn', aus dem die von der patriarchalischen Gewalt sich lösende Liebesfreiheit des Sohnes sich entbindet, sondern die beklemmende Photographie der Eltern, leitmotivisch wiederkehrend und die Entfaltung des Helden lähmend:

Dann nahm er die Photographie der Eltern zur Hand, auf der der kleine Vater hoch aufgerichtet stand, während die Mutter in dem Fauteuil vor ihm ein wenig eingesunken da saß. Die eine Hand hielt der Vater auf der Rückenlehne des Fauteuils, die andere zur Faust geballt, auf einem illustrierten Buch, das aufgeschlagen auf einem schwachen Schmuck- tischchen ihm zur Seite lag. Es gab auch eine Photographie, auf welcher Karl mit seinen Eltern abgebildet war, Vater und Mutter sahen ihn dort scharf an, während er nach dem Auftrag des Photographen den Apparat hatte anschauen müssen. Diese Photographie hatte er aber auf die Reise nicht mitbekommen.

Desto genauer sah er die vor ihm liegende an und suchte von verschiedenen Seiten den Blick des Vaters aufzufangen. Aber der Vater wollte, wie er auch den Anblick durch verschiedene Kerzenstellungen änderte, nicht lebendiger werden, sein wagrechter starker Schnurrbart sah der Wirklichkeit auch gar nicht ähnlich, es war keine gute Aufnahme. Die Mutter dagegen war schon besser abgebildet, ihr Mund war so verzogen, als sei ihr ein Leid angetan worden und als zwinge sie sich zu lächeln. Karl schien es, als müsse dies jedem der das Bild ansah, so sehr auffallen, daß es ihm im nächsten Augenblick wieder schien, die Deutlichkeit dieses Eindrucks sei zu stark und fast widersinnig. Wie könne man von einem Bild so sehr die unumstößliche Überzeugung eines verborgenen Gefühls des Abgebildeten erhalten. Und er sah vom Bild ein Weilchen lang weg. (KKA V I 134 f.)

Nicht das antiödipale Prinzip der 'entsagenden Väter' vermag sich Geltung zu verschaffen, sondern die starre, statuarische Machtkonstel- lation der Familie. Mit einer solchen, die Blickkonstellation der Familie für immer befestigenden Erfahrungsstruktur wird dem Sohn der Übergang vom natürlichen Prinzip der Zeugung zum kulturellen der Adoption, wie es Goethes Roman in der Grundformel der Entsagung noch zu entfalten vermag, unmöglich gemacht. Während Wilhelm Felix 'adoptiert', ist vom Sohn Karl Roßmanns nie wieder die Rede; er bleibt 'verschollen' wie schließlich sein Vater auch. Karl selbst wird nicht befreienden Oheim-Figuren gegenübergestellt, wie dies Wilhelm Mei- ster widerfährt, sondern gerade in den scheinbar ihn ins Leben geleitenden außerfamilialen Garanten der Lebenswelt (dem Onkel, Herrn Green, Herrn Pollunder, dem Oberkellner, dem Oberportier) immer neuen übermächtigen Vater-Gestalten ausgeliefert, die seine freie Entfaltung hemmen oder letztlich unmöglich machen. Er kann nicht 'Bruder' seines Sohnes werden wie Wilhelm Meister,[15] sondern bleibt selbst 'Sohn' bis zuletzt, in argloser und blinder Abhängigkeit.

3. Auch der dritte Problemzusammenhang des Goetheschen Romans wird von Kafkas _Verschollenem_-Fragment in Anspruch genom- men: als Thema der identifikatorischen Beziehung des Mannes zur Frau, als die Frage nach der Liebe und ihrer möglichen sozialen Codierung. Auch hier bleibt die Urszene solcher Erfahrung an das Sozialritual des

Weihnachtsfestes gebunden; freilich in umgekehrter Weise wie bei Goethe. Die Mutter öffnet Karl nicht den Mund (wie das die Großmutter Wilhelms tut), sondern verschließt ihn dem Kinde gleichsam für immer. Sie verweigert ihm seine Mündigkeit.

In vergleichbarer Umkehrung vollzieht sich auch die erste sexuelle Begegnung Karls mit der Köchin Johanna Brummer; die Liebesbegegnung wird ihm nicht zum Keim einer erzählbaren Lebensgeschichte, sondern zu deren dumpfer, verstummen machender Verhinderung: 'Dann legte sie sich auch zu ihm und wollte irgendwelche Geheimnisse von ihm erfahren, aber er konnte ihr keine sagen . . .' (KKA V 1 42).

Auch hier, wie im *Wilhelm Meister*-Roman, folgt eine Reihe von Begegnungen mit anderen Frauen: mit der Oberköchin, mit Klara, mit Brunelda. Aber in keiner dieser Begegnungen gelingt die Umsetzung einer Liebeserfahrung in zeichenbildende sozialisierende Kraft; vielmehr wiederholt sich in stereotypem Gleichmaß die 'Urszene' der Vergewaltigung des Mannes durch die Frau. Die unbewußte Zeugung des Sohnes führt bei Karl nicht wie bei Wilhelm schließlich zu dessen Adoption, sondern zu gänzlichem Vergessen. Es ist Karl unmöglich, aus dem Augenblick der Liebesbegegnung eine sinnvolle Geschichte zu entwickeln, wie dies der Onkel, von außen und zu Karls Erstaunen, vermag: 'Das war alles gewesen und doch verstand es der Onkel, daraus eine große Geschichte zu machen' (KKA V 1 43).

Die Hilflosigkeit Karls, die ihm angetane 'Liebe' zur Sprache zu bringen und die Souveränität des Onkels, die fremde Intimität zu versprachlichen und gewissermaßen 'öffentlich' zu machen, führen zu keiner Vermittlung, Liebe als soziales Faktum ist für Kafkas Roman nicht existent.

Dies wird vielleicht dort am deutlichsten, wo Kafka satirisch zu verkehren scheint, was Goethe als höchste Stufe möglicher 'Augen-Blicke' zwischen Mann und Frau gestaltet hatte: das Erwachen Wilhelms auf der Sternwarte aus dem Traum von Makaries Astral-Existenz zu deren realer Vergegenwärtigung im Abendstern. Bei Kafka degeneriert diese Situation zur Balkon-Szene mit Brunelda, die Zug um Zug widerruft, was Goethe als vollendetes Gleichgewicht zwischen innerer und äußerer Wahrnehmung vergegenwärtigt:

'Wie gefällt es dir, Kleiner?' fragte Brunelda, die sich eng hinter Karl hin- und herdrehte, um mit dem Gucker möglichst alles zu übersehen. Karl antwortete nur durch Kopfnicken. Nebenbei bemerkte er, wie Robinson dem Delamarche eifrig verschiedene Mitteilungen offenbar über Karls Verhalten machte, denen aber Delamarche keine Bedeutung beizumessen schien, denn er suchte Robinson mit der Linken, mit der Rechten hatte er Brunelda umfaßt, immerfort beiseite zu schieben. 'Willst du nicht durch den

Gucker schauen?' fragte Brunelda und klopfte auf Karls Brust, um zu
zeigen, daß sie ihn meine.
'Ich sehe genug', sagte Karl.
'Versuch es doch', sagte sie, 'du wirst besser sehen.'
'Ich habe gute Augen', antwortete Karl, 'ich sehe alles.' Er empfand es nicht
als Liebenswürdigkeit, sondern als Störung, als sie den Gucker seinen
Augen näherte und tatsächlich sagte sie nun nichts als das eine Wort 'du!'
melodisch, aber drohend. Und schon hatte Karl den Gucker an seinen
Augen und sah nun tatsächlich nichts.
'Ich sehe ja nichts', sagte er und wollte den Gucker loswerden, aber den
Gucker hielt sie fest und den auf ihrer Brust eingebetteten Kopf konnte er
weder zurück noch seitwärts schieben.
'Jetzt siehst du aber schon', sagte sie und drehte an der Schraube des
Guckers.
'Nein, ich sehe noch immer nichts', sagte Karl und dachte daran, daß er
Robinson ohne seinen Willen nun tatsächlich entlastet habe, denn Bruneldas
unerträgliche Launen wurden nun an ihm ausgelassen.
'Wann wirst du denn endlich sehen?' sagte sie und drehte — Karl hatte nun
sein ganzes Gesicht an ihrem schweren Atem — weiter an der Schraube.
'Jetzt?' fragte sie.
'Nein, nein, nein!' rief Karl, trotzdem er nun tatsächlich, wenn auch nur sehr
undeutlich, alles unterscheiden konnte. Aber gerade hatte Brunelda irgend
etwas mit Delamarche zu tun, sie hielt den Gucker nur lose vor Karls Gesicht
und Karl konnte, ohne daß sie es besonders beachtete, unter dem Gucker
hinweg auf die Straße sehen. Später bestand sie auch nicht mehr auf ihrem
Willen und benützte den Gucker für sich. (KKA V 1 327 f.)

Hier, in Kafkas Roman, gelingt die doppelte Öffnung des Blicks in Seele
und Kosmos, in Traum und Wachsein nicht mehr, es wiederholt sich
nur jene stummachende, den Blick verschließende Gebärde der Mutter
aus der Szene auf dem Weihnachtsmarkt; Brunelda hält Karl gewaltsam
den Operngucker vor die Augen und Karl sieht nun gar nichts mehr, es
erfolgt keine Öffnung des Blicks mehr, sondern dessen gänzliche
Blockierung. Es gelingt Karl an keiner Stelle des Romans, die bedrängende Körperlichkeit der Frau mit deren Blick zu vermitteln, zu
einer 'Geschichte' zu machen und damit zu sozialer Geltung zu führen,
wie dies Wilhelm mit Hilfe der Turmgesellschaft schließlich möglich
wird; nämlich Natur und Kultur, Blut und Schrift, Körper und Sprache,
Leidenschaft und Eheformel im Zeichen 'heiterer Entsagung' zu
höherer Einheit zu verbinden. Für Karl gibt es keine Instanz mehr, die
eine solche Versöhnung zu leisten vermöchte. Auch diese Unversöhn-
barkeit wird in zwei Szenen exemplarisch verdichtet: bei der Waschung
des Riesenkörpers Bruneldas, der hinter einem Wandschirm verborgen
bleibt, während für Karl nur die Stimme der Frau zu hören ist; bei der
'Ausreise Bruneldas' sodann, wo diese mit zugedecktem Körper auf
einem Karren von Karl durch die Straßen geführt wird und sich

unvermittelt durch Vorweisen der Legitimationspapiere gegenüber einem Polizisten namhaft zu machen sucht:

So streng er aber Karl angesehen hatte, so mußte er doch lächeln, als er die Decke lüftete und das erhitzte ängstliche Gesicht Bruneldas erblickte. 'Wie?' sagte er. 'Ich dachte Du hättest hier zehn Kartoffelsäcke und jetzt ist es ein einziges Frauenzimmer? Wohin fahrt Ihr denn? Wer seid Ihr?' Brunelda wagte gar nicht den Polizeimann anzusehn, sondern blickte nur immer auf Karl mit dem deutlichen Zweifel, daß selbst er sie nicht werde erretten können. Karl hatte aber schon genug Erfahrungen mit Policisten, ihm schien das ganze nicht sehr gefährlich. 'Zeigen Sie doch Fräulein', sagte er, 'das Schriftstück, das Sie bekommen haben.' 'Ach ja', sagte Brunelda und begann in einer so hoffnungslosen Weise zu suchen, daß sie wirklich verdächtig erscheinen mußte. 'Das Fräulein', sagte der Polizeimann mit zweifelloser Ironie, 'wird das Schriftstück finden.' 'Oja', sagte Karl ruhig, 'sie hat es bestimmt, sie hat es nur verlegt.' Er begann nun selbst zu suchen und zog es tatsächlich hinter Bruneldas Rücken hervor. Der Polizeimann sah es nur flüchtig an. (KKA V 1 380 f.)

Stimme und Körper, Blick und Körper, Schrift und Körper der Frau bleiben unvermittelt nebeneinander, keine soziale Instanz vermag Liebe als Wechselidentität von Mann und Frau zu etablieren. Am Ende des Romans verzichtet Karl auf seinen Namen, sein Körper verschwindet in der Weite des amerikanischen Kontinents.

4.   Auch der vierte Bereich, in dem Goethe bürgerliche Identität zu gewährleisten sucht, wird von Kafka ins Zwielicht gerückt: Es ist die Welt jener sozialen Legitimationsinstanzen, die zeichenhafte Identität zu verbürgen vermöchten. Während bei Goethe der private Mythos der weihnachtlichen Schenkung für Wilhelm nach einem langen Weg der Prüfungen und Begegnungen in die Bürokratie der Turmgesellschaft überführt wird, bleiben beide Welten, die der mythischen Garantiein- stanz und die der modernen, durch Medien getragene Zivilisation, bei Kafka von Anfang an gespalten und für immer unversöhnt. Was die Urszene am amerikanischen Schreibtisch präfiguriert — die unvermit- telte Verwandlung der Vision einer perfekten Technologie, die als Klassifikationsmaschine funktioniert, in den Weihnachtsmythos von der Geburt des Helden, damit aber die letztliche Unvereinbarkeit von Mythos und Technik zu einer identifikatorischen Instanz — repro- duziert sich im Roman immer von neuem und vollendet sich in seiner ganzen Ausweglosigkeit schließlich im Theater von Oklahoma. Dieses Theater — als Ort des Lebensspiels —, ist zugleich aber auch ein Raum perfekter Bürokratie — eine universelle Klassifikationsmaschine, die für jedes zu subsumierende Subjekt eine eigene Aufnahmekanzlei bereithält, es aber gerade dadurch nicht zu sich selbst befreit, sondern vernichtet.

Der gesamte ungeheuere Apparat dieses 'Theaters' entpuppt sich zuletzt als eine doppelte Parodie jenes Mythos von der Identifikation des Subjekts aus der Erfahrung von Liebe und der Anwendung archivalischer Verwaltung, wie ihn der *Wilhelm Meister*-Roman noch aufrecht zu erhalten sucht. Zwar wird auch bei Kafka noch das Mann-Frau-Thema inszeniert, abwechselnd erscheinen Frauen als Engel, Männer als Teufel, Trompete blasend, auf den Podesten vor dem Theater; aber diese Inszenierung führt durch die Machinationen totaler Klassifikation schließlich zur Auslöschung des Namens des Helden — Karl nennt sich schließlich 'Negro' — und zum Verschwinden seines Körpers. Während das Archiv der Turmgesellschaft noch zum allzeit befragbaren Garanten der in ihm niedergelegten Lebensgeschichten wird und umgekehrt durch vorsichtige 'Leitung' Leben zu regeln vermag, führt hier in Kafkas Roman das sinnlose und falsche Archivieren zu einem leeren Vollzug und zu gleichzeitiger gänzlicher Abwesenheit aller Legitimation: Blinde Subsumption zerstört die Subjektqualität des Helden und läßt ihn erlöschen.

Die archivierte Schrift kann keine legitimierende Kraft mehr beanspruchen, sondern erscheint als blinde Parodie eines leeren bürokratischen Apparates, ihr Ort ist ein perspektiveloses Theater, in dem Bühne und Loge ununterscheidbar, Held und Zuschauer beliebig verwechselbar werden:

Dieses Bild stellte die Loge des Präsidenten der Vereinigten Staaten dar. Beim ersten Anblick konnte man denken, es sei nicht eine Loge, sondern die Bühne, so weit geschwungen ragte die Brüstung in den freien Raum. Diese Brüstung war ganz aus Gold in allen ihren Teilen. Zwischen den wie mit der feinsten Scheere ausgeschnittenen Säulchen waren nebeneinander Medaillons früherer Präsidenten angebracht, einer hatte eine auffallend gerade Nase, aufgeworfene Lippen und unter gewölbten Lidern starr gesenkte Augen. Rings um die Loge, von den Seiten und von der Höhe kamen Strahlen von Licht; weißes und doch mildes Licht enthüllte förmlich den Vordergrund der Loge, während ihre Tiefe hinter rotem, unter vielen Tönungen sich faltendem Sammt der an der ganzen Umrandung niederfiel und durch Schnüre gelenkt wurde, als eine dunkle rötlich schimmernde Leere erschien. Man konnte sich in dieser Loge kaum Menschen vorstellen, so selbstherrlich sah alles aus. (KKA V 1 412 f.)

IV

Dieser im Vergleich beider Romane angedeutete Befund zeigt: Kafka wie Goethe beziehen sich auf bestimmte Konstellationen psychischer und sozialer 'Identifikationsspiele'. Aber ihre Spielregeln haben sich geändert. Auf der einen Seite Goethe, der sein Konzept — durch politische und naturwissenschaftliche Erfahrungen beeinflußt — immer wieder verwandelt und modifiziert, um zu einer aus Entsagung entbundenen Utopie der Exterritorialität zu gelangen: Amerika als einen Ausweg denkbar zu machen, in dem freie, Natur und Kultur vermittelnde Identität sich realisiert. Auf der anderen Seite Kafkas, der alle vier — schon von Goethe in Anspruch genommenen — Dispositive von Identität umkehrt, parodistisch entwertet und das europäische Subjekt im Dunkel des Wilden Westens schließlich verlorengehen läßt.

Das Subjekt als 'Wanderer' und als 'Verschollener': resignative Utopie im Werk Goethes, das Versagen der identifikatorischen Kraft im Werk Kafkas — ich versuche eine kurze Bilanz.

1. Die Kernfrage beider Autoren knüpft sich an das abendländische Anagnorisis-Ritual: Wer sind Sie eigentlich? fragt der Onkel Karl Roßmann im ersten Kapitel des *Amerika*-Romans:

'Wollten Sie nicht den jungen Mann hier etwas fragen, Herr Jakob?" sagte der Kapitän unter allgemeiner Stille zu dem Herrn mit dem Bambusstöckchen.
'Allerdings', sagte dieser mit einer kleinen Neigung für die Aufmerksamkeit dankend. Und fragte dann Karl nochmals: 'Wie heißen Sie eigentlich?' (KKA V 1 35)

Während aber Wilhelm Meister auf seinem Weg vom falschen zum wahren Namen gelangt und sein Körper schließlich durch die Schrift des Archivs sozial identifiziert wird, ergeht es Karl Roßmann genau umgekehrt: Im Theater von Oklahoma, das zur Rekognoszierung seiner Identität durch die Feinheit des Aufnahmeapparats geradezu prädestiniert erscheint, verliert er gerade seinen wahren Namen, sein Körper verschwindet — wie der Josefines im Volk der Mäuse — in der Weite Amerikas.

2. Bei der Frage 'wer bin ich eigentlich?', die das Erzählen der Lebensgeschichte bei Goethe wie bei Kafka regelt, orientieren sich beide Autoren an der Definition des modernen Subjekts nicht vom Tode her (wie dies bis zum Siebzehnten Jahrhundert gegolten hatte), sondern von der unveräußerlichen Erfahrung der Liebe,[16] wie sie in der Beziehung der Geschlechter sich darstellt. Die Frage nach dem Ich wird an die Sexualität gestellt. Beide Autoren gehen von einer mythisch gestalteten Zeugungssituation aus, dem Sozial-Ritual der 'Weihnacht', beide supponieren nach der 'natürlichen' eine zweite, soziale Geburt des Helden. 'Die ersten Tage eines Europäers in Amerika seien ja einer Geburt vergleichbar' (KKA V 1 56), gibt der Onkel seinem Neffen zu bedenken. Beide, Goethe wie Kafka, sehen diese zweite Geburt als die Vermittlung der Intimität an die Öffentlichkeit an — 'Karl erhoffte in der ersten Zeit viel von seinem Klavierspiel und schämte sich nicht wenigstens vor dem Einschlafen an die Möglichkeit einer unmittelbaren

Beeinflussung der amerikanischen Verhältnisse durch dieses Klavierspiel zu denken' (KKA V 1 60)—, als die Gewinnung einer sozial
kodierten 'Sprache der Liebe'. Beide trauen der Familie als Vermittlungs-
instanz bei der zweiten Geburt des Subjekts in die Gesellschaft nicht;
beide inszenieren Adoptionsspiele: Goethe indem er den Harfner,
Mignon und Felix als 'kleine Familie' Wilhelms apostrophiert (VII, 215),
Kafka indem er Karl als 'Kind' dem amerikanischen Onkel, Herrn
Pollunder, dann der Familie Delamarche-Robinson-Brunelda zuordnet.
Beide Autoren suchen diese Form kulturell erworbener Identität in
höhere Instanzen der Subjekt-Garantie zu überführen. Für beide ist das
Theater als Institut ästhetischen Rollenspiels der Weg dorthin. Während
aber Goethe den Weg Wilhelms als Überwindung des Theaters zeigt
und dieses durch Archiv ('Turm') und pädagogische Provinz zu ersetzen
strebt, zeigt Kafkas Roman die Zersetzung des als Identitätsgarantie
beanspruchten Theaters durch blinde Archivierung und leere Disziplin.

Das partielle Glücken der sozialen Codierung von Liebe bei Goethe,
deren gänzliches Scheitern bei Kafka gehören wohl im historischen
Prozeß wie Frage und Antwort zueinander. Beide Autoren sehen die
Geburt des Subjekts aus der Erfahrung der Liebe in der Familiensitua-
tion als deren 'Urszene' begründet: Goethe als Begabung des Kindes mit
dem Spiel der Wünsche durch die weibliche Instanz der Familienkon-
stellation; als die Begabung des Kindes mit der Möglichkeit heiterer
Entsagung durch die männliche Instanz dieser selben Familie. Für Kafka
dagegen verkehren sich beide emanzipatorischen Instanzen in deren
Gegenteil: als Erstickung des Spiels der Wünsche durch die weibliche
Instanz; als bedingungslose Unterwerfung des entstehenden Subjekts
durch die Gewalt der männlichen Familieninstanz, die diesem keinen
Spielraum mehr eröffnet.

3. Als Grundbedingung für die Identitätserfahrung beider
Romanhelden, Wilhelms wie Karls, gilt die Regel der Exterritorialität:
das Fremde als Bedingung des Eigenen zu erkennen ('Amerika') und
sich in diesem Anderen Subjektivität zu erarbeiten. Während aber
Wilhelm Meister sich sein Subjekt durch Ausmessung des Raumes
'erwandert', 'Distanz' als identifikatorische Erlernung von Entsagung
definiert, verliert sich Karl Roßmann in der Unermeßlichkeit des
Raums und muß 'Distanz' als definitive Selbstentfremdung erfahren.

4. Bei dem Übergang von der Familie in die Gesellschaft suchen
beide Romanhelden einen Weg aus der väterlichen Gewalt; als mögliche
Garanten solchen Auswegs fungieren auf der einen Seite die 'Onkel'-
Figuren (im *Wilhelm Meister* der Abbé, Montan, der Oheim; im
Verschollenen der Onkel, Pollunder, der Oberkellner, der Oberportier);
auf der anderen die 'Institutionen', wie sie sich im *Wilhelm Meister* — das
Theater ersetzend — als Turmgesellschaft und pädagogische Provinz

etablieren, im *Verschollenen* als Hotel und als Theater von Oklahoma in die Lebensgeschichte Eingang finden. Während aber Goethe eine allmähliche Integration dieser Instanzen in die Lebensgeschichte seines Helden gelingt, verwandeln sie sich bei Kafka in ihre bedrängende Urgestalt zurück: Die Onkel-Figuren entpuppen sich zunehmend als neue Figurationen der Vatergestalt, das Theater von Oklahoma, das allen Bewerbern Identität durch Arbeit zu versprechen schien, verkehrt sich unversehens wieder in ein leeres, funktionsloses Ritual. Was bei Goethe zur Herstellung des Subjekts durch Entsagung führt, bewirkt bei Kafka nur noch dessen Zerstörung.

5. Das 'Erzählen' der Geschichte des Subjekts wird damit gleichzeitig aber für beide Autoren auch zu einer Frage nach der 'Lesbarkeit' der Dinge als Zeichen und nach der Möglichkeit ihrer erzählerischen Integration. Dies gelingt Goethe auf kunstvolle Weise: Kästchen, Schleier, Instrumententasche und viele andere Objekte beginnen unaufdringlich, aber entschieden im Laufe des Romans ihre identifikatorische Kraft zu entfalten. Bei Kafka dagegen führt das Dazwischentreten der Dinge in der Geschichte des Helden zu gänzlicher Diffusion: Koffer, Photo, Mütze und Regenschirm verkommen zu blinden Zeichen des Selbstverfalls.

Der Prozeß, dessen Anfang und Ende Goethe und Kafka mit ihren Romanen bezeichnen, spiegelt die aporetische Situation des nachrevolutionären 'Subjekts', sich doppelt begründen zu müssen: aus der eigentümlichen und unveräußerlichen Wahrheit des Körpers zum einen, aus dem sozial begründeten Spiel der Zeichen der Sprache und ihrer Wahrheit beanspruchenden Kraft zum anderen. Goethe führt dieses Spiel zum Kompromiß der Entsagung; bei Kafka wird der Held 'strafweise umgebracht'.

Es ist ein Dilemma, dessen Ausprägungen im neunzehnten Jahrhundert ihre Schärfe gewinnen, dessen tötliche Konsequenzen erst das zwanzigste Jahrhundert auszumessen vermochte: daß 'Identität' nämlich in paradoxer Weise Insistenz des Körpers und Sprache des Anderen beanspruchen muß, um sich ihrer 'Ganzheit' versichern zu können. Kleist, in der *Familie Schroffenstein*, hat den kritischen Punkt dieser Erfahrung bezeichnet, als Augenblick des Verstehens und als Ewigkeit des Selbstzerfalls:

> Zwei Werte hat der Mensch: Den einen
> Lernt man nur kennen aus sich selbst, den andern
> Muß man erfragen.[17]

ANMERKUNGEN

1 Michel Foucault, *Die Ordnung der Dinge. Eine Archäologie der Humanwissenschaften* (Frankfurt/M., 1971).

[2] Hierzu Hannelore Schlaffer, *Wilhelm Meister. Das Ende der Kunst und die Wiederkehr des Mythos* (Stuttgart, 1980).

[3] Für diesen Zusammenhang entscheidende Anregungen gibt vor allem der Aufsatz von Friedrich A. Kittler, 'Über die Sozialisation Wilhelm Meisters', in Gerhard Kaiser/Friedrich A. Kittler, *Dichtung als Sozialisationsspiel. Studien zu Goethe und Gottfried Keller* (Göttingen, 1978), S. 13–124.

[4] Das reduzierte, auf Innerlichkeit gestellte Gegenmodell eines weiblichen Lebenslaufs, die 'Bekenntnisse einer schönen Seele', machen das nur allzu deutlich. Auch Kafka wird solche reduzierten Gegenmodelle weiblicher Lebensläufe in die Lebensgeschichte seines Helden einspielen: Therese im *Verschollenen*, die Brükkenhofwirtin, Amalie, Pepi und in gewissem Sinne Frieda — 'Du hast mich niemals nach meiner Vergangenheit gefragt' (KKA S I 392) — im *Schloß*-Roman.

[5] Die Bewertung dieses Vorgangs der 'Sozialisierung von Liebe' erfolgte in der Goethezeit von sehr verschiedenen Positionen aus. Kants *Metaphysische Anfangsgründe der Rechtslehre* (1797) innherhalb der *Metaphysik der Sitten* und Fichtes *Grundlage des Naturrechts nach Principien der Wissenschaftslehre* (1796) stehen am Anfang der Entwicklung dieses Gedankens, Hegels *Grundlinien der Philosophie des Rechts* (1820) an deren Ende. Kant zitiert nach: *Immanuel Kants Werke*, hg. von Ernst Cassirer, Band VII, *Die Metaphysik der Sitten*, hg. von Dr. Benzion Kellermann (Berlin, 1922); Fichte zitiert nach: *Fichtes Werke*, hg. von Immanuel Hermann Fichte, Band III, *Zur Rechts- und Sittenlehre I* (Berlin, 1971 = Photomechanischer Nachdruck der Ausgabe von 1845/46); Hegel zitiert nach: *Sämtliche Werke*, Jubiläumsausgabe in 20 Bänden, hg. von Hermann Glockner, Band VII, *Grundlinien der Philosophie des Rechts oder Naturrecht und Staatswissenschaft im Grundrisse* (Stuttgart, 1952). Während Kant 'Sozialisierung der Liebe' aus dem Gesetz ('*lege*', als 'Verbindlichkeit wechselseitigen Besitzes' (84)) zu begründen sucht, indem er die Ehe als 'Verbindung zweier Personen verschiedenen Geschlechts zum lebenswierigen wechselseitigen Besitz ihrer Geschlechtseigenschaften' definiert (81) und 'Genuß, zu dem sich ein Teil dem andern hingibt' nur 'unter der einzigen Bedingung' gelten läßt, 'daß, indem die eine Person von der anderen *gleich als Sache* erworben wird, diese gegenseitig wiederum jene erwerbe' (82), also letztlich auf die 'natürliche Gleichheit eines Menschenpaares' (83) zielt, sucht Fichte die Ehe von der 'juridischen Gesellschaft' (304; 317) abzugrenzen, indem er sie aus der wesentlich verschiedenen 'Natur' von Mann und Frau ableitet. 'Im Manne ist *ursprünglich* nicht Liebe, sondern Geschlechtstrieb' (310); im 'unverdorbenen Weibe äußert sich kein Geschlechtstrieb . . . sondern nur Liebe' (311). Daher vermag die Frau weder zu 'freien' (309), noch mehrere Männer zu besitzen: 'Die sich einmal ergibt, giebt sich auf immer' (312). Die Liebe (als 'Natur') ist das Geschenk, das die Frau dem Manne macht, und ihn 'ganz' zu machen. Die Frau ist 'durch ihre Verheiratung für den Staat ganz vernichtet', der 'Mann tritt ganz an ihre Stelle' (325). Eine Frau *will* kein Beamter sein (349): 'Denn sie ist bestimmt zu lieben, und die Liebe kommt ihr von selbst . . .' (349). Hegel begreift die Ehe dagegen weder wie Kant als Vertrag, noch wie Fichte als Natur, sondern als aus einem Widerspruch, dem der Liebe als Empfindung, geboren: 'Das erste Moment in der Liebe ist, daß ich keine selbstständige Person für mich seyn will, und daß, wenn ich dieß wäre, ich mich mangelhaft und unvollständig fühle. Das zweite Moment ist, daß ich mich in einer anderen Person gewinne, daß ich in ihr gelte, was sie wiederum in mir erreicht.' Daraus folgert Hegel: 'Die Liebe ist daher der ungeheuerste Widerspruch, den der Verstand nicht lösen kann, indem es nichts Härteres giebt, als diese Punktualität des Selbstbewußtseyns, die negirt wird, und die ich doch als affirmative haben soll,' (238). Liebe als Empfindung, das heißt aber: als Instabilität, hat im Staat keinen Platz: '. . . im Staate ist sie nicht mehr: da ist

man sich der Einheit als des Gesetzes bewußt, da muß der Inhalt vernünftig seyn, und ich muß ihn wissen' (238). Dort kann nur Ehe sein: als das 'unmittelbare sittliche Verhältniß' (239). Liebe aber, als Hervorbringung des Widerspruchs, ist gleichzeitig (gut Hegelisch) auch dessen Auflösung: als 'sittliche Einigkeit' (238), Verwandlung der 'Einheit der natürlichen Geschlechter in *geistige*, in selbstbewußte Liebe' (239).

6 Vgl. hierzu meinen Aufsatz 'Die Anfänge deutscher Novellistik. Schillers *Verbrecher aus verlorener Ehre* — Goethes *Unterhaltungen deutscher Ausgewanderten*', in *Das Commercium. Goethes und Schillers Literaturpolitik*. (Veröffentlichungen der Deutschen Schillergesellschaft, Stuttgart, 1984), pp. 390–417.

7 Die Umgestaltungen der zweiten Fassung von 1829 mögen hier außer Acht bleiben.

8 Vgl. hierzu meinen Aufsatz, 'Wissen und Liebe. Der auratische Augenblick im Werk Goethes', in Christian W. Thomsen und Hans H. Holländer, *Augenblick und Zeitpunkt. Studien zur Zeitmetaphorik in Kunst und Wissenschaften* (Darmstadt, 1984), pp. 282–305.

9 In den *Lehrjahren* tritt an die Stelle der Großmutter die Mutter; Kittler, a.a.O. diagnostiziert dies zutreffend als Symptom eines Paradigmenwechsels in der Auffassung der Familie.

10 Die problematische Verknüpfung von individueller und nationaler Identität wird von Jürgen Habermas plausibel gemacht in *Zur Rekonstruktion des historischen Materialismus*, suhrkamp taschenbuch wissenschaft, 154 (Frankfurt/M., 1976), namentlich S. 63–126.

11 In der reich dokumentierten Tradition des Motivs sind beide Argumente enthalten: daß der Vater zugunsten des Sohnes auf die 'Braut' und daß er auf die 'Frau' verzichtet. Vgl. hierzu Goethes *Werke*, Hamburger Ausgabe, VII, 720 ff. Erich Trunz hat dort die Überlieferung dieses Motivs rekapituliert.

12 Vgl. hierzu Michel Foucault, *Histoire de la sexualité I. La volonté de savoir* (Paris, 1976).

13 Goethes Werke werden künftig im Text mit Bandzahl und Seitenzahl zitiert nach: *Goethes Poetische Werke*, Vollständige Ausgabe (Stuttgart, o.J., J.G. Cotta'sche Buchhandlung Nachfolger).

14 Vgl. hierzu den o.g. Aufsatz 'Wissen und Liebe'.

15 Als Wilhelm Felix nach dessen Wassersturz wieder ins Leben ruft, heißt es: 'So standen sie fest umschlungen wie Kastor und Pollux, Brüder die sich auf dem Wechselwege vom Orkus zum Licht begegnen' (VII, 1233).

16 Vgl. hierzu Foucaults *Histoire de la sexualité*: 'C'est par le sexe en effet, point imaginaire fixé par le dispositif de sexualité, que chacun doit passer pour avoir accès à sa propre intelligibilité (puisqu'il est à la fois l'élément caché et le principe producteur de sens), à la totalité de son corps (puisqu'il en est une partie réelle et menacée et qu'il en constitue symboliquement le tout), à son identité (puisqu'il joint à la force d'une pulsion la singularité d'une histoire)' (a.a.O., S. 205 f.).

17 Heinrich von Kleist, *Sämtliche Werke und Briefe*, hg. von Helmut Sembdner (Darmstadt, 1962), I, 79.

Edward Timms

KAFKA'S EXPANDED METAPHORS:
A FREUDIAN APPROACH TO *EIN LANDARZT*

Kafka is a great writer. I start with this truism because so much Kafka criticism has been concerned to establish the opposite: not his greatness as a writer, but his inadequacy as a human being. This is particularly evident in Freudian criticism. From the earliest stages, psychoanalytical approaches to Kafka have been bedevilled by heavy-handed forms of vulgar Freudianism. Kafka's texts have been interpreted as confessional statements, thinly disguised. They are seen as transcriptions of a Freudian father complex or a Jungian fixation at the stage of adolescence. They are read as expressions of his sexual anxiety and fear of marriage. The symbolic motifs in his writings are decoded according to a Freudian scheme and their ambiguities resolved in terms of the familiar biographical data. Computer enthusiasts have even been at work on Kafka's thirty-seven recorded dreams and established by 'quantitative' methods that he suffered from 'castration anxiety' and 'found in writing a compensation for his castrated condition'.[1] Such arguments, whatever their value, clearly point in the wrong direction: away from Kafka's extraordinary artistic achievements and back into the sphere of his rather dismal private life.

A more fruitful perspective emerges when the methods of dream analysis are redirected. The Freudian approach is more illuminating when it is applied not biographically (to Kafka's personal anxieties) but textually — as a means of access to his fiction. In Walter Sokel's study (1964) Kafka's characteristic idiom is identified as 'eine traumhafte Bildersprache' ('a dreamlike language of images').[2] And Friedrich Beißner signposted this same direction when he endorsed Kafka's own definition of his work as 'die Darstellung meines traumhaften innern Lebens' ('the presentation of my dreamlike inner life'; T 300).[3] There is ample evidence to show that Kafka did indeed assign both to dreams and to dreamlike literary narratives quite exceptional powers of revelation. Thus in a letter to Felice Bauer of December 1912 he writes of his dreams during the previous night:

Es waren schreckliche Wahrheiten aufdringlich und überdeutlich in ihnen, so wie sie in dem mattern Tagesleben niemals zum Durchbruch kommen können. (BrF 165)

There were frightening truths in them, more insistent and vivid than could ever break through in the duller life of everyday.

And in the conversations recorded by Gustav Janouch he makes a similar point about his own use of dream-narrative as a literary technique:

Der Traum enthüllt die Wirklichkeit, hinter der die Vorstellung zurückbleibt. Das ist das Schreckliche des Lebens — das Erschütternde der Kunst.[4]

The dream reveals the reality, which has outdistanced rational conception. That is the frightening thing about life — the shattering effect of art.

There has been some debate about how consciously Kafka composed these dreamlike narratives. Did he habitually write in a trancelike state (as in the case of *Das Urteil*), or was his use of dream motifs more rationally contrived? But it seems clear that Kafka consciously cultivated his gift for dreamlike discourse.

Thus a certain consensus has emerged (summarized by Beißner, pp. 133 and 140): Kafka's narratives characteristically unfold, not according to the logic of rational causality, but by means of subtle dream-associations ('leichte Traumassoziationen'); and much of the action takes place, not on an objectively constituted narrative plane, but in the subjective consciousness of the hero ('im traumhaften Bewußtsein des Helden'). This is a real advance. We need no longer agonize over the question which so perplexed me when I first read *Das Urteil* years ago: Does the friend in St Petersburg really exist? The friend is a function of the conflicting subjective perspectives of father and son.

However, this approach also has its limitations. To say that Kafka's narratives are 'dreamlike' is a hazy generalization whose precise implications remain unclear. This is particularly the case when the generalization is linked with a dismissive attitude towards the most influential of all theories of the dream: the theory of Freud. Beißner (evidently with Freud in mind) dismisses modern depth-psychological theories as irrelevant to the understanding of Kafka's narrative style (p. 131). This position is untenable. The researches of Hartmut Binder have shown that Kafka had access to a wide range of information about psychoanalysis from 1911 onwards, and that in two periods (1911–13 and again in 1917) he immersed himself in the lively contemporary debate about Freud's theories.[5] It is true that Kafka dismissed certain aspects of psychoanalysis — or rather, not of psycho*analysis* but of psycho*therapy*:

Ich . . . sehe in dem therapeutischen Teil der Psychoanalyse einen hilflosen Irrtum. Alle diese angeblichen Krankheiten, so traurig sie auch aussehen, sind Glaubenstatsachen, Verankerungen des in Not befindlichen Menschen in irgendwelchem mütterlichen Boden. (BrM 246).

I . . . see in the therapeutic aspect of psychoanalysis a hopeless error. All of these supposed illnesses, however tragic they may appear, are matters of belief, ways that human beings in distress anchor themselves in some kind of maternal soil.

There can be no therapy for what Kafka perceived as an ontological malaise. But this discriminating formulation also suggests that his knowledge of psychoanalysis was quite sophisticated. It is not known what psychoanalytical writings he had read. But it is clear that he familiarized himself (perhaps at second hand) with the basic theories, and it is likely that the writing not only of *Das Urteil* but also of subsequent works was inspired by 'Gedanken an Freud natürlich' ('thoughts of Freud, naturally'; T 210). The stimulus received from Freud's ideas seems to have contributed to the qualitative change which occurred in Kafka's work around 1912. Indeed, not only in the work of Kafka but in the wider field of European narrative fiction after 1910, Freud's ideas contributed to a paradigm change: the displacement of a naive conception of mimesis by what James Joyce called 'the aesthetic of the dream'.[6]

Drawing on Freud's ideas, we may thus explore with greater precision the implications of Kafka's remark that dreams 'reveal reality'. What is the nature of these truths which only become apparent through the heightened perception of the dream? Psychoanalysis offers the answer that they are the unconscious impulses of inner life, impulses which have become unconscious as a result of censorship and repression. These impulses are of course not merely sexual, but may relate to any profound emotion which we dare not openly acknowledge: ambition, aggression and guilt, anxiety and insecurity, the fear of death and the longing for some primal source of consolation or authority. But how are these dimensions of experience to be revealed? How *can* they be revealed, when by definition they are unconscious and elude rational perception? Again psychoanalysis offers an answer: through language. Certain linguistic forms may become so charged with emotional energy that they elude rational controls and become bridges to the unconscious — 'Wortbrücken zum Unbewußten'.[7] The extraordinary suggestiveness of Freud's early writings derives from the ingenuity with which he explored these verbal bridges: puns and interferences, the free association of words and images, their symbolic suggestiveness and implicit dramatic force. Above all, through his scrutiny of the *metaphorical* character of language he reveals the link between innocent linguistic surface and latent emotional depths. Thus in advocating a 'Freudian approach' to Kafka's writings, I mean above all an approach informed by Freud's exceptional sensitivity to language.

At this point my argument intersects with that of one of the earliest works of Kafka exegesis: the study by Günther Anders published in 1951 under the title *Kafka Pro und Contra*. This book, originally conceived in Paris in the 1930s, interprets Kafka's work in existentialist theological terms as an expression of 'verschämter Atheismus' ('shame-faced atheism').[8] But the most suggestive part of the book is a short section (no more than five pages) dealing with the language of Kafka's narratives. Kafka's style (he argues) is not allegorical or symbolic, but metaphorical. Kafka takes the metaphorical element in language literally. His imagination seizes one of the submerged metaphors of everyday speech and transforms it into a scene or a story. Anders gives a number of examples. At the beginning of *Das Schloß* the hero has a lot to learn: 'er muß "zur Schule gehen"' ('he must "go to school"'). So he moves with Frieda into one of the classrooms of the local school and sets up house there. In the eyes of ordinary people Gregor Samsa may be regarded as 'ein dreckiger Käfer' ('a filthy insect'). This metaphor is expanded to form the whole narrative structure of *Die Verwandlung* (*Metamorphosis*). Similarly the metaphor 'am eigenen Leib etwas erfahren' ('to experience something personally' — literally 'on one's own body') is identified as the germ of the story *In der Strafkolonie* (*In the Penal Settlement*; Anders, pp. 39–44). These metaphors (to borrow a phrase from Formalist poetics) are 'foregrounded' so that they fill much of the space of the narrative.

The ideas which Anders puts forward have filtered through into subsequent Kafka criticism; but they have not received the full attention they deserve, for a number of reasons. First. Anders failed to develop his own line of argument. He treats Kafka's expanded metaphors rather externally, so that they appear to be an arbitrary literary device without any deeper justification. Secondly, Kafka did not himself emphasize language as a source of inspiration. In contrast to Austrian contemporaries like Kraus and Hofmannsthal, he did not elaborate a theory of language as a value centre or a source of insight. Thirdly, his style is not in any obvious sense metaphorical. It is characterized, on the contrary, by a remarkable sobriety and freedom from verbal ornament. Finally, the concept of metaphor itself has tended to be treated rather externally by literary criticism. It is seen merely as a device whereby a banal word may be replaced by a more 'poetic' one on the basis of a perceived similarity. Thus a sentence like 'Ships crossed the sea' may be enhanced by substituting 'Ships ploughed the sea' in order to achieve poetic effect.[9]

The case which I want to argue is that the function of metaphor in Kafka's writings is far more profound than this. For it is necessary to deepen our conception of metaphor. Metaphors are not a kind of linguistic 'Sunday best', which one wears only on special occasions.

They saturate the language of everyday speech and continuously shape our modes of perception and communication. When a moment ago I used the phrase 'The case which I want to argue', I don't suppose anyone consciously envisaged a Court of Law, with a judge and jury and myself in the robes of an advocate. For the metaphorical source of this phrase has become submerged and invisible. But such unconscious metaphors permeate our language, perhaps even our way of life. This point has been cogently argued by George Lakoff and Mark Johnson in a book called *Metaphors We Live By*. They suggest that some of the most fundamental experiences, like love or argument, do not have an intrinsic structure of their own, but acquire one only through metaphorical articulation.[10]

We must also take account of the expansive power of metaphor (which Vico identified over two hundred years ago). We have already seen a kind of drama in miniature beginning to emerge from the phrase 'arguing a case'. In Kafka's writings this technique of imaginative expansion is even more dramatic. The implicit metaphor may not even be a phrase, but simply a preposition (Anders, p. 41). The most celebrated example occurs in the story *Vor dem Gesetz*. The word 'vor' does not mean 'in front of'. It is a metaphor. The English equivalent would be 'in the eyes of the law': 'In the eyes of the Law all men are equal' — 'Vor dem Gesetz sind alle Menschen gleich'. Kafka's imagination seizes on this metaphorical 'vor', takes it literally and expands it into a scene actually set in front of the doorway leading to the Law. The scenic vividness of his parable has its source in a conventional metaphor.

This view of metaphor acquires greatest explanatory power when we take account of a further dimension: the Freudian conception of metaphor as a source of unconscious revelation. Freud's achievement (as Lionel Trilling puts it) is to show that in a scientific age 'we still feel and think in figurative formations'. Psychoanalysis can therefore be defined as 'a science of tropes, of metaphor and its variants'.[11]

An example can be taken from *Die Traumdeutung* (*The Interpretation of Dreams*) to show how expanded metaphors function in Freud's theory of dreams. One of Freud's patients tells how, in pursuit of an erotic adventure, he took lodgings in a small hotel: 'Er war in einem kleinen Hotel *abgestiegen*' ('He had put up [literally stepped down] at a small hotel'). The disreputable nature of the hotel had surprised even the cab driver, who remarked: 'Wie kann man aber da absteigen!' ('How could anyone put up at such a place'). Freud suggests that this conventional metaphor was one of the sources of a complex dream which the patient later had, involving being in a low position (in a house at the bottom of a hill) and struggling to climb up again. The dreamwork had transposed the metaphor into the literal action of climbing. At the same time its secondary metaphorical dimension becomes apparent: 'absteigen' in the sense of descending to a lower level of social intercourse (the lady was only an actress). [12]

To take full measure of Kafka's expanded metaphors, it is necessary to combine the suggestive insights of Günther Anders with Freud's more systematic account of metaphor as a mode of access to the unconscious. In Kafka's finest writings a synthesis occurs between verbal sensitivity and depth-psychological insight. Indeed, it is only by adopting this approach that we can make sense of one of Kafka's greatest achievements — the story *Ein Landarzt* (*A Country Doctor*).

Ein Landarzt appears to have been written in January or February 1917 and was first published in an almanach towards the end of that same year. It is by general consent one of the most dreamlike of Kafka's narratives, and its surrealistic imagery has sometimes seemed to defy comprehension. According to Heinz Politzer this story consists of 'incoherent fragments' and is 'basically unintelligible'. Its incoherence (he argues) is an 'artistic deficiency', because 'language failed Kafka' in this story. [13] In more recent structuralist criticism, on the other hand, it has been argued that such indeterminacy is a positive merit, since it undermines facile assumptions about the construction of meaning. Meaning in Kafka's writings, like the access to Castle, Court or Law, is eternally 'deferred', and Freud himself is cited to justify the view that dreams are 'untranslatable' into other modes of discourse. [14] But the Freudian approach to *Ein Landarzt* which is here proposed leads to very different conclusions. For I shall argue that the story *is* coherently structured; that this is an artistic merit, since it generates a cogent pattern of meaning; and that Kafka succeeds in articulating unconscious dimensions of experience with exceptional linguistic sensitivity.

The opening scene of the story seems realistic enough. Set in the courtyard of the doctor's house, it is narrated by the doctor himself in first-person form in the imperfect tense. He has been called out at night in the middle of a snowstorm to attend a patient ten miles away. But his horse had died the previous night, and his maid has been unsuccessful in trying to borrow one from a neighbour. The eruption of uncanny forces into this familiar scene only occurs when the doctor, in his distraction and distress, kicks open the dilapidated door of the pig-sty, which has been out of use for years.

'Pig-sty' ('Schweinestall') is of course a word replete with metaphorical associations. But this is one of many points where English translations of Kafka are likely to lead the reader astray. For 'pig' in English or American usage has different associations from 'Schwein' in German. We speak of 'behaving like a pig', 'being a filthy pig' or 'being greedy as a pig'. The pig is the emblem of gluttony, dirt, obnoxiousness and disorder. An American commentator on *Ein Landarzt*, invoking the

Judaic prohibition against eating pork, has suggested that the pig-sty must represent 'unclean' and 'materialistic' attitudes.[15]

In German, however, the associations are different. The word 'Schwein' may connote dirt and disorder, but we enter a different realm of experience when we use phrases like 'sich wie ein Schwein benehmen' ('to behave like a pig'), 'Schweinereien begehen' ('to commit obscene acts') or 'schweinische Witze erzählen' ('to tell obscene jokes'). For these phrases allude to indecent behaviour in the sexual sphere.

The word 'Schweinestall' thus has sexual associations. Moreover Kafka exploits these associations in a manner reminiscent of Freud's own analysis of how metaphors betray suppressed erotic impulses. An interesting parallel can be found in *Zur Psychopathologie des Alltagslebens* (*The Psychopathology of Everday Life*; 1904) in the section on slips of the tongue. Freud quotes an account of a person trying to describe feelings of which he was ashamed. Wishing to present his conduct in a favourable light, he had intended to say: 'But then the facts came to light . . .' What he actually said was: 'Dann aber sind Tatsachen *zum Vorschwein* gekommen'. He had of course intended to say: 'zum Vorschein gekommen'. But as he then ruefully admitted, he had at the back of his mind an uneasy awareness that the facts really were 'Schweinereien' — 'indecencies'. Against his conscious intention this awareness had betrayed itself linguistically in the conflated metaphor 'zum Vorschwein kommen' (Freud, IV, 65).

It seems likely, not that Kafka necessarily had read this passage by Freud (though he may have done), but that his imagination worked in a similar way. Kafka dramatizes what Freud analyses: the sudden eruption of repressed feelings though the medium of metaphor. But he doesn't use the long-hand method of discursive narrative. A more prosaic author would have written: 'Die Schweinereien, deren auch ein pflichtbewußter Landarzt fähig ist, kamen schließlich zum Vorschein' ('The indencencies of which even a conscientious country doctor is capable eventually came to light'). In Kafka's imaginative vision the door of the actual 'Schweinestall' opens and from it emerge the bearers of repressed sexual energies: the two magnificent horses that carry the doctor away, and the bestial groom who pursues and rapes his maid. In place of narrative long-hand we have a method which expands metaphor into miniature drama. Features of this method are linguistic condensation, the displacement of the action on to a symbolic plane, and the visual representation of intangible emotions. These are of course the three primary methods which Freud identifies in his chapter on 'Dreamwork' in *Die Traumdeutung*.

Against the potent metaphor of the 'Schweinestall' Kafka immediately sets a second which is of equal importance (the two indeed structure the whole story). The doctor's maid responds to the spectacle of horses and groom with the words: 'Man weiß nicht, was für Dinge man im eigenen Hause vorrätig hat' ('One never knows what's at hand in one's own house'; E 147). Again we have a potent metaphor concealed in a familiar phrase. For the word 'Haus' has deep-rooted associations with the idea of establishing an ordered identity: 'ein Haus bauen' ('to build a house'), 'sich wie zu Hause fühlen' ('to feel at home'), 'Herr im Hause sein' ('to be master of the house'), 'das Haus bestellen' ('to put one's house in order'). It is even possible (in a figure of speech more current in Kafka's day than it is now) to use the word as a colloquial form of address: 'Wie geht es dir, altes Haus?' ('How are things, old boy?') If groom and horses have been lurking 'im eigenen Hause', they must embody forces latent within the doctor's own personality. Or rather, doctor and groom may be taken to represent two aspects of a single personality: the dutiful, self-sacrificing servant of the community on the one hand, the repressed sexual self on the other. It is as if Kafka were transcribing into imaginative terms those 'Two Principles of Mental Functioning' which Freud had identified in a celebrated essay of 1911: the primitive self ('das Lust-Ich') guided only by the appetite for pleasure; and the socially adjusted self ('das Real-Ich') which conforms to the demands of the environment (Freud, VIII, 230–38).

The antithesis of 'Haus' and 'Schweinestall' gives *Ein Landarzt* its structural coherence. The house is associated with the doctor's official identity, his sense of duty and self-sacrifice, his sexual abstemiousness, his clothing, instruments and carriage, and his care for his patient. The pig-sty is linked with groom and horses, the release of pleasurable energies and the eruption of sexual lust, the motif of nakedness and climbing into bed, and the rape of the maid. Kafka's expanded metaphors do not in this story 'collide' and generate incoherence, as is the case with some of his artistically less accomplished narratives.[16] Time and again the word 'Haus' recurs within a consistent pattern as the image of an apparently secure identity which has been destroyed from within — by groom-energies which the doctor-self can no longer control. And the structure of the narrative is closed by this image in the final paragraph: 'Niemals komme ich so nach Hause' ('I shall never get home this way'; E 153). Separated from his house, his carriage and his clothes, clinging naked to one of his unearthly horses, the doctor perceives his situation as irretrievable.

This dualistic structure is held together by a remarkable feat of imaginative condensation. Both the doctor's visit to the patient and the groom's assault on the maid are enclosed within the image of the house. It is inside the house that both the maid is raped and the doctor discovers the wound in his patient's side. In appearance they may be two separate houses ten miles apart, but in psychic time they are separated by a journey which lasts 'nur einen Augenblick, als öffne sich unmittelbar vor meinem Hoftor der Hof meines Kranken' ('only a moment, as if the farmyard of my patient opened directly in front of my gate'; E 148). It is possible to take the two houses, and indeed the two actions, as identical: as one-and-the-same action viewed from two angles of mental functioning. The pleasure-self exults in raping the maid, while the reality-self is horrified by the consequences: the deep dark wound which suddenly appears in the body of his patient.

This condensation of two dimensions of emotional experience is completed by the central and most overtly Freudian metaphor of the whole story — Rosa, the name of the doctor's maid. None of the characters in the story has a personal name apart from Rosa. They are identified by their functions: a country doctor, the groom, the patient, the parents, the father, the mother, the boy, the children. Indeed, if the doctor had his way, the maid would not have a personal name either. Throughout the first page of his recollected narrative he refers to her as 'mein Dienstmädchen' ('my maidservant') and 'das Mädchen' ('the maid'). The young woman is thereby reduced to a servant — of the reality principle, not simply of the doctor. Her female personality has been subordinated to her neutral function, as even the pronoun 'es' (for 'das Mädchen') perhaps suggests. Her physical beauty (as he later ruefully acknowledges) has been ignored by him — 'jahrelang von mir kaum beachtet' ('hardly noticed by me from one year to the next'; E 150). Her personal name only erupts in the narrative when it is suddenly pronounced by the groom: 'ich bleibe bei Rosa' ('I am staying with Rosa'; E 147). From this point onwards the maid is emphatically female: 'Rosa' or 'sie', rather than 'es'. And the narrative accelerates into the continuous present tense of stream of consciousness.

Kafka's use of allegorical speaking names has often been remarked on. A recent study has shown how systematically he exploits this realm of suggestive ambiguity.[17] But no other name in his œuvre has quite the expressive resonance of 'Rosa' in this story. We may recall the ingenuity with which Freud explored the concealed meanings of names in his most widely read early writings, *Die Traumdeutung*, *Zur Psychopathologie des Alltagslebens* and *Der Witz und seine Beziehungen zum Unbewußten* (*Jokes and their Relation to the Unconscious*). It is with a similar ingenuity that Kafka plays upon the name Rosa in this story. The name becomes the matrix of its meaning, giving the story not only its inner coherence but also a deeper archetypal resonance.

Rosa is of course a common name (or was common in this period, particularly among German-Jewish families). But Kafka achieves a Freudian condensation of two planes of meaning by punning on 'Rosa' (the name of the girl being raped) and 'Rosa' (the colour of the wound which appears in the patient's side):

Rosa, in vielen Schattierungen, dunkel in der Tiefe, hellwerdend zu den Rändern, zartkörnig, mit ungleichmäßig sich aufsammelndem Blut, offen wie ein Bergwerk obertags. (E 151)

Rose-red, in many shades, dark in the depths, growing lighter toward the edges, softly granulated, with blood collecting here and there, open like a mine to the light of day.

The pun is clearly 'Freudian' not only in its verbal subtlety but also in its symbolic associations. The links between flowers, fertility and sexuality are repeatedly stressed in *Die Traumdeutung*, and the description of the wound makes the sexual associations rather explicit. It is located 'in der Hüftengegend' ('in the region of the hips'; E 151), a polite way of saying 'in the genital area', and certain details are suggestive of the bleeding which occurs after a woman has been deflowered. Before the doctor's fascinated gaze, wound and vulva seem to have become interchangeable.

Kafka later remarked that this description of the wound had been 'zusammenphantasiert' ('phantasized together', 'amalgamated through phantasy'), implying an absence of conscious intention.[18] But the fact that he placed the word 'Rosa' first in his sentence, giving it a capital letter which unmistakably echoes the maid's name, suggests considerable literary sophistication. If, however, we take Kafka at his word and assume that the description of the wound was the result of free creative phantasy, this provides further confirmation of our Freudian hypothesis. Kafka phantasized in ways that Freud analysed. Starting from what was perhaps initially an unconscious pun on the name Rosa, he expands its metaphorical and symbolic content by means of a chain of associations: girl–flower–pinkness–wound–blood.

Our ultimate concern, however, is not with Kafka's intentions but with the effect of his text on the reader. And one feature of this description of the wound is likely to fill any reader with bewilderment, perhaps even revulsion. This is the graphic picture of the worms which are crawling around inside the wound:

Würmer, an Stärke und Länge meinem kleinen Finger gleich, rosig aus eigenem und außerdem blutbespritzt, winden sich, im Innern der Wunde festgehalten, mit weißen Köpfchen, mit vielen Beinchen ans Licht. (E 151).

Worms, the breadth and length of my little finger, themselves rosy pink and also flecked with blood, while held fast in the depths of the wound, are wriggling with little white heads and many tiny legs towards the light.

No wonder critics like Politzer have found such details unfathomable. Clearly, any literal reading will be inadequate. But we may again be better served by metaphorical modes of interpretation. To take first the possibility of expanded metaphor: a whole group of German expressions associates the word 'Wurm' with bad conscience and an uneasy sense of something being rotten inside: 'da steckt der Wurm' ('there's something fishy here'), 'etwas trägt den Wurm in sich' ('something has a canker within'), 'der Wurm des schlechten Gewissens' ('the pangs of a bad conscience') and even 'das wurmt mich' ('that nettles me!'). In these terms the worms become the physical expression of the doctor's bad conscience about sexuality.

This reading is confirmed when we link the metaphorical dimension of Kafka's image with its symbolic associations. Is the 'worm in the wound' a recognizable symbol? Yes and no. For the wound is not simply a wound. It is also (by the logic of the doctor's free associations) a flower: 'Ich habe deine große Wunde aufgefunden; an dieser Blume in deiner Seite gehst du zugrunde' ('I have uncovered your great wound; this flower in your side will be the end of you'; E 151). The 'worm in the wound' thus finds its displaced meaning in the image of the worm in the flower: 'der Wurm in der Blüte' (in English: 'the worm in the bud'). The 'worm in the bud' is one of the fundamental, even archetypal symbols of frustrated sexuality. It expresses (as in Blake's poem 'The Sick Rose') that 'invisible worm' which gnaws away at the human capacity for love and destroys it before it can flower.[19] It occurs also in a passage from Shakespeare's *Twelfth Night* which may well have been familiar to Kafka in German translation. The Duke is inquiring about a woman frustrated in love:

> Duke: And what's her history?
> Viola: A blank, my lord. She never told her love,
>   But let concealment, like a worm i' the bud,
>   Feed on her damask cheek.[20]

Shakespeare, like Kafka, foregrounds his image, so that we no longer think of the abstraction 'concealment', nor even primarily of the woman's cheek. The woman has become identified with the closed flower within which the worm of repressed feeling is gnawing away, destroying her beauty.

Where Shakespeare foregrounds his image, Kafka goes one stage further. He describes the worms as if they were real: the worms in the flower — which is a wound — which is pink — which is a girl; Rosa, whom the doctor has ignored until it is too late. Or rather, it is not simply in the mind of Kafka that this chain of association evolves but in the mind of the doctor which is registering the sequence of events. And if there were any doubt that through the image of the worms Kafka is hinting at the doctor's attenuated sexuality, it is surely dispelled by the way the doctor records this motif: 'Würmer, an Stärke und Länge meinem kleinen Finger gleich' (E 151). In the doctor's mind there is the most intimate connection between the wound and his own body. Appropriately, he soon finds himself undressed and lying in bed beside his patient. Of course, at the level of consciousness represented in the figure of the doctor, these sexual implications cannot be fully apprehended. Still clinging to his status as 'Amtsarzt', he tries to console the patient as to the nature of his wound: 'deine Wunde ist so übel nicht' ('your wound is not so dreadful'; E 152).

Even the doctor grasps, however, that this wound cannot be healed by medical means. It has existential implications which exceed his competence ('Immer das Unmögliche vom Arzt verlangen' ('Always asking the impossible of the doctor'), E 151). The wound of sexuality is not a fortuitous injury but an existential endowment, as the patient's words imply: 'Mit einer schönen Wunde kam ich auf die Welt; das war meine ganze Ausstattung' ('I came into the world with a beautiful wound; that was my whole endowment'; E 152). Through a remarkable act of imaginative condensation the wound becomes simultaneously the image of birth ('auf die Welt kommen'), intercourse ('Rosa . . . in der Hüftengegend') and sickness unto death ('zugrundegehen'). The Freudian story also carries undertones of Kierkegaard.[21] By focusing on the Freudian dimension, we are thus also able to elucidate its existential implications. Kafka's subject, here as in so many of his writings, is a crisis of identity and the existential insecurity it reveals. The distinctive quality of this story (as I hope my argument has shown) is that here his theme is centred on sexuality; and that we gain a deeper insight into the story if we adopt a Freudian approach to Kafka's expanded metaphors.

Ein Landarzt may constitute the extreme case — more explicitly Freudian in form and theme than other stories. But the notion of expanded metaphor can also be fruitfully be applied to other narratives. The structure of *Das Urteil* hinges on a rather similar pun on the word 'Korrespondenzverhältnis' ('correspondence relationship'), which links Georg Bendemann to his friend in St Petersburg on the psychological plane. And the final sentence of the story, which forms his epitaph, concludes with an even more Freudian pun on the word 'Verkehr' (meaning both 'traffic' and 'intercourse'; E 56 and 68). To explore this method fully would require another paper. But one only needs to think of the first sentence of *Der Prozeß* (*The Trial*) to become aware of its potential:

Jemand mußte Josef K. verleumdet haben, denn ohne daß er etwas Böses getan hätte, wurde er eines Morgens verhaftet. (P 9)

Someone must have maligned Josef K., for without having done anything wrong, he was arrested one morning.

'Verhaftet sein' also carries metaphorical overtones — the idea of being at an 'arrested' stage of emotional development. And the 'process' described in the novel is essentially a psychological one. Readers of this novel too might have been less perplexed if they had been less literal-minded and more alert to the resonance of metaphor.

NOTES

[1] Calvin S. Hall and Richard E. Lind, *Dreams, Life and Literature: A Study of Franz Kafka* (Chapel Hill, 1970), p. 85. The mechanistic decoding of 'Freudian' symbols is exemplified by Charles Neider, *Kafka: His Mind and Art* (London, 1949).

[2] Walter H. Sokel, *Franz Kafka: Tragik und Ironie* (Munich, 1964), p. 270.

[3] Friedrich Beißner, *Der Erzähler Franz Kafka* (Frankfurt, 1983), pp. 125–48.

[4] Gustav Janouch, *Gespräche mit Kafka* (Frankfurt, 1951), p. 27.

[5] Hartmut Binder, *Motiv und Gestaltung bei Franz Kafka* (Bonn, 1966), pp. 92–114.

[6] Richard Ellmann, *James Joyce*, revised edition (New York, 1982), p. 546.

[7] Sigmund Freud, *Gesammelte Werke* (London, 1942), II/III, 380. References to Freud's writings in the text of this article refer to this edition of the *Gesammelte Werke*.

[8] Günther Anders, *Kafka Pro und Contra* (Munich, 1951), p. 71.

[9] David Lodge, *The Modes of Modern Writing: Metaphor, Metonymy, and the Typology of Modern Literature* (London, 1977), p. 75. Lodge's book is a contribution to the structuralist debate about metaphor and metonymy initiated by Roman Jakobson.

[10] George Lakoff and Mark Johnson, *Metaphors We Live By* (Chicago, 1980), pp. 81, 110.

[11] Lionel Trilling, 'Freud and Literature', in *Freud: A Collection of Critical Essays*, ed. Perry Meisel, Twentieth Century Views (Englewood Cliffs, 1981), pp. 95–111 (p. 108).

[12] Freud, II/III, 291–95. The translation of this phrase as to 'put up' at a hotel in the Standard English edition of Freud obscures the metaphorical associations.

[13] Heinz Politzer, *Franz Kafka: Parable and Paradox*, revised edition (New York, 1966), p. 89.

[14] Jacques Derrida, *Writing and Difference* (London, 1978), especially pp. 196–231: 'Freud and the Scene of Writing'.

[15] Richard H. Lawson, 'Kafka's "Der Landarzt"', *Monatshefte*, 49 (1957), 265–71 (p. 267). For a more promising approach see Herman Salinger, 'More Light on Kafka's "Landarzt"', *Monatshefte*, 53 (1961), 97–104; and Eric Marson and Keith Leopold, 'Kafka, Freud and "Ein Landarzt"', GQ, 37 (1964), 146–60.

[16] Anders, p. 47: 'Metaphernverschlingung oder Metaphernkollision verdunkelt oft den Sinn Kafkascher Geschichten'.

[17] Elizabeth M. Rajec, *Namen und ihre Bedeutung im Werke Franz Kafkas* (Berne, 1977).

[18] Hartmut Binder, *Kafka-Kommentar zu den sämtlichen Erzählungen* (Munich, 1975), p. 210.

[19] William Blake, *Songs of Innocence and Experience*, Facsimile, ed. Geoffrey Keynes (London, 1967), plate 39.

[20] Shakespeare, *Twelfth Night*, II, iv, 110–13. The physical effect of the image is retained in the Schlegel/Tieck translation, *Shakespeares Werke in vierzehn Teilen*, ed. Wolfgang Keller (Leipzig, n.d.), XII, 40:

> Und ließ Verheimlichung wie in der Knospe
> Den Wurm, an ihrer Purpurwange nagen.

[21] Kierkegaard, *The Sickness unto Death*, translated by Howard V. Hong (Princeton, 1980). Kafka acknowledged a certain affinity with Kierkegaard (T 227), but his treatment of the 'wound in the side' motif precludes Kierkegaard's Christian solution.

J. J. White

THE CYCLICAL ASPECT OF KAFKA'S SHORT STORY COLLECTIONS

Frequent reference has been made in recent years to the care and deliberation with which Kafka planned his three short story collections, *Betrachtung* (*Observation*), *Ein Landarzt* (*A Country Doctor*) and *Ein Hungerkünstler* (*A Hunger Artist*). Yet almost all relevant interpretations have concentrated on single stories in them, each viewed in isolation. The collections as such have, altogether, been the subject of less than half a dozen readings;[1] and as a result many cyclical features remain under-explored. In particular, we still need to know much more about the contribution made by individual stories to the larger ensemble effect, about the way they change their meaning and acquire fresh nuances in the wider context of a structured cycle, and just what that structure might be. Only then will it be possible to decide whether the various collections actually cohere into successful 'Einheiten' ('unities'), as Kafka explicitly hoped they would.

Some modern writers publish their stories in collections which make little or no pretence to being logically constructed cycles — or where sequence is at most of marginal importance. Kafka's work, on the other hand, belongs to an older tradition of ordering tales in deliberately significant patterns. Whether the resultant collections are also 'cyclical' in the other sense of operating with quasi-circular structures is something that will be touched upon later. But at least we have ample evidence that Kafka envisaged his collections as meaningful arrangements, where the impact of the whole was intended to be greater than that of the parts.

Sequence, as one kind of supra-segmental coherence, was evidently a major preoccupation in all Kafka's collections. Writing to Brod about *Betrachtung*, he wonders in retrospect whether the chosen order is right: 'ich stand gestern beim Ordnen der Stückchen unter dem Einfluß des Fräuleins [Felice], es ist leicht möglich, daß irgendeine Dummheit, eine vielleicht nur im Geheimen komische Aufeinanderfolge dadurch entstanden ist. Bitte, schau das noch nach' ('yesterday when putting the pieces in order I was under the influence of the woman [Felice]; it is very possible that as a result some stupid mistake or other has arisen, a progression which is comic, if only in some hidden way. Please, look over it again'; Br 102). Kafka's preoccupation with the possibilities created by publishing in collections is demonstrated by the fact that after the *Betrachtung* collection two further cyclical projects were mooted: the trilogy *Die Söhne* (*The Sons*), which was to have contained *Der Heizer* (*The Stoker*), *Die Verwandlung* (*Metamorphosis*) and *Das Urteil* (*The Judgement*); and another — *Strafen* (*Punishments*), combining *Das Urteil*, *Die Verwandlung* and *In der Strafkolonie* (*In the Penal Settlement*). 'Diese Geschichten', Kafka notes of the *Strafen* stories, 'geben eine gewisse Einheit, auch wäre natürlich ein Novellenband eine ansehnlichere Veröffentlichung gewesen' ('These stories yield a certain coherence, and naturally a novella volume would have been a more respectable publication'; Br 149). When weighing the principal advantage of publishing stories separately ('daß nämlich jede Geschichte selbständig angesehen werden kann und wirkt', 'that is, that every story works, and can be viewed, independently; Br 148), against the merits of collective publication, Kafka was more than once influenced by the attraction of producing something substantial enough to compensate for his various setbacks with the novels. Thus, although aware that *Der Heizer* 'could well be published on its own', he is soon persuaded that, together with *Die Verwandlung* and *Das Urteil*, it would make 'quite a good book': the three works 'belong together' ('sie gehoren äußerlich und innerlich zusammen'; Br 116). The failure of *Die Söhne* and *Strafen* to materialize was more due to his publisher's disinclination than to any waning of enthusiasm on Kafka's own part. In his own words: 'Mir liegt eben an der Einheit der drei Geschichten nicht weniger als an der Einheit einer von ihnen' ('I set no less store by the coherence of the three stories together, than by the coherence of any one of them'; Br 116).

That Kafka could stress the intrinsic coherence of the *Söhne* stories and yet at almost the same time argue for the inclusion of *Das Urteil* in another collection is characteristic of the complex process of creative 'Segmentieren, Kombinieren und wieder Segmentieren' ('segmenting, combining, and again segmenting') that Wolf Kittler and Gerhard Neumann have recently described while discussing the problems of reflecting it in the new critical edition.[2] For example, eleven of the fourteen *Landarzt* stories had been prepublished in other contexts, two even appearing in *Der Jude* yoked together as *Zwei Tiergeschichten* (*Two Animal Stories*). Before the collection itself was published, Kafka had toyed with at least five permutations of stories for it;[3] and even after 1919, three of its pieces still remained as integral parts of larger narratives. What Neumann has called the 'Problematik der "doppelten Situierung" seiner Texte' ('the problematics of the "double siting" of his texts') is, as he shows, a symptom of Kafka's continual vacillation between bibliophile publication of his work and private jottings.[4] The

published collections that emerge from such a process often seem to
acquire a less permanent, interim quality. In this respect, Kafka's works
are seen to stand at variance to a whole tradition of writing: 'das
Werkprinzip . . ., das die europäische Kulturtradition ihm nahelegte:
Werketappen als Durchgangszustände auf das Telos des vollendeten
Werks hin zu begreifen' ('the principle of the work, suggested to him by
the European cultural tradition: to conceive of the stages of a given work
as transitional phases leading to the telos of the completed work'; 'Der
verschleppte Prozeß', p. 107). Recent concern with the peculiarities of
Kafka's 'Schaffensprozeß' ('creative process') and with the problems
thus posed for the organization of the new critical edition have served to
highlight this unusually extreme vacillation between 'Schreibstrom und
Werkidol' ('the stream of writing and the work as idol') — to use
Neumann's terms. It is as if, in the light of this fluid process, a more
transient status is to be attributed to the published collections, with them
consequently appearing as merely one among various tentative group-
ings, rather than representing *the* definitive creative goal.

Yet a measure of caution is called for here. Kafka's sense of a correct
order for his stories was, for a start, often less tentative than the state of
affairs I have just been describing might be assumed to imply. For
instance, we find him quite emphatically declaring to his publisher that
the first *Betrachtung* story must be *Kinder auf der Landstraße* (*Children on
the Country Road*); clearly, he sees, he should have sent Wolff a table of
contents (Br 110). For the *Landarzt* cycle (a project which, as Joachim
Unseld has shown,[5] dominated Kafka's relations with Wolff for well-
nigh three years) a specific order had already been determined by August
1917, even though the work was not to appear for almost another two
and a half years. From then on, Kafka adhered to this as, in his own
words, 'die richtige Reihenfolge' ('the correct order'; Br 245). When
Meyer proposed joint publication of *Das Urteil* and *In der Strafkolonie*,
Kafka was adamant that this would make a dreadful combination
('abscheuliche Verbindung'; Br 149); *Die Verwandlung* was needed to
mediate. After Kafka's death, the proofs of *Ein Hungerkünstler* were
returned by Brod with a note about the necessary reordering of the
material (Dietz, p. 129). In all these cases, one sees the permutational
possibilities of a sequence of texts soon giving way to a sense of an
appropriate arrangement. Modifications were of course still possible
(for example, the removal of *Der Kübelreiter* (*The Bucket Rider*) from *Ein
Landarzt* or the addition of *Josefine* to *Ein Hungerkünstler*). But an overall
order nevertheless rapidly established itself as preferable. The prior and
subsequent history of the component stories may be a chequered one,
but at a certain stage Kafka does appear to have conceived his cycles in
relatively conventional terms. In any case — and this is the more

compelling reason for not being unduly constrained by Kafka's continually evolving work-complexes — the published collections always remain *one* possible way of experiencing certain stories (some would say: *the* most fruitful way). Even a critical edition presenting the stories within various combinations and matrices will still have to allow for a reading of *Betrachtung*, *Ein Landarzt* and *Ein Hungerkünstler* as integrated cycles. And it is their logic as such that interests me here.

In his comments on his work, Kafka unfortunately never indicates why particular stories come where they do or what kinds of relationship he wishes to establish between them. Nor does he reveal which of the various possible principles of ordering (e.g. complementary, variational, contrastive, progressive or circular) or which criteria of effect he had in mind. Once one has crystallized, his attitude to a 'richtige Reihenfolge' seems to be largely intuitive; hence he is willing to invoke 'a secret connection' (Br 116) or reject a combination out of hand as 'dreadful' (Br 149). The order of the stories is usually neither governed by the date a work was written, nor, where appropriate, by that of prior publication. The eventual sequence of the *Landarzt* stories, for example, bears no detectable relationship to either set of dates. And with regard to *Betrachtung*, Kafka once tellingly asked Felice: 'Ob Du wohl erkennst, wie sich die einzelnen Stückchen im Alter voneinander unterscheiden. Eines ist z. B. darunter, das ist gewiß 8–10 Jahre alt' ('Whether you do recognize how the individual pieces differ from one another, in terms of age. There is one among them, for example, that is certainly 8–10 years old'; BrF 175).

At one time it did look as if Kafka was preparing to present the *Landarzt* stories as variations on a single stated theme (which is, of course, just about the simplest form of coherence a writer can give a collection). In April 1917 he sent Martin Buber a selection of his recent work. 'Alle diese Stücke und noch andere', he wrote, 'sollen später einmal als Buch erscheinen unter dem gemeinsamen Titel: "Verantwortung"' ('All these pieces, and others besides, should some time later appear as a book with the general title: "Responsibility"').[6] Since this remark was published in the early seventies, various attempts have been made, the most detailed being that by Robert Kauf, to relate the *Landarzt* collection to this theme. In Kauf's opinion: 'The fact that . . . Kafka seriously considered the title *Verantwortung* indicates the need to view the *Landarzt* stories as exponents of the responsibility theme'.[7] But does it? If they had actually been published under the collective title 'Verantwortung' (which, Dietz suggests, p. 107, may in any case have been a deliberately ethical sounding title, chosen with an eye to the stories' recipient, Buber), then certainly the stories would have necessitated such a reading. However, since Kafka did *not* retain this umbrella title, there is no reason at all why the theme of responsibility should acquire any more special significance as a framework for interpretation than, say, the themes of 'dehumanization', 'salvation' and 'Botschaft' ('message') (all of which have in turn been proposed as *the* main link between the various stories).[8] Given that the title Kafka eventually chose represents a positive refusal to relate all the tales to one single concept, it remains possible to construe a whole range of thematic and motif-links between the constituent stories. In fact, the change in type of title brings about a change of reading process, for a title giving explicit thematic unity to a collection forces the reader to conceptualize the stories in that light, whereas the title *Ein Landarzt* allows for a more subtle set of refractions between the title-story and the others. It is doubtful whether Kafka abandoned 'Verantwortung' simply, as Kauf suggests, because he 'realized that it did not fit all the stories equally well'. The addition of *Ein Traum* (*A Dream*) to the collection may well have created accommodation problems in this respect, but this would not have been unprecedented: many have, after all, felt that the collective title *Ein Hungerkünstler* makes *Eine kleine Frau* (*A Little Woman*) a difficult inclusion to justify as a consequence. In rejecting an almost allegorical title in favour of naming his second collection after one of the major tales in it, Kafka was primarily opening the way for the same kind of multiple relationships between title and parts of the collection as one finds in the other two cycles. *Betrachtung*, as a title, merely indicates a stance; it scarcely straitjackets the first collection in the way that 'Verantwortung' would have done to the second one (even granting that many different kinds of responsibility figure in the *Landarzt* collection). And while the next two projected titles, *Die Söhne* and *Strafen*, would have suffered from the sort of obviousness Kafka goes on to reject in the case of 'Verantwortung', his later strategy — of using a key work as title-story — shows more inventiveness; the work in question achieves emblematic status without over-conceptualizing the cycle, it foregrounds one situation and yet allows a whole range of relationships to colour one's reading of the entire collection. (A further factor may have led to the rejection of a thematic title like 'Verantwortung': for a collection containing fourteen stories to have been constructed in relation to just one explicit concept would have risked becoming mechanical. Recent collaborative experiments by writers all treating a shared topic have shown how artificial variations-on-a-theme can easily become as a genre.)

But of course, if coherence is not explicitly thematic, it can still be a matter of implicitly shared themes and common situations; it can still be observed as the product of very generalized common denominators in the subject matter. Yet to read the few existing commentaries on the collections, one would think that it was no more than a product of local linking devices — merely connecting adjacent stories or sub-groups of tales, and even then not always in a very vital way. Thus it has been argued that the first three *Betrachtung* stories 'stehen in einer zeitlichen Folge; es wird immer später am Abend' ('stand in a temporal sequence; it becomes later and later in the evening'), after which this form of temporal linking is assumed to give way to other kinds. Hence, *Entschlüsse (Decisions)* is linked to the preceding *Plötzlicher Spaziergang (A Sudden Walk)* by no more than the formulation 'wenn man sich am Abend endgültig entschlossen zu haben scheint' ('when in the evening one finally seems to have decided'; *Kafka-Handbuch*, 209). Sometimes the suggested connection is a shared motif: 'Sowohl *Ein altes Blatt* als auch *Vor dem Gesetz* tragen Überlieferungen aus alter Zeit vor', according to Binder, 'in beiden gibt es ein zum Absoluten führendes Tor, vor dem das Geschehen spielt' ('Both *An Old Page* and *Before the Law* present traditions from much earlier times; in both there is a gate leading to the Absolute; the action takes place before this gate'; *Kafka Kommentar*, p. 235). Sometimes echoes in vocabulary link two stories: for example, a simile in *Ein Brudermord (A Fratricide)* ('der über dem Ehepaar sich wie der Rasen eines Grabes schließende Pelz'; E 181) is taken up by the literal image of a grassy mound ('Grabhügel') in *Ein Traum*, according to Binder (*Kafka Kommentar*, p. 235). A particular story may be seen to elaborate thematic aspects of its predecessor. Thus in *Auf der Galerie (In the Gallery)* Richter sees a portrayal of the impossibility of individual intervention, '*Ein altes Blatt* dagegen zeigt die Machtlosigkeit einer ganzen Klasse [read: 'Gruppe'] gegenüber dem unmittelbaren Zugriff der Barbarei' ('*An Old Page*, on the other hand, shows the powerlessness of an entire group faced with the immediate onslaught of barbarism'; *Franz Kafka*, p. 138). Here the link supplied is in the shape of a notional progression from specific to general helplessness. Yet most links that commentators have so far concentrated on have not involved such progressions, they have simply been associative or loosely thematic. At times the connexions posited have been central (for instance, the frustrations and despair of the artist-figures in the *Hungerkünstler* collection). More often than not, though, proposed common denominators have been — at best — peripheral. Whether most readers would see *Schackale und Araber (Jackals and Arabs)* and *Ein Besuch im Bergwerk (A Visit to the Mine)* as being persuasively linked by the idea of visiting or whether many would consider the staircase motif ('die Vorstellung, dauernd auf Treppen zu leben'; *Kafka-Handbuch*, II, 213) as an illuminating parallel between *Eine kaiserliche Botschaft (An Imperial Message)* and *Die Sorge des Hausvaters (The Cares of a Family Man)* seems unlikely. Any link that exists via staircases between Odradek and the imperial messenger is probably at most an arabesque.

Obviously, a whole spectrum of links, covert and explicit, major and minor, agreed by consensus or part of an idiosyncratic interpretation, can obtain between individual stories in a collection. They can reinforce thematic consistency; or they can even be there in its stead. Rather than treating essential binding elements alongside arabesques and giving apparently equal status to aspects that must feature in any serious reading and to eccentric analogies, any serious account of cyclical coherence needs first to discern what a text's overall strategy is, if one is going to see the wood for the trees. It is necessary to decide just what kind of textual combination one is dealing with before one can distinguish major contributory devices from those which are, at most, of local tactical significance. (By contrast, there is a telling moment in the *Kafka-Handbuch* where we are informed, in all seriousness: 'daß es nicht nur zwischen unmittelbar benachbarten Texten . . . Motiv-verknüpfungen gibt' ('it is not only between immediately adjacent texts that thematic connexions exist'; II, 213). One might well wonder what reader would assume that connexions in a cycle could be restricted to those between adjacent stories, if it were not for the persistent way in which this assumption has dogged discussions of coherence in these three cycles!)

Each of Kafka's collections, I would suggest, is substantially different. By comparison with *Ein Landarzt*, the sketches of *Betrachtung* are loosely connected and appear in a less sacrosanct arrangement. (One indication of this is the number of differences between the *Hyperion*, *Bohemia* and Rowohlt Verlag versions of the cycle — differences so great, in fact, as to create three almost completely independent works.) Given the more free-floating structure of the *Betrachtung* stories, the intermittent, arabesque links that have been detected are not so much there to underline crucial structural and thematic coherences of the first order; they are often the only connexion we have. The *Hungerkünstler* collection, by contrast, is even more tightly structured than *Ein Landarzt* (a feature which must partly be the result of having a substantially smaller corpus of stories to operate with). In this case, local links tend merely to reinforce the more essential patterns of coherence we shall be looking at later.

If one accepts that the collections are each different, then it follows that even seemingly comparable structural features can have dissimilar functions within them. Without making anything of the point, both Binder's *Kafka Kommentar* (p. 235) and the *Kafka-Handbuch* (II, 213) note that in all three of his collections Kafka chooses to put his longest story last. (Or, even less helpfully, Binder argues that *Ein Bericht für eine Akademie*, 'der längste Text, mußte das Ende bilden' (*A Report for an Academy*, 'the longest text, had to form the conclusion') — on grounds of analogy, that is, between *Ein Landarzt* and the other collections, when argument-by-analogy becomes a most inappropriate approach to Kafka's cycles.) Length on its own would, in any case, seem a very rough-and-ready measure of anything. *Josefine* may be the longest story in *Ein Hungerkünstler*, but (with all due respect to J. P. Stern's spirited defence of it in the present volume) it hardly plays the crucial role within its cycle that we shall find *Ein Bericht*, also the longest story, does in *Ein Landarzt*. In various respects *Josefine* is the 'Satyrspiel' to the preceding title-story, and in many readings it remains little more than elaborate parodistic postscript to it. In the case of *Betrachtung*, it would seem less instructive simply to note that the last story, *Unglücklichsein* (*Unhappiness*), is the longest, than to relate this to the equally striking fact that the second-longest, *Kinder auf der Landstraße*, is in first position. It is the 'framing' of a series of often remarkably brief sketches by these two more substantial items that is a key feature of *Betrachtung*. For the disjointed recollections of a strangely isolated childhood in *Kinder auf der Landstraße* are taken up in the final encounter with the child-ghost in *Unglücklichsein*, though the bleakness of the final sketch means that we do more than just come full circle: 'diese Angst bleibt . . . weil ich mich so verlassen fühlte, ging ich . . . hinauf und legte mich schlafen' ('this anxiety remains . . . because I felt so abandoned, I went up and went to bed'; E 49 f.) — a contrast to the people who never sleep and the wish to travel with them evoked at the end of the first tale.

The two longest stories are also at each end of the *Landarzt* collection, although here the pattern is not as simple as the one in *Betrachtung*.

In January 1918, Kafka wrote concerning the *Landarzt* cycle to the Kurt Wolff Verlag: 'Das Buch soll aus 15 kleinen Erzählungen bestehn, deren Reihenfolge ich Ihnen vor kurzer Zeit in einem Brief angegeben habe. Wie diese Reihenfolge war, weiß ich augenblicklich nicht auswendig, jedenfalls war aber "Landarzt" nicht das erste Stück, sondern das zweite; das erste . . . war "Der neue Advokat"' ('The book should consist of fifteen small stories, the order of which I indicated to you in a letter a short time ago. At the moment I don't remember precisely what this order was; in any case, though, "A Country Doctor" was not the first piece, but the second; the first was "The New Advocate"').[9] Kafka is here emphasizing what might look like an obvious anomaly to the arrangement: his much-prized title-story is in *second*, not (as one might have expected) in first position — which is taken by the more modest *Der neue Advokat*. (In fact, even Kafka's earliest list of possible *Landarzt* stories has a number one against the third title, *Der neue Advokat*; of the other tales, only *Ein Traum* has a number (viz. eleven) against it — which suggests that the longest-last principle does not figure in Kafka's thinking, at least at this stage.)[10]

One possible interpretation of this structure is that *Der neue Advokat* is intended as an overture to the collection, introducing, *inter alia*, the contrast between 'Former times' and an impoverished present, the theme of frustrated messianic hopes and the contrast between deeds and words that pervade much of *Ein Landarzt*. (On this there is already a measure of critical agreement, and arguably a comparable role is played by *Erstes Leid* (*First Sorrow*) in the next collection.) Such an overture function is common enough in story-cycles;[11] one finds it, for instance, in both Sherwood Anderson's *Winesburg, Ohio* and Hemingway's *In Our Time*. But what is substantially different in *Ein Landarzt* is the way in which a more specific overture plus title-story sequence — when combined with the fact that the title-story and the final one are so evidently related — establishes a more complex link between the collection's beginning and its ending.

Recent suggestions that *Ein Landarzt* is 'framed' by two stories in which animals change into human beings (*Kafka Kommentar*, p. 235, *Kafka-Handbuch*, II, 212) are not strictly accurate, for the whole point about *Der neue Advokat* and *Ein Bericht* is that their protagonists *do not* completely become human beings. Still, a variation on the metamorphosis motif does clearly connect them. First and last stories are inevitably brought together in the reader's mind by certain similarities between Bucephalus and Rotpeter. But there is a double 'framing' here. The main pairing, if one treats *Der neue Advokat* as essentially an overture, is that between the second and the last stories in the *Landarzt* structure.

The individual stories *Ein Landarzt* and *Ein Bericht* are both thematically and quantitatively more substantial than the intervening tales they 'frame'. They form part of a symmetrical structure, having at its centre the shortest piece in the whole collection: *Das nächste Dorf* (*The Next Village*). This six-line parable embodies the truth that all action is vanity, a truth illustrated by most of the tales on either side of it. Other symmetries emerge as well, once one hives off *Der neue Advokat* as an overture to the collection proper. And what we shall see, as we explore the relationships between some of the individual stories, is that position often adds further significance to various *Landarzt* tales (which is hardly surprising, given the care that Kafka took in ordering his material). This is not the place for a detailed structure-oriented reading of the entire collection, but even the following brief consideration of the relationships between the first two stories and the last two should indicate the lines along which such an interpretation would proceed.

Whereas the 'framing' in *Betrachtung* tended on the whole to bring out essential similarities between the first and last stories in the cycle, giving an impression of circularity or even a deterioration of predicament, an analogous structure in *Ein Landarzt* is used for contrastive reasons. If *Der neue Advokat* and *Ein Bericht für eine Akademie* are similar, in that both have animal protagonists obliged to break with their pasts and accommodate themselves to the world of modern men, it is nevertheless the *differences* between Bucephalus and Rotpeter that determine the cycle's overall meaning. In *Kafka's Narrators*, Roy Pascal makes out a persuasive case for seeing Rotpeter's story as one of positive achievement: the ape displays a welcome pragmatism, he survives against the odds. Not only is he realistic enough in his contentment with a 'way out' rather than searching for some ideal freedom (which, the cycle shows elsewhere, is elusive), he is also a sociable creature.[12] The contrast between the lugubrious Dr Bucephalus, sitting in lone contemplation of the lawbooks (perhaps he is doing the best thing, the narrator opines in a spirit of luke-warm conciliation) and the gregarious Rotpeter reporting his successful act of assimilation to the 'hohe Herren der Akademie' ('gentlemen of the Academy') (clearly his inferiors) is the measure of the ground that has been covered by the end of *Ein Landarzt*. *Der neue Advokat* is an elegiac tale; it looks back to a golden time of heroic grandeur. But by the end of *Ein Landarzt*, thanks largely to *Ein Traum*, immortality such as Alexander enjoyed and K. dreams of (N.B. the image of having his name engraved in gold letters) has been rejected as no more than a dream, another false 'night-bell'. Rotpeter's solution, by contrast, smacks of a healthy realism in confronting the present.

Various connexions between *Der neue Advokat* and the stories that follow it appear to reinforce this idea of a progression within the *Landarzt* cycle: for the early negative images clearly form a contrast to the final story in the collection. Until recently, Kafka's much-interpreted country-doctor story had only been viewed in isolation. However, Binder's *Kafka Kommentar* rightly points to one crucial motif it shares with the works around it: '*Landarzt* und *Kübelreiter* — dieses Stück sollte ursprünglich an dritter Stelle der Sammlung erscheinen — schließen als Reitergeschichten gut an Bucephalus an und haben überdies ein sehr ähnliches Ende. *Auf der Galerie* als nächster Text ist über die Kunstreiterin natürlich mit dem Kübelreiter, aber dann auch . . . mit dem auf einem Pferd reitenden Landarzt motivisch gut verbunden' ('*Country Doctor* and *Bucket Rider* — this piece was originally meant to appear as the third story in the collection — link up well with Bucephalus as stories of riders, and have moreover a very similar ending. As following text, *In the Gallery* is naturally connected, via the acrobat on horseback, to the bucket rider, but then in addition can be firmly linked with the country doctor, who also rides a horse'; II, 235). Provided that one is primarily interested in common denominators and one acts as if *Der Kübelreiter* were still part of the collection,[13] then this is certainly so. But the whole point about the horse-motif in *Ein Landarzt* is surely the fact that the doctor does *not* have a horse to ride: it is not a 'Reitergeschichte' ('das Pferd fehlte' ('the horse is missing'), E 146). Hence the impossible combination of 'earthly carriage' and 'unearthly horses' (E 153). *Der neue Advokat* prepares us for this predicament by showing that the ideal combination of horse and controlling rider, Bucephalus and Alexander, is a thing of the past ('Heute [. . .] gibt es keinen großen Alexander' ('Today . . . there is no great Alexander'), E 145). The elegiac concluding image of the former 'Streitroß' without his master then becomes contrasted with that of the country-doctor, a rider without a horse (a man who falls sadly short of being an Alexander, even if inordinate hopes are invested in him). Instead of the oneness of horse and rider recalled in the first tale, we now have a carriage and two uncontrollable horses; and contrasting with the myth of Alexander's showing the way with his 'royal sword' comes the image of the doctor's interminable, directionless wandering. Answering the false summons of the night-bell is the opposite of having a legendary Alexander to follow. The perspective supplied by *Der neue Advokat*, in short, serves to intensify our sense of the doctor's shortcomings; even if the gods *do* send horses, he is no Alexander, able to control them. (Little would have been added to the cycle, in this respect, by the retention of *Der Kübelreiter*, whereas *Auf der Galerie* develops the idea — to the stage where wandering infinitely has been reduced to the absurdity of being forced to ride in a circle ('monatelang ohne Unterbrechung im Kreise herum'), where not being in charge, as Alexander was, becomes being 'driven [. . .] by the relentless ringmaster cracking his whip' (E 154), and where golden legend has given way to deceptive tinsel. *Auf der Galerie* is, of course, bleak enough when read on its own. In the context of the preceding stories it inevitably becomes even more so.

Both *Der neue Advokat* and *Ein Landarzt* sound the notes of frustration and despair which are to characterize so many of the middle stories in their collection, a mood which is most concentratedly presented in the brief central piece, *Das nächste Dorf*. But in its entirety, the cycle is more than a series of restatements of a fixed set of themes. One only has to consider the relationship between the initial stories and *Ein Traum* and *Ein Bericht* to appreciate this.

Robert Kauf sees *Ein Traum* as the story whose 'inclusion . . . in a collection called *Verantwortung* would perhaps have been hardest to justify' (p. 432). But once one abandons the assumption that the *Landarzt* collection offers a series of explorations of the responsibility theme, *Ein Traum* becomes easier to integrate. The country-doctor's story itself centres on the question of whether his patient's wound is fatal or something shared by everyone (and by that token 'so übel nicht' ('not so bad'), E 152). The final two stories juxtapose a similar pair of possibilities: death as a solution or, as an alternative, a sense of bond with others. The choice between death and possibly posthumous fame (the gold letters on K.'s tombstone are more monumental than horrific) and assimilation into a world of humans is surely decided in favour of Rotpeter's 'way out'. He too could have chosen death; he knows that if he had tried to escape, he would in all probability have been shot. So he decides upon a more modest 'way out'. *Ein Traum* presents the rewards of posterity as a mere dream from which one wakes up, hence the ape's decision seems a sensible one. No doubt, *Ein Traum* could have been interpreted within the *Verantwortung* framework, if that had been the collection's overall title. But in the cycle as it is, the story has a different function: it raises (only to reject) the possibility of death as a response to the predicaments so far evoked. And in doing so, it ensures that we read the final story more positively.

When seen in the light of the earlier tales, Rotpeter's contrast between 'way out' and absolute freedom becomes more acceptable. 'Freiheit wollte ich nicht. Nur einen Ausweg . . . Ich meine nicht dieses große Gefühl der Freiheit nach allen Seiten. Als Affe kannte ich es vielleicht und ich habe Menschen kennengelernt, die sich danach sehnen [such idealism has, after all, been one of the recurrent themes of the central stories], mit Freiheit betrügt man sich unter Menschen allzuoft!' ('I did not want freedom. Only a way out . . . I don't mean this great feeling of freedom on all sides. Perhaps I knew it as an ape, and I have come to know men who yearn for it; with freedom one all too often deceives oneself among men!'; E 188). The new advocate Dr Bucephalus may claim to feel free ('unbedrückt von den Lenden des Reiters', 'unhampered by the thighs of the rider'; E 146), but he has paid a high price for this spurious sense of freedom and he does not seem all that convinced by his own boast. Certainly by the end of the cycle it is Rotpeter's 'way out' that emerges as 'really perhaps the best thing' (E 146), not Bucephalus's.

The first and last stories in the *Landarzt* collection, we can conclude, mark a progression: from lonely resignation to an affirmation of a relatively social existence. Whereas the structure of *Betrachtung* was essentially non-progressive, that of *Ein Landarzt* is far from being so: not only is Rotpeter's achievement a contrast to the frustrations of his predecessors (the jackals, those unable to drive out the nomads, the person waiting for a message from the Emperor or the one before the gates of the Law), there is also a progression in mood. For whereas the title-story verges on nightmare and the image in *Ein altes Blatt* of the nomads devouring a living ox strikes a distinctly horrific note, by the end of the cycle we have entered into a very different register, with

Rotpeter's amusing performance before the allegedly learned academicians.

In the planned *Strafen* collection, as Kittler has shown, the outlook was to have become progressively gloomier, as one moved from *Der Heizer* via *Das Urteil* to *Die Verwandlung*. Yet even if the final optimistic note sounded in *Ein Landarzt* is not mirrored in the general development of *Ein Hungerkünstler*, even here the addition of *Josefine* (in contrast to *Der Bau* (*The Burrow*), which Kafka was reputedly considering at one time as the final story) takes the cycle eventually in roughly the same direction. Just as the second collection would be very different if it ended with the title-story instead of with *Ein Bericht*, so the *Hungerkünstler* collection would change radically, if *Josefine* came before the story about the hunger-artist instead of after it.

Many of the features of the *Hungerkünstler* collection give it a relatively 'closed' form. Indeed, Kafka's cycles move progressively from openness towards closedness, with *Betrachtung* being the most loosely structured of the three, and *Ein Landarzt*, as I have tried to indicate, moving — despite its having an equally large number of stories — in the direction of closure, and, through *Ein Bericht*, offering something of an antidote to the predicaments previously described.

In the *Hungerkünstler* collection, the various ways in which first and third and second and fourth stories are cross-linked has been commented on by both Binder and Kittler. Not only do *Erstes Leid* and *Ein Hungerkünstler* seem the closest works in the cycle in their comparable treatment of the theme of the artist's dissatisfactions; they are also the collection's two third-person texts. *Eine kleine Frau* and *Josefine* concern 'difficult' female protagonists and are first-person narratives (the one singular, the other plural). This method of linking alternate stories — which is also quite frequently to be found in the *Landarzt* collection — is just one structure to the cycle; and it is one that often engenders ironic relationships between neighbouring works. I have already suggested that the title-story's pathos is off-set by the tone and dominant motifs of *Josefine*; the suffering of the trapeze-artist is similarly transposed into a different realm of values when externalized as the attitude of the 'kleine Frau' towards the protagonist of the next story. But this ironic alternation is only one pattern to the cycle. There is also a temporal progression between the stories, as we begin with the idea of *first* suffering and proceed, via progressively older protagonists to end with thoughts of what Josefine's standing will be in the eyes of posterity.

What is more, the overall structure of *Ein Hungerkünstler* is also open to at least one further interpretation. Rather than progressing in any meaningful sense from shortest to longest story (which would seem little more than a mannerism, if it really was an intentionally operative feature in the author's view), *Ein Hungerkünstler* can be seen to display the same pattern of overture plus main stories that is to be found in *Ein Landarzt*. Moreover, since length on its own is no reliable indicator of relative importance within the collection, other — less superficial — factors must become more instrumental in determining relationships between the component stories. The title-story (by common consent the most artistically successful and complex in the collection) comes this time in third position. (Let us discount for the purposes of this analysis the possibility that this is simply a result of the last-minute incorporation of *Josefine* into the collection.) While the other stories were already set up in print before *Josefine* was added, it seems clear that Kafka had been intending to include one more story (probably *Der Bau*), if he had been able to finish it to his satisfaction. What we have then, either way, is a collection of three main stories (preceded by an overture), where the key story is at the centre of the cycle, flanked by two lesser works, both of which in their various ways ironize the central story. This is, I would suggest, an extension into cyclical structure of the kind of ironic effect Kafka indulges in in some of his individual story-endings. Just as the concluding sentence of *Das Urteil*, the last few pages of *Die Verwandlung* and the final paragraph of *Ein Hungerkünstler* introduce an ironic counter-perspective into one's reading experience of events, so individual stories within a cycle can counterbalance one another. Critical attention has been so concentrated on the unifying elements in Kafka's collections that one of their other major features — contrastive and ironizing effects — has scarcely received any consideration at all.

There is, however, one respect in which the discontinuity in the *Hungerkünstler* collection has been acknowledged, and that is in the case of *Eine kleine Frau*, which has generally been felt not to be thematically well integrated into the cycle. The *Kafka-Handbuch*, for example, describes it as a work with a completely different theme from the other stories (II, 214), by contrast to the other tales in the cycle it does not centre on an artist-figure. Yet there is nothing accidental here. *Eine kleine Frau* was always intended as part of a collection entitled *Ein Hungerkünstler*. Even if the fourth story had been *Der Bau*, *Eine kleine Frau* would still have been the exception, thematically speaking. For Malcolm Pasley has shown the extent to which the problems and terminology of the burrowing hero have aesthetic overtones, so *Eine kleine Frau* would still have remained the 'non-artist' anomaly. It is therefore more prudent to assume that any contrast between it and the other stories is a deliberate feature of the collection's significance. Not only does the collection then colour our reading of *Eine kleine Frau*, but, equally importantly, this story gives a new complexion to our interpretation of the other stories. A work surrounded by three artist-stories, and one where the protagonist is very much concerned with his public reputation ('ich [bin] der Öffentlichkeit nicht unbekannt' ('I am not unknown to the public'), he admits at one point, E 253), is likely to seem like a 'Verfremdung' of the artist-problems — the frustrations of being misunderstood, the parallels between self-image and public persona and the neurotic vacillation between confidence and angst — that we have in the other tales, rather than simply a maverick. And the corollary of this is that the inclusion of *Eine kleine Frau* should also encourage the reader to reassess the neighbouring artist-stories. Are the idealism, perfectionism, self-questioning and frustrations depicted there peculiar to the artist? Whenever artists appear in literature, there is a natural tendency to assume that the author is speaking *pro domo*, rather than to allow for a symbolic function. Kafka's final collection would seem to be trying to counteract this literalizing tendency by juxtaposing the artist-tales with *Eine kleine Frau*.

The handful of interpretations we have of Kafka's collections are almost exclusively concerned with *integrating* devices and with showing how the parts add up to a greater unity. (Kittler's section in Volume II of the *Kafka-Handbuch* on 'Die Erzählsammlungen als Einheit' ('The Collections of Stories as a Unity') in fact forms part of a larger survey-section entitled 'Integration'.) Such approaches radiate outwards from the individual stories towards some notional cyclical wholeness. But viewed hermeneutically, the effect is a two-directional one. If the individual parts add up to some greater whole, then that whole, in turn, must affect the way we read the individual stories. Although we rejoice in numerous interpretations of the individual *Landarzt* and *Hunger-künstler* stories, each still needs to be re-examined in the light of its cyclical context. To take the most famous example: *Vor dem Gesetz* (which in any case is likely to have a different meaning when it forms part of *Der Prozeß* than when read as a separate parable) becomes a different work again within the framework of the *Landarzt* collection. To cite a small, but telling detail, one could scarcely imagine a greater contrast than that between the opening myth of the great Alexander spurring his charger on to India and the man–insect relationship we have here: '[er bittet] auch die Flöhe, ihm zu helfen und den Türhüter umzustimmen' ('he also asks the fleas to help him by persuading the guard at the door'; E 159). Within the context of *Der Prozeß* (especially the 'Untersuchung' ('interrogation') sequence in Chapter Two), it may seem as if all the man has to do is walk in, anyway. But when *Vor dem Gesetz* comes within the pattern of repeated frustration that one has with *Ein altes Blatt*, *Eine kaiserliche Botschaft*, *Ein Landarzt* and *Schackale und Araber*, the impasse assumes an air of inevitability, rather than appearing of the man's own making. The last paragraph of the preceding *Ein altes*

Blatt is relevant here, for it reads: 'Der kaiserliche Palast . . . versteht es nicht, [die Nomaden] wieder zu vertreiben. Das Tor bleibt verschlossen . . . Wir sind einer solchen Aufgabe [scil. der Rettung des Landes] nicht gewachsen . . . wir gehen daran zugrunde' ('The Imperial Palace has no idea how to drive the nomads away again. The gate remains locked. We are unequal to such a task [i.e. the salvation of the country] . . . that will be the end of us'; E 157 f.). Pressure of context such as this makes the Mann vom Lande's chances seem even more hopeless, though by the same token Rotpeter's *faute de mieux* solution of a 'way out' becomes all the more understandable.

Textual environment also changes or sharpens some of the associations of *Schackale und Araber*. For a messianic hope that had still been imbued with a sense of heroic leadership (in *Der neue Advokat*) and religious healing (in *Ein Landarzt*) has now been reduced to its own caricature. The pathetically symbolic rusty scissors, the contrast between the misplaced hopes of deliverance and the jackals' baser instincts, and the Arab's final mocking words are a sad postscript to both individual and communal hopes expressed in other stories. The jackals are the *reductio ad absurdum* of the 'salvation' theme depicted elsewhere in the cycle. After *Ein Besuch im Bergwerk* (with its resigned conclusion: 'wir werden die Rückkehr der Herren nicht mehr mit ansehen' ('we will not accompany the gentlemen any further on their return journey'), E 168), it is a short, logical step to the most negative piece in the collection, *Das nächste Dorf*. The grandfather's declaration (borne out by the next story) that life is too brief even for the short ride to the next village would, were it not for the cycle's concluding story, be an apt epitaph for all the vain endeavours we witness in *Ein Landarzt*. *Das nächste Dorf* may be at the centre of the collection and it may offer in quintessential form the truths of most of the stories around it, but it will eventually be relativized by Rotpeter's 'report'.

After the polemics the story has generated in recent years, one feels hesitant to mention 'Elf Söhne' ('Eleven Sons') within this framework. But it too must assume a more contextual and less extrinsically enigmatic meaning, when sandwiched between *Die Sorge des Hausvaters* and *Ein Brudermord*. Even if one were to accept Malcolm Pasley's elaboration of Kafka's remark that the eleven sons are simply eleven stories and assume that the eventual removal of the story from final 'commentary'-position is an instance of Kafka's including a private allusion and yet covering his tracks,[14] one would still have to allow for a less genetic meaning in the final collection, as Pasley himself points out. Compared with the total incomprehension the caretaker shows Odradek (whom he treats 'like a child') and by comparison with the fratricide to follow, the father's behaviour here assumes relatively human proportions. Within the catalogue of relationships described in *Ein Landarzt* — between jackals and Arabs, rulers and subjects, performers and public (not to mention ring-masters), workers and superiors — this paternal ambivalence is by no means the worst. Context again relativizes, position gives rise to new meanings and associations.

Kafka has offered two conflicting metaphors which might conceivably sum up the achievements of his short story collections. The one is the so-called 'Teilbausystem' ('piecemeal system of construction') of *Beim Bau der Chinesischen Mauer* (*Building the Great Wall of China*), where the individual parts being laboured away at in frustrating isolation never cohere into something 'zusammenhängend' ('cohesive'). The other comes at the end of a contemplation on the indivisibility of truth: 'Erst im Chor mag eine gewisse Wahrheit liegen' ('In the chorus alone there may be a certain truth'; H 343). Kafka's general success in making more complex statements through his carefully conceived collections is, I think, better expressed by the second image. *Betrachtung* may in some respects be closer to the discontinuities of the 'Teilbausystem', but the two later collections do surely sing with a voice that is richer than those of their individual members.

NOTES

[1] It was Max Brod who originally stressed the importance of the cycles for Kafka's view of his writings (see *Über Franz Kafka*, Frankfurt/M., 1966, passim). In recent years, the point has been substantially reinforced by Ludwig Dietz, *Franz Kafka. Die Veröffentlichungen zu seinen Lebzeiten (1908–1924). Eine textkritische und kommentierte Bibliographie*, Repertoria Heidelbergensia, 4 (Heidelberg, 1982), and Joachim Unseld, *Franz Kafka. Ein Schriftstellerleben. Die Geschichte seiner Veröffentlichungen. Mit einer Bibliographie sämtlicher Drucke und Ausgaben der Dichtungen Franz Kafkas 1908–1924* (Munich, 1982). The earliest, and in many respects (for all its Marxist distortions) most detailed study of the cyclical aspect of Kafka's story collections is Helmut Richter, *Franz Kafka. Werk und Entwurf*, Neue Beiträge zur Literaturwissenschaft (Berlin, 1962), especially pp. 52–81 and 127–66 (although Richter does not subject the *Hungerkünstler* collection to the same analysis as the earlier cycles receive). The cyclical aspect receives brief coverage in Hartmut Binder, *Kafka Kommentar zu sämtlichen Erzählungen* (Munich, 1975), pp. 116–22, 333–36, and in Wolf Kittler, 'Die Erzählsammlungen als Einheit', in the *Kafka-Handbuch*, ed. Hartmut Binder, vol. II: *Das Werk und seine Wirkung* (Stuttgart, 1979), pp. 209–14. Although the latter is, by Kittler's own admission, strongly indebted to Binder's *Kafka Kommentar*, it does have the merit of including a helpful analysis of the logic of Kafka's projected cycles *Die Söhne* and *Strafen*.

[2] Wolf Kittler and Gerhard Neumann, 'Kafkas "Drucke zu Lebzeiten". Editorische Technik und hermeneutische Entscheidung', *Freiburger Universitätsblätter*, 78 (December, 1982), 65.

[3] In his notes to *Hochzeitsvorbereitungen auf dem Lande*, Brod records: 'Im ersten Oktavheft folgt hier [i.e. at the end] noch eine Seite, die die erste Zusammenstellung der für den *Landarzt*-Band bestimmten Erzählungen enthält. Die Titel der

damals also wohl schon fertig vorliegenden Erzählungen lauten: Auf der Galerie—
Kastengeist—Kübelreiter—Ein Reiter—Ein Kaufmann—Ein Landarzt—Traum
— Vor dem Gesetz — Ein Brudermord — Schackale und Araber — Der neue
Advokat. Die Skizze "Ein Reiter" könnte mit dem im *Landarzt*-Band stehenden
Stück "Das nächste Dorf" identisch sein. "Kastengeist" ließe sich vielleicht als "Ein
Besuch im Bergwerk" agnoszieren. "Ein Kaufmann" ist vielleicht das Stück, das ich
im Band *Beschreibung eines Kampfes* unter dem Titel "Der Nachbar" veröffentlicht
habe' (H 440). The further title-list that Brod notes appeared at the end of the Sixth
Oktavheft (see H 447) gives the order as: 'Ein Traum — Vor dem Gesetz — Eine
kaiserliche Botschaft—Die kurze Zeit—Ein altes Blatt—Schackale und Araber—
Auf der Galerie — Der Kübelreiter — Ein Landarzt — Der neue Advokat — Ein
Brudermord — Elf Söhne'. Kafka's letter of 20 August 1917 to Kurt Wolff (Br 159)
gives the actual final contents of the published collection, with the one difference that
'Der Kübelreiter' is still included in the planned collection in third place. In fact, as
Pasley and Wagenbach have shown, Oktavhefte One and Six are consecutive. See:
'Datierung sämtlicher Texte Franz Kafkas' in Jürgen Born et al., *Kafka-Symposion*
(Munich, 1969), pp. 59 f. Here Heft B (= what Brod calls the First Oktavheft) is
dated January–February 1917 and Heft C (= Brod's Sixth Oktavheft) is dated
March–April 1917. Dietz has pointed out, however, that these datings may not in
fact apply to the concluding title-lists themselves. Both lists use the title 'Ein
Brudermord', whereas (according to Dietz, p. 107) Kafka was still referring to this
work as 'Der Mord' as late as July 1917; so the title-lists may well have been entered at
a later date. In addition to these well-known title-lists, there are, according to
Joachim Unseld (p. 276) further unpublished lists of titles for the *Landarzt* collection
in the Max Brod Archives in Tel Aviv.

4 'Der verschleppte Prozeß. Literarisches Schaffen zwischen Schreibstrom und
   Werkidol', *Poetica*, 14 (1983), 83.

5 *Franz Kafka. Ein Schriftstellerleben*, pp. 129 f.

6 Martin Buber, *Briefwechsel aus sieben Jahrzehnten* (Heidelberg, 1972), I, 491 f.

7 '*Verantwortung*. The Theme of Kafka's *Landarzt* Cycle', *MLQ*, 33 (1972), 420–32.

8 See, respectively, Heinz Politzer, *Franz Kafka. Parable and Paradox* (Ithaca, 1962),
   p. 92; Malcolm Pasley, 'Semi-private games', in *The Kafka Debate. New Perspectives
   for our Time*, ed. Angel Flores (New York, 1977), p. 197; and Kittler and Neumann,
   pp. 79 f.

9 Kurt Wolff, *Briefwechsel eines Verlegers 1911–1963* (Frankfurt/M., 1980), p. 46.

10 A facsimile of this list appears on p. 18 of the *Kafka-Symposion*.

11 On generic features of the modern short story cycle, see Forrest L. Ingram,
   Representative Short Story Cycles of the Twentieth Century. Studies in a Literary Genre,
   De Proprietatibus Litterarum, 19 (The Hague, 1971), and Dieter Meindl, 'Der
   Kurzgeschichtenzyklus als modernistisches Genre', *GRM*, 33 (1983), 216–28.

12 Roy Pascal, *Kafka's Narrators. A Study of his Stories and Sketches* (Cambridge, 1982),
   pp. 192–201.

13 It may be, as Dietz has suggested (pp. 110 ff.), that the Kurt Wolff Verlag had also
   mislaid the *Kübelreiter* MS, in addition to its various other blunders in the preparation
   of the *Landarzt* collection for publication. Nevertheless, I feel that there is a strong
   case for charitably assuming that Kafka actually realized that the inclusion of *Der
   Kübelreiter* at this juncture would have represented an over-determination of the
   rider-motif.

14 See Malcolm Pasley, 'Drei literarische Mystifikationen Kafkas' (*Kafka-Symposion*,
   pp. 17–21) where this allusion is described as 'offenbar absichtlich verdunkelt' in the
   sequence of the eventual collection (p. 21). The point is elaborated more fully in
   Pasley's 'Semi-private games' (pp. 197 f.).

Helmut Heißenbüttel

SANCHO PANSAS TEUFEL.
DIE UMKEHRUNG ALS DENKFIGUR
IM WERK FRANZ KAFKAS

ABSTRACT

Kafka's prose-piece 'The Truth about Sancho Panza' (1917) is shown to involve a complex reversal of the Don Quixote–Sancho Panza relationship with which Kafka can assume his readers to be familiar. Sancho Panza is not only the dominant character now, but he is a free man and Don Quixote is both his 'devil' and his creation. Detailed exploration of the meanings, associations and historical and cultural possibilities triggered off by the text's individual statements also reveals the work to be a reversal of a narrative tradition in a more fundamental sense. Like Kafka's aphorisms, 'The Silence of the Sirens' and 'Prometheus', with which it is here compared, 'The Truth about Sancho Panza' is shown not to be a story in the conventional sense. Instead of an aesthetic play or quasi-allegorical variation on the preformed material, 'The Truth about Sancho Panza' is viewed as a tentative exploration of a sequence of ideas, a train of thought pursued 'without recourse to system, goal or preconceived pattern'. More significant than any demonstrable reversals of surface detail or specific meaning of the original text is the change in literary genre involved. This shift, associated with several pieces written in 1917, to a kind of text involving trains of thought, where the whole relationship between vehicle and meaning has evidently changed, is seen to mark a new stage in Kafka's creative development.

Im Oktober 1917 schrieb Franz Kafka, vierunddreißig Jahre alt, ein paar kurze Texte, die erst aus dem Nachlaß, zuerst 1931, sieben Jahre nach seinem Tod, veröffentlicht wurden. Zusammen mit den Aphorismen, denen Max Brod den Titel gegeben hat *Betrachtungen über Sünde, Leid, Hoffnung und den wahren Weg*, aufgeschrieben zwischen Oktober 1917 und Februar 1918, bezeichnen sie so etwas wie eine Zäsur in der literarischen Produktion Kafkas.

Einer dieser Texte vom Oktober 1917 ist gedruckt unter dem Titel: 'Die Wahrheit über Sancho Pansa'. Er lautet:

Sancho Pansa, der sich übrigens dessen nie gerühmt hat, gelang es im Laufe der Jahre, durch Beistellung einer Menge Ritter- und Räuberromane in den

98

Abend- und Nachstunden seinen Teufel, dem er später den Namen Don Quixote gab, derart von sich abzulenken, daß dieser dann haltlos die verrücktesten Taten aufführte, die aber mangels eines vorbestimmten Gegenstandes, der eben Sancho Pansa hätte sein sollen, niemandem schadeten. Sancho Pansa, ein freier Mann, folgte gleichmütig, vielleicht aus einem gewissen Verantwortungsgefühl dem Don Quixote auf seinen Zügen und hatte davon eine große und nützliche Unterhaltung bis an sein Ende.

Zwei literarische Figuren, Sancho Pansa und Don Quixote, werden zitiert, die man ohne Kommentar zitieren kann, weil ihre Bekanntheit allgemein vorauszusetzen ist. Man kann sogar voraussetzen, daß das genaue Verhältnis, in dem diese Figuren zueinander stehen, bekannt ist. Der *Don Quixote*-Roman von Cervantes wird als etwas genommen, das den Charakter des von einem Einzelnen verursachten literarischen Werks bereits überschritten hat, sozusagen zum Allgemeinbesitz geworden ist, sich zwar nicht in einen Mythos verwandelt hat, aber dadurch, daß die Figuren sich aus ihrem konkreten literarischen Zusammenhang herausgelöst haben, mythenähnlich geworden ist. Die Figuren Don Quixote und Sancho Pansa stehen auf einer Stufe mit Figuren der antiken Sage, wie Odysseus oder Poseidon, aber auch mit Akteuren der Fabel oder der Gegenwartsanekdote (*Kleine Fabel* und *Ein alltäglicher Vorfall*).

Dieser erste Punkt ist insofern wichtig, als er ein Referenzmodell andeutet, das der Autor benutzen kann, ohne sich in langwierige Ausführungen einlassen zu müssen. Das Modell setzt voraus, daß der Leser weiß, Don Quixote ist die Hauptperson und Sancho Pansa Sekundärakteur, genauer gesagt, überhaupt kein Akteur, sondern lediglich der auf die Taten der Hauptperson Reagierende. Nicht ganz so, dies als Anmerkung, wie in Diderots *Jacques le Fataliste*, wo der Diener in seiner Dienerrolle dem Herrn folgt, doch, in der vielleicht genialsten Verschränkung, die das von Cervantes erfundene Modell erfahren hat, durch seine Taten dem Herrn das Gesetz des Handelns vorschreibt, ohne je den Versuch zu machen, sich selber die Rolle des Herrn anzumaßen. Was Cervantes in seinem Paar an Geschichtserfahrung zusammenfaßt und zur Wahrheit bringt über das Verhältnis von gesellschaftlichem Oben und Unten, wird bei Diderot korrekt auf den Stand des Jahrzehnts vor der Französischen Revolution gebracht, ohne das Gleichgewicht aufzuheben.

Kafka dagegen, in eben dem Zeitpunkt, an dem die Revolutionen des zwanzigsten Jahrhunderts anfangen, Wirkung zu zeigen, kehrt das vorgefundene Bekannte ohne Umstände um. Sancho Pansa ist nicht nur die Hauptperson, er ist im Grunde die einzige Person, Don Quixote lediglich sein Teufel. Dieser Teufel muß ihn geplagt haben, denn sonst hätte er nicht den Versuch gemacht, ihn von sich abzulenken. Welcher

Art die Teufeleien dieses Teufels waren, wird nicht gesagt. Ob er Sancho Pansa gequält hat im theologischen, psychologischen oder sozialen Sinn, bleibt offen. Wie aber hat Sancho Pansa den Teufel abgelenkt? 'Durch Beistellung einer Menge Ritter- und Räuberromane in den Abend- und Nachtstunden.' Das heißt, er hat den Teufel vollgestopft mit Lektüre über Ritter und Räuber. Er hat ihn, so könnte man ausmalen, belehrt und aufgeklärt über die historische Vergangenheit als einer Ritter- und Räubergeschichte. Diese Belehrung und Aufklärung hat dann Sancho Pansa so weit getrieben, daß sein Teufel sich mit Rittern und Räubern identifizierte und nun nicht mehr 'seinen vorbestimmten Gegenstand, der eben Sancho Pansa hätte sein sollen', plagte, sondern 'haltlos die verrücktesten Taten aufführte'.

Sancho Pansa befreit sich also von seinem Quälgeist, er emanzipiert sich, so könnte man in einer aktuellen Ausdrucksweise sagen, nicht, indem er ihn besiegt, beseitigt, totschlägt, unterdrückt, sondern indem er ihn verführt, durch Beschäftigung mit den Verrücktheiten der Vergangenheit selber verrückt zu werden. Das ist sehr wichtig. Auch im Verrücktmachen übt Sancho Pansa keinen Druck aus, wendet keine Gewalt an. Er unterlegt dem Teufel etwas, er schiebt ihm was unter, das im Grunde von diesem selber stammt. Denn er, Don Quixote, ist ja der letzte der Ritter und Räuber, deren Geschichten ihn verrückt machen. Er wird, so könnte man vorschnell sagen, zum Bewußtsein der vererbten eigenen Verrücktheit gebracht. Nur wird er sich dessen nicht bewußt, sondern versinkt gleichsam im Meer der eigenen Verrücktheit.

So weit der erste Satz des Textes von Kafka. Der zweite Satz beginnt: 'Sancho Pansa, ein freier Mann, folgte gleichmütig'. Vielleicht ist hier der Schlüssel zu suchen, zu suchen nämlich in der Feststellung, Sancho Pansa sei ein freier Mann. Das Herr-Knecht-Verhältnis, sei es in der historischen Konstellation bei Cervantes, sei es in der bei Diderot, ist aufgehoben. Der letzte Rest davon besteht darin, daß der Geplagte nun, nachdem er seinen Teufel von sich abgelenkt hat, ein gewisses Verantwortungsgefühl für diesen verspürt. Aber er ist frei, sich, wenn er wollte, auch abzuwenden. Er ist frei und gleichmütig. Sein Quälgeist ist verrückt. Ist dies das neue historisch-gesellschaftliche Referenzmodell, das Kafka mit diesem Text in Vorschlag bringt? Dauern die Verrücktheiten des Teufels an in alle Ewigkeit?

Vielleicht. Der zweite Satz des Textes jedoch endet: 'und hatte davon eine große und nützliche Unterhaltung bis an sein Ende'. Sancho Pansa, der freie Mann, der von Herrschaft Emanzipierte, hat Unterhaltung von den verrückten Taten seines früheren Herrn, seines Teufels. Diese Unterhaltung ist groß, das heißt, sie belebt und beschäftigt ihn. Sie ist aber auch nützlich, er lernt aus ihr. Was lernt er aus dieser Unterhaltung durch die verrücktesten Taten seines Teufels? Obwohl es nicht ausdrücklich gesagt wird, kann man mit Fug annehmen, er lerne, wie man sich nicht verrückt benimmt. Oder dient das Verrückte ihm, dem Freien, Unverrückten, Gleichmütigen, zur Erbauung, gleichgültig, was fernerhin noch an Verrücktheiten geschieht? Oder zeigt diese Momentaufnahme nur den einen Aspekt, den Gleichmut zu bieten vermag, egal, wie schwer er errungen sein mag?

Oder hat diese 'Wahrheit über Sancho Pansa' ihr wahres Äquivalent, ihr schreckliches Gegengesicht, erst im neunten Abschnitt von Walter Benjamins von Adorno so genannten *Geschichtsphilosophischen Thesen*? Dort heißt es:

Der Engel der Geschichte . . . hat das Antlitz der Vergangenheit zugewendet. Wo eine Kette von Begebenheiten vor uns erscheint, da sieht er eine einzige Katastrophe, die unablässig Trümmer auf Trümmer häuft und sie ihm vor die Füße schleudert. Er möchte wohl verweilen, die Toten wecken und das Zerschlagene zusammenfügen. Aber ein Sturm weht vom Paradiese her, der sich in seinen Flügeln verfangen hat und so stark ist, daß der Engel sie nicht mehr schließen kann. Dieser Sturm treibt ihn unaufhaltsam in die Zukunft, der er den Rücken kehrt, während der Trümmerhaufen vor ihm zum Himmel wächst. Das, was wir den Fortschritt nennen, ist dieser Sturm.

Gehe ich zu weit, wenn ich so unmittelbar dem Sancho-Pansa-Teufel Kafkas den Geschichtsengel Benjamins entgegensetze, die große und nützliche Unterhaltung, die sich bei Kafka aus den verrücktesten Taten von Sancho Pansas Teufel ziehen läßt, gleichsetze mit Benjamins Trümmerhaufen, der deshalb zum Himmel wächst, weil der Sturm des Fortschritts es zu keiner vernünftigen Korrektur der zertrümmernden Untaten kommen läßt? Noch einmal: Vielleicht. Meine Absicht war, eine Möglichkeit aufzudecken, den zweisätzigen Text Kafkas versuchsweise in eine Perspektive zu stellen, die das Harmlose und Spielerische, das ihm scheinbar anhaftet, gar nicht erst zu Wort kommen läßt. Kafka hat nicht mit dem Cervanteschen Referenzmodell ein Gedankenspiel getrieben, das noch viele andere und vielleicht sogar lustigere Varianten zuließe. Er hat das, was er referiert, entschieden in einen veränderten Bezug gebracht, der nun definitiv und unauflösbar erscheint. Was täuscht, ist nicht Harmloses oder Spielerisches, sondern Einfachheit der Redeweise und Lapidarität der Bezugnahme. Das, was dabei herauskommt, ist von ungeheuerlicher Unwiderlegbarkeit.

Benjamins Sturm, der vom Paradies her weht, ist übrigens nicht ohne Zusammenhang mit Vorstellungen bei Kafka. Der Jäger Gracchus, dessen Ankunft in der Stadt Riva in dem Fragment von 1917 geschildert wird, sagt: 'Ich bin hier, mehr weiß ich nicht, mehr kann ich nicht tun. Mein Kahn ist ohne Steuer, er fährt mit dem Wind, der in den untersten Regionen des Todes bläst.' Die ewige Wiederkehr, deren Genealogie Benjamin über Nietzsche hinweg zu Blanqui verfolgt hat, setzt den Tod

des Jägers Gracchus aus. Sein Nichtsterbenkönnen ist gleichsam die
Ewigkeit der Todesangst. 'Mein Todeskahn verfehlte die Fahrt', sagt
der Jäger: 'eine falsche Drehung des Steuers, ein Augenblick der
Unaufmerksamkeit, eine Ablenkung durch meine wunderschöne
Heimat, ich weiß nicht, was es war, nur das weiß ich, daß mein Kahn
seither die irdischen Gewässer befährt.' Wie Sancho Pansa seinen Teufel
Don Quixote durch Ritter- und Räuberromane von sich ablenkt, so
wird der Todeskahn des Jägers Gracchus durch, er weiß nicht was, von
der Überquerung des Styx, der Leben und Tod trennt, abgelenkt. Das
andere Ufer erscheint unerreichbar.

Legt man so die Folgerichtigkeit der wörtlichen Interpretation mit
dem Anklang der Bilder zusammen, erkennt man überrascht, daß es
hier nicht um eine besondere Art des Erzählens geht, aber auch nicht
darum, daß bestimmte Inhalte theologischer, psychologischer, philo-
sophischer, soziologischer Art in eine Erzählform verschlüsselt werden
sollen, Parabeln einer veränderten Art, sondern daß es sich in den beiden
bisher zitierten Texten um eine neue und veränderte Art des Denkens
handelt. Ein Denken, das nicht aus der Auflösung von Erzählzusam-
menhängen oder der Entschlüsselung von Metaphern und Bildern
hervorgeht, also erst aus dem literarischen Text in den Gang des
Gedankens übersetzt werden müßte, sondern das sich ihrer unmittelbar
bedient.

Die Verschiebung des Referenzmodells Don Quixote Sancho Pansa
mithilfe von Wörtern wie Teufel, verrückteste Taten, freier Mann,
Unterhaltung bedeutet nicht die Entlarvung eines Erzählmusters in
einen verborgenen Zusammenhang, der dem übernommenen Modell
unterlegt wird. Kafka stülpt nicht den Entwurf des Cervantes um zu
einer Fabel, einer erzählerischen Kurzform, die seinen speziellen Beitrag
zu den literarischen Erfindungen des zwanzigsten Jahrhunderts darstellt. Er setzt vielmehr einen Denkprozeß in Gang, der sich nicht der
Begriffe und ihrer logischen Verknüpfung, sondern einer Mischung aus
Bedeutungsebenen bedient, der der wörtlichen und der des Umfelds,
das aus Zusammenhängen genommen wird, für die diese Wörter stehn.
Man könnte auch sagen, indem Kafka Sätze bildet, syntaktisch und
semantisch vollkommen durchschaubare Sätze, die sich gleichzeitig
vokabulärer und allegorischer Bedeutung bedienen, bildet er Verknüp-
fungen aus, die nicht literarischer, also veranschaulichender, sondern
gedanklicher, also abstrahierender Art sind.

Die kürzesten Beispiele für derartige Denkprozesse finden sich in der
Aphorismensammlung, auf deren Zusammenstellung und Abschrift
Kafka ja besonderen Wert gelegt hat. Hier zeigt sich nun, auf welche
Weise der von Max Brod formulierte Titel, *Betrachtungen über Sünde,
Leid, Hoffnung und den wahren Weg*, irreführt. Es handelt sich in keinem

Fall, auch nicht bei den längeren Beispielen, um Betrachtungen, sondern immer um Sätze, Sätze in dem Sinn, in dem Ludwig Wittgensteins *Philosophische Bemerkungen* aus Sätzen bestehen. Die Tatsache, daß von Kafka theologisch abgeleitete Wörter verwendet werden wie Herr, Gott, Teufel usw., hat Brod dazu verleitet, das Konvolut insgesamt theologisch zu lesen, und sei es auch im Sinne einer negativen Theologie. Kafka hat jedoch offensichtlich solche Wörter gewählt, weil sie einen weiten und vorgeprägten Bedeutungshof haben, nicht weil er sie inhaltlich vertrat, als Lehre, als Offenbarung, als Hinweis auf 'den wahren Weg'. Schon der zweite Satz sollte dem einen Riegel vorschieben: 'Alle menschlichen Fehler sind Ungeduld, ein vorzeitiges Abbrechen des Methodischen, ein scheinbares Einpfählen der scheinbaren Sache'. Wobei man auch diesen Satz nicht absolut als Maxime verstehen, sondern das Augenmerk auf die Vokabel 'scheinbar' legen sollte.

Ein Beispiel mit scheinbar theologischem Inhalt kann weiter als Erläuterung dienen, Aphorismus 64.65:

Die Vertreibung aus dem Paradies ist in ihrem Hauptteil ewig: Es ist also zwar die Vertreibung aus dem Paradies endgültig, das Leben in der Welt unausweichlich, die Ewigkeit des Vorganges aber (oder zeitlich ausgedrückt: die ewige Wiederholung des Vorganges) macht es trotzdem möglich, daß wir nicht nur dauernd im Paradies bleiben könnten, sondern tatsächlich dort dauernd sind, gleichgültig ob wir es hier wissen oder nicht.

Dieser Satz verknüpft die biblische Vorstellung von der Vertreibung aus dem Paradies mit dem Begriff der Ewigkeit und der Feststellung der Unausweichlichkeit der Existenz. Von dieser Unausweichlichkeit her ist die Vertreibung endgültig. Dreht man jedoch die theologische Prämisse um, verwandelt sich die Endgültigkeit in eine Ewigkeit, in die ewige Wiederholung des Vorgangs der Vertreibung, die das Verbleiben im Paradies nicht nur zur Möglichkeit macht, sondern als Dauerzustand erscheinen läßt. Die, wie man sagen könnte, existentielle Auflösung des Satzes wird aufgehalten dadurch, daß am Ende noch einmal der Gegensatz von dort und hier erscheint. Der Satz stellt auch nicht ein Paradoxon dar, in dem sich dann wieder der Inhalt festklemmen läßt. Es handelt sich um ein versuchsweises Denken in Sätzen, die, gebildet, vor der Auflösung wieder verschwinden, ein experimentelles Denken ohne den Rückhalt von System, Ziel oder noch Entwurf.

Dies dokumentiert sich, so meine ich in jenen Aphorismen, und hier wird auch die Grenze erkennbar, die es wiederum verbietet, einen Begriff wie den des Aphorismus zu verwenden, die in ihrer Gedrängtheit, Unauflösbarkeit, Undurchdringbarkeit in Ursätze zurückführen: 'Ein Käfig ging einen Vogel suchen' (16); 'Das Gute ist in gewissem

Sinne trostlos' (30); 'Es gibt kein Haben, nur ein Sein, nur ein nach letztem Atem, nach Ersticken verlangendes Sein' (35); 'Lächerlich hast du dich aufgeschirrt für diese Welt' (44); 'Was ist fröhlicher als der Glaube an einen Hausgott!' (68); 'Ein Glaube wie ein Fallbeil, so schwer, so leicht' (87); 'Zum letztenmal Psychologie!' (93); 'Die Sünde kommt immer offen und ist mit den Sinnen gleich zu fassen. Sie geht auf ihren Wurzeln und muß nicht ausgerissen werden' (101); 'Es ist nicht notwendig, daß du aus dem Haus gehst. Bleib bei deinem Tisch und horche. Horche nicht einmal, warte nur. Warte nicht einmal, sei völlig still und allein. Anbieten wird sich dir die Welt zur Entlarvung, sie kann nicht anders, verzückt wird sie sich vor dir winden' (109).

Die Umkehrung des Verhältnisses von Sancho Pansa zu Don Quixote, welche 'Die Wahrheit über Sancho Pansa' darstellt, ist ein Gedanke, der sich nicht der begrifflichen Verkürzung und seiner logischen Ableitung bedient, sondern der konkreten verbalen, nominalen, mythologischen, kulturellen, historischen, literarischen Bezüge, aus deren Feldern die Sprache ihr wirksames Leben bezieht. 'Das Schweigen der Sirenen' ist ein anderer Text vom Oktober 1917. Er beginnt mit dem Satz: 'Beweis dessen, daß auch unzulängliche, ja kindische Mittel zur Rettung dienen können'. Im Prinzip besteht dieser Text aus einer Kurzerzählung der Vorüberfahrt des Odysseus an den Sirenen. Kafka durchlöchert jedoch die bekannte Geschichte durch Korrekturen und Zusätze. Er sagt, das Verstopfen der Ohren und die Fesselung des Odysseus sei sinnlos gewesen, da der Gesang der Sirenen alles durchdrang und alle Ketten sprengte. Sodann wird eingefügt, daß das Schweigen der Sirenen eine noch schrecklichere Waffe gewesen sei als ihr Gesang. 'Und tatsächlich sangen sie nicht, als Odysseus kam.' Odysseus aber hörte weder Gesang noch Schweigen, sah über die Verführerinnen hinweg, sodaß diese ihrerseits verführt wurden durch 'den Abglanz vom großen Augenpaar des Odysseus'. Hätten sie Bewußtsein gehabt, wären sie vernichtet worden. Möglich aber auch, so Kafkas Schluß, Odysseus sei ein solcher Fuchs gewesen, daß er auch das Schweigen bemerkt, aber den Göttern, dem Schicksal den beschriebenen Scheinvorgang vorgespielt habe.

Man könnte den Versuch machen, die Kafkasche Nacherzählung aufzulösen als eine Version, die die bekannte Sage in Richtung auf eine Allegorie der Libido verschiebt. Das Durchdringen des ohrenverstopfenden Wachses (das der biographische Kafka in der Form von Ohropax zeitweise Tag und Nacht verwendete), das Sprengen von Mast und Ketten durch die Leidenschaft der Verführten, das schreckliche Schweigen, die Wendungen der Hälse, das tiefe Atmen usw., die Umkehr der Verführungsmacht vor dem seelenvollen Fernblick des Unverführten, in dem sie 'schöner als jemals' sich streckten und drehten, all dies spricht für eine Interpretation in Richtung auf das Libidinöse. Was aber soll der Scheinvorgang, den Göttern 'gewissermaßen als Schild entgegengehalten'? Eine sublimierende Verankerung des Lustprinzips in der Mythologie, eine scherzhafte Schleife, ein zusätzlicher Schnörkel, mit dem Kafka lediglich seine Lust am exquisit Kuriosen befriedigen wollte?

Auch hier kann man, so meine ich, den Text besser und konsequenterweise als einen probierenden, versuchsweisen Gedankengang auffassen mit den Mitteln konkreter Wortbedeutungen und Vorstellungen. Einen Gedankengang, der mehrschichtig abläuft, sich an den Ausstrahlungen seiner Bezugsfelder inspiriert und orientiert. Einen Gedankengang, der einen Weg bahnt, eine Schneise schlägt in Unbegangenes, Ungedachtes, Ungesagtes. Die psychoanalytischen oder existenziellen Züge und Vorgriffe, die als anklingend zu erkennen sind, bleiben nur ein Hinweis. Das Unbegangene, Ungedachte, Ungesagte läßt sich nicht einfach in solche, inzwischen geläufig gewordene Bahnen ablenken. Vielmehr wird in entscheidender Weise das ganze Konkrete der metaphysischen und geschichtlichen Vorexistenz mit hineingezogen, hineingezogen in eine akute Situation, die als Ort der Desorientierung erfahren wird. Ein Ort der Desorientierung deshalb, weil alle die angesprochenen Bezüge, alle die benannten prähistorischen, historischen, kulturellen, ästhetischen Wirkungsmächte noch ihre Wirksamkeit ausüben, sie jedoch zugleich auch schon in entscheidendem Maße verloren haben. Wirksamkeit und Unwirksamkeit ineins sind das Fatum, unter dem der Versuch Kafkas steht, neu ins Ungewußte voraus- und hinauszudenken.

Ein weiteres Beispiel, 'Prometheus', zu datieren auf den 17. Januar 1918:

Von Prometheus berichten vier Sagen: Nach der ersten wurde er, weil er die Götter an die Menschen verraten hatte, am Kaukasus festgeschmiedet, und die Götter schickten Adler, die von seiner immer wachsenden Leber fraßen. Nach der zweiten drückte sich Prometheus im Schmerz vor den zuhackenden Schnäbeln immer tiefer in den Felsen, bis er mit ihm eins wurde. Nach der dritten wurde in den Jahrtausenden sein Verrat vergessen, die Götter vergaßen, die Adler, er selbst. Nach der vierten wurde man des grundlos Gewordenen müde. Die Götter wurden müde, die Adler wurden müde, die Wunde schloß sich müde. Blieb das unerklärliche Felsgebirge. —Die Sage versucht das Unerklärliche zu erklären. Da sie aus einem Wahrheitsgrund kommt, muß sie wieder im Unerklärlichen enden.

Diese, so könnte man sie nennen, mythologische Glosse scheint auf Anhieb einfach nur unsinnig zu sein. Wieso vier Sagen, handelt es sich doch eher um Folgerungen aus der einen gegebenen? Wie kann das Felsengebirge unerklärlich sein, wenn es als der topographische Ort

Kaukasus, in jedem Lexikon zu finden, zur Prämisse der Sage dient? Der Fehler, wenn ich so frage, liegt in der Logik des Fragens. Die Benennungen der Prometheussage, aus denen sich der Text aufbaut, sind gleichsam die Stichworte für den Gedanken, der das Wesentliche des Sagenhaften wie in einer konkreten Schleife zu umfassen sucht. Wenn die Sage tatsächlich das Unerklärliche erklären würde, würde Kafkas Paraphrase, die Auffächerung in vier Varianten, die Erklärung des Unerklärlichen noch einmal erklären. Das wäre nicht nur überflüssig, das wäre Unsinn. Ist diese Paraphrase dazu da, das Unsinnige des Unsinns herauszustellen, sozusagen im syntaktisch-logischen Unsinnigwerden das Ganze als Unsinn zu entlarven? Man könnte eine solche Erklärung annehmen. Aber Kafka geht doch noch einen Schritt weiter. Da das unerklärliche Felsgebirge als der geographische Ort Kaukasus nominal vorausgesetzt worden ist, erklärt die Sage es auch nicht. Eben dies, das Nichterklären des garnicht Erklärbaren, Unerklärlichen, aber wird als aus einem Wahrheitsgrund kommend bezeichnet. Da es aus dem Wahrheitsgrund kommt, muß es wiederum im Unerklärlichen enden.

Man könnte dies als die Kernformel, ja als eine der möglichen Definitionen des Absurden auffassen. Wäre ein Text wie dieser über die Prometheussage nicht ein Beleg dafür, daß Kafka der erste Autor und Meister des Absurden war? Ist die Idee des Absurden, Jahrzehnte später, nicht in die Literatur eingedrungen, weil Autoren das unerklärte Unerklärliche zur Wahrheit, zur einzig noch möglichen, alle früheren Wahrheiten übertreffenden erklärt haben? Wiederum möchte ich zurücklenken und darauf bestehen, daß es sich nicht um einen solchen, mythologisch-literarischen Stoff manipulierenden Vorgang handelt, sondern um eine Denkbewegung. Eine Denkbewegung, die sich der Daten des tatsächlich Unerklärlichen, des Sagenhaften bedient (Verrat der Götter an die Menschen, von Göttern entsendete Adler, die lebendige Leber fressen, eine Leber die überdies ununterbrochen nachwächst, das Hineindrücken in den Felsen, das Vergessen der Götter und des Gepeinigten, die Müdigkeit der Götter, der Adler, der Wunde), um eine Überlegung durchzuspielen, die in diesen Daten enthalten ist. Nicht eigentlich darin verborgen, denn die Stichworte werden ja benannt. Vielmehr als Denkpanorama in den Vorstellungspartikeln der Überlieferung. Dessen Aspekte, vielleicht Stufen, wären: Streit zwischen Göttern und Menschen, Bestrafung und Mumifizierung der Straftat, Vergessen der Götter in doppeltem Sinn, Müdigkeit selbst der Wunde der Erinnerung. Bleibt der Kaukasus, dessen Topographie dieses alles zugeordnet worden ist. Ihm ist nichts abzulesen. Und erst dies, dieses Nichtmehrablesen können ist Wahrheit und Unerklärlichkeit ineins.

Dies möchte ich ergänzen durch den dritten Text, den Kafka im Oktober 1917 niederschrieb, einen Text, der sich nicht der mythologisch oder literaturgeschichtlich vorgeprägten Stichworte bedient, sondern in der Gegenwart ansetzt. Er beginnt: 'Ein alltäglicher Vorgang: sein Ertragen eine alltägliche Verwirrung'. Es geht um ein Geschäft zwischen zwei Personen, A und B genannt, die nicht im gleichen Ort wohnen, der Ort, in dem B wohnt, wird H genannt. Vorgegeben wird eine normale Zeitangabe. Zur Vorbesprechung benötigt A für Hin- und Rückweg je zehn Minuten. Für den Weg zum Abschluß des Geschäfts jedoch benötigt A, obwohl er sehr früh weggeht und alle Bedingungen seiner Ansicht nach gleich sind, zehn Stunden. B ist weg. A legt den Rückweg 'geradezu in einem Augenblick zurück'. Zu Hause erfährt er, er habe doch B noch beim Weggehn getroffen, ihn jedoch nicht anhören wollen, da er keine Zeit habe. B befinde sich noch, wartend, in As Zimmer. A stürzt auf der Treppe, 'fast ohnmächtig vor Schmerz' hört er, wie B, 'undeutlich ob in großer Ferne oder knapp neben ihm — wütend die Treppe hinunterstampft und endgültig verschwindet'.

Zwei Interpretationen bieten sich an der Oberfläche an: es kann eine Traumerzählung sein, in der die bekannten Verhinderungen und Überkreuzungen die Handlung bestimmen; es kann die Übersetzung der Redewendung: Zeit haben oder keine Zeit haben, wörtlich genommen, in Erzählhandlung sein, A hat einmal Zeit und braucht infolgedessen keine Zeit, das zweitemal braucht er Zeit und hat infolgedessen keine. Zweifellos spielen beide Aspekte eine Rolle. Traumlogik und Traumrealität spielen jedoch, so wenig wie in dem Romanfragment *Das Schloß*, das man hier vielleicht am ehesten zum Vergleich heranziehn könnte, die Hauptrolle. Das Zeitspiel hängt an einer Ausdrucksweise, die auf den ersten Blick wie ein zusätzlicher Scherz aussieht: zehn Minuten werden zehn Stunden entgegengehalten und beiden wiederum ein Augenblick. Dies sind die drei Kennmarken, auf denen der Gedankengang, den die Erzählung darstellt, aufbaut. Hinzu kommt, daß diese drei Zeitangaben allein für A gelten, er braucht zehn Minuten, zehn Stunden und einen Augenblick. B, so sagt die Erzählung, befindet sich innerhalb einer normalen, realen Zeitrechnung, allerdings muß er bereits ungeduldig sein Warten abgebrochen haben, ehe A überhaupt aufbrach. Auch diese Verschränkung steht rein in der Perspektive von A. B existiert nur in A.

Der Gedanke, den Kafka hier versuchsweise, konkret, in beschreibenden Sätzen, in Gang setzt, springt aus einer der Grundvoraussetzungen der Welterfahrung heraus und nennt dieses Herausspringen zweimal alltäglich, einmal als Vorfall, einmal als Verwirrung: der Voraussetzung nämlich, daß Raum und Zeit die nicht veränderbaren Gegebenheiten der Realität sind. Eben dies hebt Kafka auf. Er setzt ein

Raum-Zeit-Verhältnis bei gleichbleibendem Raum einmal mit zehn Minuten, einmal mit zehn Stunden, einmal mit einem Augenblick fest. Was geschieht? Der Testfall ist ein Grundmodell menschlicher Kommunikation, bei dem Zeit eine Rolle spielt, das Geschäft. Dieses Geschäft läßt sich abschließen unter der sozusagen normalen Raum-Zeit-Bedingung: Hin- und Rückweg je zehn Minuten. Bei Dehnung wie Schrumpfung, zehn Stunden und Augenblick, jedoch kommt nichts mehr zusammen. Es findet keine Kommunikation mehr statt. Der Unfall auf der Treppe ist nur die dritte Konkretion der Veränderung der Zeit-Raum-Relation: die Zeit, die zum Treppensteigen benötigt wird, verschiebt sich nahe unendlich. Das Subjekt A, an das die Verschiebungen gebunden sind, wird absolut isoliert. Auch die Mitteilungen der anonymen anderen gehen über ihn hinweg.

Ich habe gesagt, es handele sich bei den zitierten Texten um Gedankengänge, nicht um Erzählungen. Warum spreche ich von Gedankengängen? Könnte ich nicht ebenso reden von einer Vermischung zwischen Anschauung und Abstraktion? Vielleicht würde das die Vorgänge, was ihre Beschreibbarkeit betrifft, besser treffen. Aber ich komme dann um eins nicht herum, das ich doch vermeiden will: ich behalte die Zweiteilung zwischen Text und Auslegung. Was ich zeigen will, ist, daß die Texte dieser Entstehungsstufe bei Kafka eine solche Zweiteilung nicht vertragen. Der Umkehrungsakt, den etwa die Bezüge auf mythologische Überlieferung erfahren, ist inhaltlich festzuhalten. Das Festhalten der Manipulation des Inhalts jedoch läßt die Texte lediglich als extreme, vielleicht verrückte Uminterpretation von eingefahrenen Überlieferungen erscheinen. Kann das alles sein? Findet nicht zugleich eine Umkehrung statt, die sich nicht auf die angesprochenen Inhalte bezieht, sondern die Art und Weise des Redens selbst betrifft, die Auffassung von dem, was literarisch machbar ist, was die Grundauffassung von Literatur betrifft?

Wenn ich 'Die Wahrheit über Sancho Pansa' lese, so lese ich nicht eine Kurzgeschichte, Fabel, Parabel, in der mir etwas erzählt wird, das diese Wahrheit in sich enthält, verbirgt, aufbewahrt. Sondern das konkret Gesagte, die Zusammensetzung aus Nomina und Bedeutungshöfen, die, zugespitzt, Algebra daraus, ist diese Wahrheit. Mehr noch, sie stellt die einzige Möglichkeit dar, diese Wahrheit sprachlich auszudrücken. Eine Wahrheit, von der sich dann nur aussagen läßt, daß sie das Unerklärliche ist oder daß das Unerklärliche die Wahrheit ist, weil aus dem Wahrheitsgrund allein Unerklärliches kommen kann. 'Ein Käfig ging einen Vogel suchen.' Diese Aussage ist weder absurd noch phantastisch noch gleichnishaft noch traumhaft, sie ist die Wahrheit. In den Aufzeichnungen von 1920, die unter dem Obertitel 'Er' publiziert worden sind, heißt es:

Alles, was er tut, kommt ihm zwar außerordentlich neu vor, aber auch entsprechend dieser unmöglichen Fülle des Neuen außerordentlich dilettantisch, kaum einmal erträglich, unfähig historisch zu werden, die Kette der Geschlechter sprengend, die bisher immer wenigstens zu ahnende Musik der Welt zum erstenmal bis in alle Tiefen hinunter abbrechend. Manchmal hat er in seinem Hochmut mehr Angst um die Welt, als um sich. Mit einem Gefängnis hätte er sich abgefunden. Als Gefangener endend — das wäre eines Lebens Ziel. Aber es war ein Gitterkäfig. Gleichgültig, herrisch, wie bei sich zu Hause strömte durch das Gitter aus und ein der Lärm der Welt, der Gefangene war eigentlich frei, er konnte an allem teilnehmen, nichts entging ihm draußen, selbst verlassen hätte er den Käfig können, die Gitterstangen standen ja meterweit auseinander, nicht einmal gefangen war er. Er hat das Gefühl, daß er sich dadurch, daß er lebt, den Weg verstellt. Aus dieser Behinderung nimmt er dann wieder den Beweis dafür, daß er lebt.

Die Belege, die ich aus dem Werk Kafkas herangezogen habe, stammen, wie gesagt, aus dem Jahr 1917. Dieses Jahr, in dem er vierunddreißig wurde, bildet in mancher Hinsicht eine Zäsur auch im Leben Kafkas. In der Nacht vom 9. zum 10. August hat er den ersten Blutsturz. Die Krankheit, an der er sterben sollte, tritt sichtbar in sein Dasein. Im Juni beginnt Kafka Hebräisch zu lernen, sein Blick und ein Teil seiner inneren Aufmerksamkeit wenden sich jenem äußeren Ausweg zu, der, hätte er sich ihm wirklich zuwenden können, vielleicht sein Leben verlängert und verändert hätte. Im Juli verlobt er sich zum zweitenmal mit Felice Bauer, am 16. Oktober schreibt er den letzten erhaltenen Brief an sie, mit dem Besuch Felices zu Weihnachten ist nicht nur diese Beziehung beendet, es wird für Kafka unwiderruflich deutlich, daß das Erreichen von Heim und Familie für ihn unmöglich ist. 1917 beginnt er die Konzeption des Briefs an den Vater. Pascal und Kierkegaard treten erneut ins Blickfeld.

1919 endet die erste Phase der Tiergeschichten und beginnt der direkte Bezug auf Mythologie und Vorgeformtes. Wie mit einem Ruck wächst das Werk aus dem Literarischen im engeren Sinne heraus, wie mit einem Ruck wendet es sich davon ab in eine neue Perspektive. Die Diskussion der Vergangenheit, der Ordnung, der Herrschaft, die bis dahin als Stoff für Literatur diente, gewinnt eine andere Dimension. *Beim Bau der Chinesischen Mauer, Das Stadtwappen, Die Abweichung, Zur Frage der Gesetze, Die Prüfung* sind Beispiele dafür. Die Tiergeschichte erfährt, etwa von der *Kreuzung* an, eine Veränderung. Zugleich wird der unvermittelt erkennbare Ausdruck des eigenen Geschicks, der Leiden der Person Franz Kafka erkennbar. Der letzte, noch selber vorbereitete Band belegt das, die Erzählungen des Bandes *Ein Hungerkünstler* sind insofern autobiographisch, als sie sich mit der Problematik des Alterns und des Künstlers beschäftigen. In drei Anläufen versucht Kafka, soetwas wie eine Summe zu ziehen: *Das Schloß, Forschungen eines Hundes* und *Der Bau*.

Wenn ich sage, die Erzählungen beschäftigen sich mit der und der Problematik, autobiographische Bezüge sind zu erkennen, die Diskussion von dem und dem gewinnt eine neue Dimension, so ist das natürlich oberflächlich formuliert. Zeigen müßte ich hier, wie das, was ich von der Umkehr, von der Veränderung der erzählerischen in eine gedankliche Abfolge anzudeuten versucht habe, allmählich eindringt in alles, was Kafka noch schreibt. So, unter der Voraussetzung einer solchen Veränderung, müßte der Leser anfangen, nicht neu zu interpretieren, sondern neu zu entziffern, was in vielen Fällen heißen kann: neu hinzunehmen. Etwa indem man *Das Schloß* nicht im Verbund mit dem *Verschollenen* und *Prozeß* liest, auf einer Ebene mit diesen, sondern gegen den Strich dieser früheren Entwürfe. Indem man die späten Tiererzählungen vergleicht und abwägt mit den früheren und gegen die früheren. Indem man auch die biographische Zäsur an der schriftstellerischen mißt.

Vielleicht zeigt sich das noch einmal in jenen späten Arbeiten, in denen philosophische Thematik direkt angesprochen wird: 'Der Steuermann', 'Der Kreisel', 'Von den Gleichnissen'. 'Ein Philosoph trieb sich immer dort herum, wo Kinder spielten', beginnt 'Der Kreisel' und endet: 'hielt er aber dann das dumme Holzstück in der Hand, wurde ihm übel und das Geschrei der Kinder, das er bisher nicht gehört hatte und das ihm jetzt plötzlich in die Ohren fuhr, jagte ihn fort, er taumelte wie ein Kreisel unter einer ungeschickten Peitsche.' Der mythologische Bezug biegt sich in die Tierfabel zurück. 'Der Geier', der den Erzähler zerfleischt wie die Adler Prometheus, holt, als ein Gutmeinender den Leidenden ermahnt, sich der Gefahr kurzer Hand zu entledigen, zum endgültigen Anlauf aus und durchstößt sein Opfer, um allerdings im gleichen Zustoß, sozusagen zu weit gehend, im Blut des Opfers zu ertrinken. Und noch einmal kommt die Gedankenfigur, die am Ende die Literatur Franz Kafkas beherrscht, zu sich selber in der *Kleinen Fabel*:

'Ach', sagte die Maus, 'die Welt wird enger mit jedem Tag. Zuerst war sie so breit, daß ich Angst hatte, ich lief weiter und war glücklich, daß ich endlich rechts und links in der Ferne Mauern sah, aber diese langen Mauern eilen so schnell aufeinander zu, daß ich schon im letzten Zimmer bin, und dort im Winkel steht die Falle, in die ich laufe'. —

'Du mußt nur die Laufrichtung ändern', sagte die Katze und fraß sie.

J. M. Rignall

HISTORY AND CONSCIOUSNESS IN
BEIM BAU DER CHINESISCHEN MAUER

Kafka's diary of his visit to Paris in 1911 contains a page of notes on Francisque Sarcey's *Le Siège de Paris* which reveal both his interest in a certain kind of historical material and his critical insight not only into the limitations of this particular work, but also, by implication, into historical writing in general. Sarcey's work is an account of his own experience of the siege of Paris in the autumn and winter of 1870–71, a memoir such as Kafka was wont to read and one that dealt with a period that held a particular fascination for him. Nor is it surprising that an account of a siege in particular should arouse his curiosity. To read Kafka noting the bizarre juxtaposition of the diurnal and the violently extraordinary in *Le Siège de Paris* is inevitably to be reminded of the condition of existence in his own fictional worlds: life lived under the shadow of a threatening power; normal existence carried on steadfastly in an entirely abnormal context; violence erupting arbitrarily into the humdrum routine of urban life.

Ein Tag aus dem damaligen Paris: Auf den Boulevards war es sonnig und schön, ruhige Spaziergänger, gegen Hôtel de Ville verändert es sich, dort ist eine Revolte der Kommunarden mit vielen Toten, Truppen, Exzessen. Am linken Ufer zischen die preußischen Granaten, Quai und Brücken sind still. Zurück zum Théâtre Français. Das Publikum kommt aus einer Vorstellung der "Mariage de Figaro". Die Abendblätter erscheinen gerade, dieses Publikum sammelt sich in Gruppen um die Kioske, in den Champs Elysées spielen Kinder, Sonntagsspaziergänger sehen neugierig einer Kavallerie-Eskadron zu, welche mit Trompeten vorüberreitet. (T 626)

A day in the Paris of that time: On the boulevards it was sunny and fine, people strolling placidly along; the scene changes near the Hôtel de Ville, where there is a revolt of the Communards with many dead, troops, excesses. Prussian shells whistle on the Left Bank; quays and bridges are still. Back to the Théâtre Français. The audience is coming from a performance of "The Marriage of Figaro". The evening papers are just appearing; the playgoers collect in groups around the kiosks; children are playing in the Champs Elysées; Sunday strollers watch with curiosity a cavalry squadron, which rides by with trumpets blowing.

But Kafka does not simply content himself with recording details of Sarcey's experience, he also comments on the nature of the writing, its changeable, inconsistent quality: 'Wechselnder Charakter des Buches selbst, während es den wechselnden Charakter von Paris beschreibt. . . . Die Ruhe von Paris nach Niederlagen ist einmal der französische Leichtsinn, einmal die französische Widerstandsfähigkeit' ('Changing character of the book itself, as it describes the changing character of Paris. . . . The calm of Paris after defeat is sometimes French frivolity, sometimes the French ability to resist'; T 626). Sarcey was not a professional historian but a theatre critic and minor novelist, and he did not claim to be writing a scholarly history, but rather one that was 'purement pittoresque, anecdotique et morale'.[1] Nevertheless Kafka's laconic note does more than simply define the particular deficiencies of a particular writer, for it indicates a general problem of historical writing, the ascription of causes to observed or recorded phenomena. In switching from one interpretation of Parisian calm in the face of defeat to another, Sarcey implies that these mutually exclusive explanations ('Leichtsinn' and 'Widerstandsfähigkeit') are equally plausible, and in the end entirely arbitrary and interchangeable. The inconsistency that Kafka observes points finally towards the elusiveness of historical truth, and it will be later echoed in *Beim Bau der Chinesischen Mauer* (*Building the Great Wall of China*), where the discourse of Kafka's narrator, another chronicler-cum-historian, is characterized by a similarly suggestive unsteadiness.

The scepticism about the writing of history implied in this passing comment of 1911 is made explicit in the notebooks of 1917, the year in which he writes *Beim Bau der Chinesischen Mauer*. Whether in response to the apparent disintegration of European civilization in a year of continuing war and erupting revolution, or in response to the crises in his own physical and emotional life, he repeatedly engages with the subject of history, casting a critical eye on its value as a written record and on the course that it was taking. In the second octavo notebook he remarks upon the disjunction between written history and human consciousness: 'Die geschriebene und überlieferte Weltgeschichte versagt oft vollständig, das menschliche Ahnungsvermögen aber führt zwar oft irre, führt aber, verläßt einen nicht' ('The traditional written history of the world often fails completely; human imagination, however, does in fact often lead astray, yet it does lead, does not abandon one'; H 65). Although history only records seven wonders of the world, he continues, the rumour of an eighth has always persisted, the implication being that the human mind remains unsatisfied and unbounded by recorded history. On other occasions his scepticism focuses not on the writing of history but on the idea of historical progress: 'An Fortschritt glauben heißt nicht glauben, daß ein Fortschritt schon geschehen ist. Das wäre kein Glauben' ('To believe in progress does not mean believing that any progress has yet been made. That would be no real belief'; H 44). Progress remains an article of faith, not a fact or a truth. Another aphorism is even more radical, denying all substance and significance to the past: 'Der entscheidende Augenblick der menschlichen Entwicklung ist immerwährend. Darum sind die revolutionären geistigen Bewegungen, welche alles Frühere für nichtig erklären, im Recht, denn es ist noch nichts geschehen' ('The decisive moment of human development is everlasting. That is why the revolutionary spiritual movements that declare everything in the past to be insignificant are correct, for nothing has yet occurred'; H 39–40). This implies a dismissal of time itself as an illusory construct, as does the well-known aphorism on the Last Judgement: 'Nur unser Zeitbegriff läßt uns das Jüngste Gericht so nennen; eigentlich ist es ein Standrecht' ('It is only our conception of time that allows us to call the Last Judgement by that name; in fact it is a permanent state of martial law'; H 43). Judgement comes not at the end of time, as the completion and fulfilment of human history, but arbitrarily, now or at any time. If the mind cannot be satisfied by recorded history, neither can it be secured by eschatology.

In these aphorisms and observations Kafka challenges not only historiography and the ideology of historical progress, but a whole series of concepts commonly associated with history — temporal progression, continuity, linearity, teleology. Walter Benjamin left a manuscript note suggesting the possibility of defining Kafka's attitude to history on the basis of the aphorism about the Last Judgement: '"Das jüngste Gericht ist ein Standrecht". Von diesem gnostischen Einschlag bei Kafka seine Stellung zur Geschichte bestimmen' ('"The Last Judgement is a permanent state of martial law." To determine from this gnostic element in Kafka's thought his relation to history').[2] Had Benjamin followed up his own suggestion, he might well have described something quite close to his own stance as revealed in the *Thesen über den Begriff der Geschichte* (*Theses on the Concept of History*) — critical of traditional history, anti-historicist, opposed to the assumption of inevitable progress, and rejecting the idea of historical continuity in favour of the discontinuous moment. In these affinities between the two writers' pronouncements on history there can be sensed the common legacy of Nietzsche and the second of the *Unzeitgemäße Betrachtungen* (*Untimely Meditations*). Kafka did not, of course, share Benjamin's commitment to the idea of political revolution, but the general effect of his aphorisms could be described in Benjamin's terms as one of 'blasting open the continuum of history' in an intellectual sense, and there is an echo of this in the discontinuities of *Beim Bau der Chinesischen Mauer*.

It is clear from these notes and aphorisms of 1917 that Kafka could as little take history and its attendant concepts for granted as he could take for granted life in general and its simplest exigencies. History is yet another problematic subject, and it is in *Beim Bau der Chinesischen Mauer* that he engages most fully with that subject in a fictional narrative, exploring and exploiting its complex nature. The term history itself is elusively overdetermined, referring without distinction to what men write and to what they make, to words and to deeds, while also bearing in many languages (among them German) the double sense of factual record and invented story. In the story of the Great Wall of China Kafka brings all these connotations of the term into play. In employing a narrator who is a kind of historian and in focusing on an historical edifice he explores the relationships between history and fiction, words and deeds, writing and truth in a characteristically sinuous and ironic way. To read the story in these terms is to avoid the interpretative extremes of ahistorical deconstruction and historical allegorizing, the one seeing textual self-reference in the structure that is never completed and the message that never arrives, the other collapsing the Chinese empire into the Hapsburg one or the Chinese into the Jews. It is, moreover, to locate the story in its literary-historical context. Adorno has pointed to the period quality of Kafka's hermetic stance towards history, seeing it as characteristic of expressionist writing around the time of the First World War,[3] but in this particular story it is rather Kafka's sceptical and ironic play with the subject of history that marks him as a writer of his time and links him, however tenuously, with contemporaries such as Musil and Mann, Conrad and Joyce. History both as lived and as written, as actions and words, becomes typically an object of irony in the writings of Modernism. The disorder of the historical world is opposed to the constructed order of art, while the claim of written history to make sense of human affairs by revealing their inherent pattern of causality is dismissed, along with the similar and related claims of traditional realism. Ironic scepticism is thus brought to bear not only on notions of historical order and progress but also on assumptions about narrative form, and there is, in modernist fiction, both a pervasive sense of a cultural ending and an experimental openness to new possibilities of fictional ending.

It is to this context that Kafka's story can be seen to belong. It employs a narrator who is not just the simple chronicler to be found in related stories such as *Ein altes Blatt* (*An Old Page*), but rather a man who is engaged in an historical enquiry, a self-proclaimed student of the comparative history of peoples ('vergleichende Völkergeschichte'), who is seeking not simply to record what he has witnessed but to understand events and institutions and make them intelligible. But having set up such a narrator, Kafka proceeds to show how his efforts at historical understanding gently and ironically undermine themselves until the point is reached where they are arbitrarily suspended. The story is, of course, unfinished, but its incompleteness is of a piece with its essential nature, a final manifestation of its ironic procedures. It fails to reach a conclusion and at the same time it repeatedly exposes to irony the narrator's readiness to leap to conclusions, showing his grander pronouncements to be without secure foundation and his certainties to be mere constructs.

The story begins with the statement of an apparently certain and unambiguous fact: 'Die Chinesische Mauer ist an ihrer nördlichsten Stelle beendet worden' ('The Great Wall of China has been completed at its northernmost point'; SE 289). The perfect tense employed here implies the grounds for that certainty, in that it suggests a link between the past event and the present in which the as yet unidentified narrative voice is speaking. In the second paragraph that implied connection is made explicit, for the narrator reveals himself to have been one of the builders of the wall as well as its unofficial historian. He has been, so to speak, a maker of history as he is now a writer of it. The autobiographical dimension of his account implies privileged access to the facts of the building process, and up to a point the narrator makes uncontentious use of this access, providing information about the wall-builders and later about his fellow-countrymen, which nothing in the narrative invites the reader to question. But in the course of his account he also reaches out for larger and more inclusive truths, or meanings, which go beyond first-hand experience and enter the realm of speculation and even metaphysics, and it is these that are exposed to gentle irony.

Irony is already at work in the structure of the first paragraph, which bears the mark of Kafka's scepticism about history.

Die Chinesische Mauer ist an ihrer nördlichsten Stelle beendet worden. Von Südosten und Südwesten wurde der Bau herangeführt und hier vereinigt. Dieses System des Teilbaues wurde auch im Kleinen innerhalb der zwei großen Arbeitsheere, des Ost- und des Westheeres, befolgt. Es geschah das so, daß Gruppen von etwa zwanzig Arbeitern gebildet wurden, welche eine Teilmauer von etwa fünfhundert Metern Länge aufzuführen hatten, eine Nachbargruppe baute ihnen dann eine Mauer von gleicher Länge entgegen. Nachdem dann aber die Vereinigung vollzogen war, wurde nicht etwa der Bau am Ende dieser tausend Meter wieder fortgesetzt, vielmehr wurden die Arbeitergruppen wieder in ganz andere Gegenden zum Mauerbau verschickt. Natürlich entstanden auf diese Weise viele große Lücken, die erst nach und nach langsam ausgefüllt wurden, manche sogar erst, nachdem der Mauerbau schon als vollendet verkündigt worden war. Ja, es soll Lücken geben, die überhaupt nicht verbaut worden sind, eine Behauptung allerdings, die möglicherweise nur zu den vielen Legenden gehört, die um den

Bau entstanden sind, und die, für den einzelnen Menschen wenigstens, mit
eigenen Augen und eigenem Maßstab infolge der Ausdehnung des Baues
unnachprüfbar sind. (SE 289)

The Great Wall of China has been completed at its northernmost point.
From the southeast and the southwest it came up in two sections that were
united here. This system of piecemeal construction was also followed on a
smaller scale by the two great armies of labour, the eastern and the western.
It was done in this way: groups of about twenty workers were formed which
had to complete a section of wall about five hundred metres long, while a
neighbouring group built a corresponding wall of similar length to meet the
first. But after the junction had been effected, the construction was not then
carried on from one end of this thousand-metre section; rather, the groups of
workers were sent off again to continue their work on the wall in altogether
different regions. Naturally in this way many large gaps arose, which were
only filled in slowly and gradually — some, indeed, only after completion of
the wall had actually been announced. In fact, there are said to be gaps which
have never been filled at all — though admittedly this assertion may be no more
than one among the many legends which have grown up around the wall, and
which, at least for a single individual with his own eyes and his own standards
of judgement, cannot be verified because of the extent of the structure.

The first sentence refers to the completion of an historical action, so that
the story could be said to begin with an ending. It is not, however, a
classically end-determined narrative such as Sartre defines in *La Nausée*,
for it moves not towards an ending implied in the opening lines, but
rather away from that openly stated ending and the certainty with which
it is invested. In a typical Kafka move the assurance of the opening
sentence and the authority of the narrative voice are progressively
undermined. The ending proves to be a qualified one; the building work
has ceased but the wall itself may still be incomplete. From a confident
statement of an apparently historical fact the paragraph moves finally
into the realm of legends, the truth of which can never be ascertained by
a single individual, unable as he is to survey the immense expanse of the
wall with his own eyes. Just as the wall is, as it were, dismantled in the
account of its piecemeal construction, so too is the authority of the
narrator. By focusing on an historical object of such physical immensity, Kafka seems to emphasize how history must dwarf the individual
mind that seeks to comprehend it. A gap opens up between history and
consciousness that is never closed. Instead of converging in a moment of
definitive understanding and unambiguous truth, the two remain
stubbornly apart, and Kafka plays on the space between them, now
stressing the limited nature of man's mental powers, now stressing his
ability imaginatively to transcend the given and known.

In the structure of the first paragraph, reversing as it does that passage
from the mists of legend to the clear light of understanding which could

be said to constitute the achievement of written history, some of the problems involved in the writing and transmissions of history are brought home to the reader. 'Unnachprüfbar' is the penultimate and crucial word. Furthermore, in so far as the piecemeal building of the wall and the narrator's attempts to understand it are both marked by discontinuity, the opening paragraph sets a pattern for the remainder of the narrative. The most striking discontinuity in the first part of the story comes at the climax of the narrator's enquiry into the building of the wall. As he reaches the question of where the idea of the wall originated, he suddenly takes leave of history and leaps into the timeless and indeterminable. As unable to determine the wall's beginning as he was to ascertain its completion, he succumbs to mystification in the notion that the high command and the decision to build the wall have existed for all time: 'Vielmehr bestand die Führerschaft wohl seit jeher und der Beschluß des Mauerbaus gleichfalls' ('Far more probably the high command has been in existence for ever, and the decision to build the wall likewise'; SE 294). The historical investigation collapses into an expression of mystical faith: the continuum of history dissolves into a timeless perpetuum.

It is not only the narrator's enquiry that suffers from indeterminacy, for he himself is a most indeterminate figure. His relationship to his fellow builders and fellow countrymen remains elusive; he is one of them yet apart from them, now identifying with them, now holding himself critically aloof. Moreover he displays at different times very different, and often contradictory, attitudes and characteristics. Sceptical and questioning for the most part, he yet appears on occasions to be smugly and complacently knowing. He is rational and matter-of-fact, yet also prepared to put blind faith in the superior wisdom of the unseen high command. Scrupulous in acknowledging the limits of his own understanding, he does not shrink from making sweeping pronouncements about human nature. He is capable of wielding irony, as in his description of the patriotic enthusiasm inspired in the wall-builders, but also apparently unaware of ironic elements in his own discourse that cast doubt on his self-knowledge and understanding: he refers, for instance, to the 'wahrheitsgetreuen Bilder' ('faithful representations'; SE 293) painted of the northern barbarians, and then proceeds to describe paintings so violent, lurid and extreme that they suggest not truth to nature but rather the expression of fear and hatred on the part of the painters and their culture. Kafka, it seems, has created a figure as teasingly elusive as the subjects he is seeking to illuminate.

A pattern can nevertheless be perceived in one aspect of the narrator's inconsistent discourse, its shifts of tone and stylistic level, its vacillation between a soberly descriptive and analytical style on the one hand, and a highly figurative and rhetorical one on the other. Whenever, in the first

9

part of the story, the narrator reaches out beyond his own experience towards larger and more inclusive certainties, towards truths of a general nature, his discourse draws attention to itself by a marked elevation or inflation of style. The truths he utters appear, under scrutiny, to be more like acts of persuasion, perhaps even self-persuasion, performed with the rhetorical resources of a high style. Describing the Tower of Babel theory he makes a sober and cautious observation: 'Es gab . . . viel Verwirrung der Köpfe damals, vielleicht gerade deshalb, weil sich so viele möglichst auf einen Zweck hin zu sammeln suchten' ('There was much confusion in people's minds at that time, perhaps precisely because so many were doing their utmost to combine forces in pursuit of a single aim'). Then in the very next sentence, he delivers himself of a grand generalization: 'Das menschliche Wesen, leichtfertig in seinem Grund, von der Natur des auffliegenden Staubes, verträgt keine Fesselung; fesselt es sich selbst, wird es bald wahnsinnig an den Fesseln zu rütteln anfangen und Mauer, Kette und sich selbst in alle Himmelsrichtungen zerreißen' ('Human nature, fundamentally changeable, as flighty as swirling dust, can endure no restraint; if it fetters itself, it will soon begin to rattle its fetters, tearing wall, chain, and even itself asunder in all directions'; SE 292). The biblical echo of 'dust' and the knowing and declarative solemnity of the prophet or preacher carry this large pronouncement, which is so out of keeping with the preceding sentence and the narrator's repeated expressions of diffident uncertainty, such as 'wenn ich mir einen solchen Gedanken . . . erlauben darf' ('if I may permit myself such a thought'; SE 294) or 'ich hüte mich vor Verallgemeinerungen' ('I am wary of generalizations'; SE 298).

The description of the unseen high command involves a similar stylistic elevation and declarative tone: 'In der Stube der Führerschaft . . . kreisten wohl alle menschlichen Gedanken und Wünsche und in Gegenkreisen alle menschlichen Ziele und Erfüllungen' ('In the office of the high command revolved all human thoughts and desires, and counter to them all human goals and fulfilments'; SE 292). The rhetorical repetition of 'all' seeks to claim assent for this propostion, whose speculative nature is still faintly acknowledged by the qualifying adverb 'wohl'. However, in the next sentence that qualifying note of the hypothetical disappears and certainty drives out speculation: 'Durch das Fenster aber fiel der Abglanz der göttlichen Welten auf die Pläne zeichnenden Hände der Führerschaft' ('Through the window, however, the reflected glory of divine worlds fell upon the hands of the leaders as they traced their plans'; SE 292). Certainty is achieved, it seems, with the aid of the high-sounding image, 'Abglanz der göttlichen Welten', which crowns this flight of the imagination with a sense of metaphysical grandeur. Of course the past tense and the context of the passage have the effect of bracketing it off as a belief held at a particular time by a particular group of people — the builders of the wall during the process of construction — but the truth of the speculation is not qualified by anything else in the story.

In at least one of these purple passages there is an indication that the narrator knows what he is up to, that he is the user of irony rather than its object. Describing the patriotic enthusiasm of the wall-builders as they set off from their homes, he mimics their thinking in free indirect speech:

> Wie ewig hoffende Kinder nahmen sie dann von der Heimat Abschied, die Lust, wieder am Volkswerk zu arbeiten, wurde unbezwinglich. Sie reisten früher von Hause fort, als es nötig gewesen wäre, das halbe Dorf begleitete sie lange Strecken weit. Auf allen Wegen Gruppen, Wimpel, Fahnen, niemals hatten sie gesehen, wie groß und reich und schön und liebenswert ihr Land war. Jeder Landmann war ein Bruder, für den man eine Schutzmauer baute, und der mit allem, was er hatte und war, sein Leben lang dafür dankte. Einheit! Einheit! Brust an Brust, ein Reigen des Volkes, Blut, nicht mehr eingesperrt im kärglichen Kreislauf des Körpers, sondern süß rollend und doch wiederkehrend durch das unendliche China. (SE 291)

> Like eternally hopeful children they then took leave of their homeland; the desire to labour once more on the communal task became irresistible. They set off from home earlier than they would have had to do; half the village accompanied them for long distances. On all the roads were groups of people, waving scarves and banners; never before had they seen how vast and rich and beautiful and worthy of love their country was. Every fellow-countryman was a brother for whom one was building a protecting wall, and who gave thanks for that throughout his life, with all that he had and all that he was. Unity! Unity! Shoulder to shoulder, a ring of one people, blood no longer confined within the narrow circuit of one body, but sweetly rolling and yet returning throughout the endless expanses of China.

The certainty or faith expressed here is clearly signalled as theirs rather than his. An ironic distance between narrator and builders is established at the beginning of the passage when he likens them to children, and the free indirect speech preserves that distance and intimates the childlike naivety of their enthusiasm. There is, too, a note of careful composition in the alliteration of 'im kärglichen Kreislauf des Körpers', and a general sense of language being manipulated to create a particular effect. The manifest irony of this passage serves to point up what is less openly at work in those cited above; the use of rhetorical devices and a highly figurative language to convey a sense of certainty and conviction which is without ultimate foundation. Certainty here is a rhetorical construct.

There is a clear parallel between this aspect of the narrator's discourse and its subject in the first part of the story; the building of the wall. The wall serves one purpose successfully, that of containment; not in the sense of containing the threat of the northern barbarians, but rather in the sense of providing a focus for the energies and aspirations of the people.[4] On the personal and psychological level this prevents individuals from drifting aimlessly into decline, like those, we are told, who completed their training before the building of the wall began. On the social and political level it creates a common sense of unity and purpose. The dangers of the uncontained existence are illustrated by the parable of the river which overflows its banks and fatally disperses itself, and it is a danger to which the narrator is expressly exposed in that the field of his investigation is an infinite one: 'das Gebiet aber, das hier zu durchlaufen wäre, ist das Endlose' (SE 293). His historical enquiry itself runs off into timelessness and infinity, but the firm ground that he fails to achieve by a strictly historical ordering, he creates in other ways, building bulwarks against levelling emptiness, constructing walls of words, buttressed by metaphor, which are designed to secure a few 'truths' from engulfing uncertainty. These rhetorical sections are, however, as discontinuous as the sections of the wall, never coming together in a coherent pattern of meaning that unites the whole narrative.

The account of the construction of the wall ends on a note of precarious knowingness, solidarity and security. Starting from what he initially acknowledges to be a personal notion of the high command — 'Vielmehr bestand die Führerschaft seit jeher und der Beschluß des Mauerbaues gleichfalls' — the narrator once again writes himself into conviction: 'Unschuldige Nordvölker, die glaubten ihn verursacht zu haben, verehrungswürdiger unschuldiger Kaiser, der glaubte, er hätte ihn angeordnet. Wir vom Mauerbau wissen es anders und schweigen' ('Innocent peoples of the North, who believed that they had caused it, worthy, innocent Emperor, who believed he had decreed it. We builders of the wall know otherwise and keep silence'; SE 294). In this rhetorical climax, the ironic distance which had earlier separated the narrator from the other builders of the wall is abandoned, and personal opinion is raised to the level of shared knowledge which sets him above and apart from ordinary men as a member of an elite endowed with privileged insight. Self-doubt and hesitation have given way to a knowing, but manifestly factitious superiority.

The second part of the story, which focuses on the institution of the empire, displays similar rhetorical procedures to the first part and similarly undermines a linear conception of history. The narrator stands once again in an uneasy relationship to his fellow countrymen, now identifying himself with the inhabitants of his native region, now distancing himself from them. As a student of comparative history he is able to perceive and put into perspective their muddled consciousness of history, their confusion of past with present and of temporal differences with spatial ones. In the popular consciousness the chronology of linear history is hopelessly scrambled: 'Längst verstorbene Kaiser werden in unseren Dörfern auf den Thron gesetzt . . . So verfährt also das Volk mit den vergangenen, die gegenwärtigen Herrscher aber mischt es unter die Toten' ('Emperors long dead are installed on the thrones in our villages . . . So the people behave towards rulers of the past; yet the present rulers they consign to the realm of the dead'; SE 296–97). Battles of the remotest past are received as the latest news, and the more past the affairs of the imperial court are, the more colourful they appear to the popular mind. History is, for the people, not a chronological succession of related events but something more like an imaginary stage on which all events are repeatedly acted out. Indeed, it comes to resemble the realm of romantic fiction, and as the narrator describes the way the popular consciousness registers historical events, his prose takes on the colouring of a lurid historical romance:

Die kaiserlichen Frauen, überfüttert in den seidenen Kissen, von schlauen Höflingen der edlen Sitte entfremdet, anschwellend in Herrschsucht, auffahrend in Gier, ausgebreitet in Wollust, verüben ihre Untaten immer wieder von neuem. Je mehr Zeit schon vergangen ist, desto schrecklicher leuchten alle Farben, und mit lautem Wehgeschrei erfährt einmal das Dorf, wie eine Kaiserin vor Jahrtausenden in langen Zügen ihres Mannes Blut trank. (SE 297)

The imperial ladies, lounging overfed among silken cushions, estranged from noble customs by wily courtiers, swollen with ambition, irritable with greed, unbounded in their lust, are forever committing their outrageous deeds anew. The more time has already passed, the more terribly all the colours glow, and with loud cries of woe the village learns, one day, how an Empress thousands of years before drank in long draughts the blood of her husband.

The narrator may stand at some distance from this romancing, but he shares the predicament from which it springs — the remoteness of his homeland from the imperial centre in Peking. Moreover his description of the imperial court, prefaced as it is by the admission that he and his compatriots can have no direct knowledge of it, smacks itself of the clichés of inferior fiction: 'Um den Kaiser drängt sich die glänzende und doch dunkle Menge des Hofstaates — Bosheit und Feindschaft im Kleid der Diener und Freunde — das Gegengewicht des Kaisertums, immer bemüht, mit vergifteten Pfeilen den Kaiser von seiner Wagschale abzuschießen' ('Around the Emperor presses the brilliant and yet sinister throng of the court — malice and enmity in the guise of servants and friends — the counterweight to the imperial power, always seeking to topple the emperor from his seat in the balance with poisoned arrows'; SE 295). The difference between scholar and simple villagers becomes hard to discern, and factual report becomes indistinguishable from fictional story-telling. Kafka's irony here points once again towards the elusiveness of historical truth and the inevitability of fabrication.

The legend of the imperial message can be read in similar terms. It involves a blurring of the distinction between spatial and temporal, geographical and historical, that occurs elsewhere in the story. The spatial distance between the narrator and Peking translates itself into a temporal one — news from the court will always arrive too late — just as the message from a distant province written in a strange dialect is mistakenly interpreted by the village people as temporally rather than spatially different, since they read the dialect not as geographically remote but as historically antiquated. Similarly the interminable journey of the messenger is described in terms not only of the territory he must cross but also of the time he must traverse: '. . . und wieder Treppen und Höfe; und wieder ein Palast; und so weiter durch Jahrtausende . . .' ('. . . and once more stairs and courts; again a palace; and so on through thousands of years'; SE 296). This shifting of categories, the way space and time slide into each other and change places, opens up a possible reading of the legend as, among other things, a parable of the failure of a specifically historical transmission, rendering in narrative terms the unbridgeable gulf that separates the original acts of history from the present. The message is, after all, 'die Botschaft eines Toten' ('the message of a dead man'). In this reading the final image of a figure, addressed as 'Du', who sits at the window when evening falls and dreams up the message, implicates the historian–narrator as well as the reader of Kafka's elusive text. His activity, too, may be no more than a dreaming into existence of what can never be certainly known.

In both parts of the story the narrator is thus shown to be involved in creating structures of meaning on the basis of uncertainty, structures over a void. However, at the end of the story as originally published by Max Brod, Kafka seems to lay stress on the opposite power of the mind to overthrow such structures and undermine the basis of a secure existence. The narrator breaks off his enquiry at the point where it threatens to do just that. He shrinks from exploring further and criticizing the Chinese people's inability to conceive clearly of the imperial authority in Peking, for to do so would be to shake the foundation of their own, and his, existence. Paradoxically it is this inability, or weakness, which unites the nation. The words he uses in defining the danger of such a criticism — 'an unseren Beinen rütteln' (SE 299) — catch an echo of an earlier scene, that episode remembered from his childhood when the schoolteacher, gathering up his skirts, ran at the wall built of pebbles by the children, who were scarcely yet steady on their legs — 'kaum unserer Beine sicher' (SE 290) — demolishing it and sending them running home in tears to their parents. This tiny incident, as he calls it, makes a connection between human, physical, and emotional unsteadiness and vulnerability on the one hand, and the unsteadiness or fragility of the structures created by human effort on the other, and it dramatizes the existential dangers that the narrator has approached at the end of his investigation.

The story concludes on a note of precarious balance and ironic suspension. Different possibilities are kept in play with regard both to the narrator's stance and the Chinese people's attitude to the empire. That institution itself seems to exist in a state of fragile equilibrium, neither commanding whole-hearted commitment nor provoking rebellion. The people's inability to conceive clearly of the imperial authority and take it to their hearts is presented by the narrator in highly ambiguous terms. He appears to define it as a weakness: 'Andererseits aber liegt doch auch darin eine Schwäche der Vorstellungs- oder Glaubenskraft beim Volke, welches nicht dazu gelangt, das Kaisertum aus der Pekinger Versunkenheit in aller Lebendigkeit und Gegenwärtigkeit an seine Untertanenbrust zu ziehen, die doch nichts besseres will, als einmal diese Berührung zu fühlen und an ihr zu vergehen' ('On the other hand, however, this attitude also conceals a weakness of imagination or of faith on the part of the people, who are incapable of rousing the imperial power from its depths in Peking, and drawing it in all its vital, living presence to their obedient breasts, when indeed they want nothing better than to feel that touch, and to be consumed by it'; SE 298–99). And yet this is another of those high-sounding assertions that raise the question of irony. Does he himself see it this way, or is he merely expressing what he assumes to be the view of those in power? This definition of the people's wishes certainly conflicts with his earlier description of them, while it is clear that to realize such wishes would be an act of profound political subservience. It would be abjectly to identify with the imperial authority, to sacrifice independence and surrender selfhood. It is understandable that the narrator hesitates to pronounce such an action desirable. Yet there is another possible view of the matter, since in maintaining their distance the people also commit themselves to a life of political quietism, never challenging the manner in which they are governed. Similarly, the narrator's decision to break off his investigation can be seen in different ways, as legitimate scholarly scrupulousness or as a timid refusal to embark on a course of action that is uncertain and potentially disturbing. The ending holds these different possibilities in suspension, making nothing explicit and leaving nothing resolved.

This ironic openness strongly suggests that the story could be continued, and Malcolm Pasley has concluded from his study of the manuscript that it actually was. His English translation follows Kafka's drafts a stage further than Max Brod, closing with the narrator's recollection of how news of the building of the wall reached his native village when he was still a child.[5] If the story began with an ending, it now ends with news of a beginning:

Such was the world into which the news of the building of the wall now penetrated. It too came belatedly, some thirty years after it had been announced. It was on a summer evening. I, then aged ten, was standing with my father on the river bank.

Once again, with the belated arrival of the news, there is a gap between the historical event and the moment at which it impinges on the awareness of the narrator and his countrymen. However, the main point of this scene is not the remoteness of that event but its impact on consciousness. The occasion is imprinted on the narrator's memory with lasting precision and clarity. He can recall his father's appearance that evening in graphic detail — the movement of his hand along the stem of his pipe, his 'long, sparse, stiff beard', and his pigtail 'rustling faintly on the gold-embroidered silk of his holiday robe'. The same clarity of detail and gesture inform the remainder of the scene:

At that moment a bark drew up before us, the boatman signalled to my father to come down the embankment, while he himself climbed up towards him. They met halfway, the boatman whispered something in my father's ear; he put his arms round him to get really close. I could not understand what was said, I only saw that my father seemed not to believe the news, the boatman tried to assure him of its truth, my father still could not believe it, then the boatman, with the vehemence of sailor folk, almost ripped apart the clothes on his chest to prove the truth of his words, whereupon my father fell silent and the boatman leapt heavily into the bark and sailed away. Thoughtfully my father turned towards me, knocked out his pipe and stuck it in his belt, stroked me on the cheek and drew my head against his. That was what I liked best, it filled me with good spirits, and thus we returned home. There the rice-pap was already steaming on the table, a number of guests were assembled, the wine was just being poured into the goblets. My father paid no attention to any of this, and while still on the threshold he began to recount what he had heard. I cannot of course remember the exact words, but the sense impressed itself on me so deeply, owing to the exceptional nature of the circumstances that were enough to entrance even a child, that I do feel able to give some version of what he said. I do it because it was so very characteristic of the popular attitude. Well, then, my father said something like this:

[A strange boatman — I know all those who usually pass here, but this one was a stranger — has just told me that a great wall is going to be built to protect the emperor. For it seems that infidel tribes, and demons among them, often gather in front of the imperial palace and shoot their black arrows at the emperor.][6]

It is gesture that is important here, and the narrator's language seems to efface itself before the remembered moment rather than drawing attention to itself with rhetorical flourishes and stylistic inflation. The scene bears the quiet authority of first-hand experience and carries no suggestion of an ironic discrepancy between what the narrator claims to know and what he is able to know. There is a certainty here that is not shown up by irony to be a rhetorical construct. It is both the certainty of remembered experience and at the same time the certainty of a secure childhood world, sheltered by the protective presence of the father. However, the arrival of the messenger appears to announce the end of that secure and certain existence, for the father's protective gesture of drawing the child towards him, his distracted thoughtfulness and inattention to the convivial domestic gathering all suggest his awareness of the threatening implications of the news. If the building of the wall is inspired by the threat of an invasion, the news of that building is itself an invasion of the peaceful provincial world of childhood. It marks the eruption of history into the life of the narrator and, implicitly, the advent of insecurity. In this respect the ending of Pasley's version, although open, implies a kind of circularity, since what may be said to begin here is that condition of uncertainty which lies behind the historical investigation of the building of the wall. *Beim Bau der Chinesischen Mauer* has here arrived, in a sense, at its source. What the narrator has been reaching vainly after in his writing is the certainty and security whose last moments this final scene so vividly describes.

This is not to say, however, that the story is complete or Kafka's preoccupation with its themes exhausted. He returns to the Chinese material in other fragments and in later years. One piece in particular, written in the autumn of 1920 and later published as 'Die Abweisung' ('The Refusal'), reveals specific parallels with *Beim Bau der Chinesischen Mauer* that throw light on the earlier story and its problematic or precarious structures. The narrator of 'Die Abweisung' is the citizen of a remote little town, unimaginably far from both the capital of the empire and its frontiers. The empire is immeasurable, but any danger of its citizens feeling lost in this immensity is averted by the figure of the imperial colonel who governs the town. Whenever the local people come to present a petition to him, he adopts a forbidding but at the same time reassuring pose: 'Wenn eine Abordnung mit einer Bitte vor ihn kommt, steht er da wie die Mauer der Welt. Hinter ihm ist nichts mehr, man hört förmlich dort weiterhin noch ahnungsweise ein paar Stimmen flüstern, aber das ist wahrscheinlich Täuschung, er bedeutet doch den Abschluß des Ganzen, wenigstens für uns' ('When a delegation comes before him with a request, he stands there like the wall of the world. Behind him there is nothing more; one still imagines one hears one or two voices whispering there, in the background, but that is probably an illusion; for indeed he signifies the end of all things, at least for us'; SE 311). Once again Kafka uses the image of the wall that contains and protects. When the colonel rejects the people's petition they go away with a sense of relief, and yet they continue to submit such petitions. They feel a need, it seems, to test the limits of their world, and are reassured when those limits are reaffirmed. As in *Beim Bau der Chinesischen Mauer* security is maintained by not overstepping limits, by not enquiring too deeply or pressing too hard. In this respect both stories appear to illustrate that 'general law' which Nietzsche postulates in the second of the *Unzeitgemäße Betrachtungen*, and which he applies indiscriminately to individuals and to peoples: 'und dies ist ein allgemeines Gesetz; jedes Lebendige kann nur innerhalb eines Horizontes gesund, stark und fruchtbar werden ; ist es unvermögend, einen Horizont um sich zu ziehn, und zu selbstisch wiederum, innerhalb eines fremden den eignen Blick einzuschließen, so siecht es matt und überhastig zu zeitigem Untergange dahin' ('. . . and this is a general law: every living creature can become healthy, strong, and fruitful only within a circumscribed horizon; if it is incapable of drawing such a horizon around itself, and conversely too egoistic to delimit its own vision within that of another, so it wastes away, feeble and overhasty, to a timely end').[7] In 'Die Abweisung' the colonel represents such an horizon for the townspeople and secures their existence. In the earlier story Kafka, aware like Nietzsche of the dangers of an overdeveloped historical consciousness, shows his historian–narrator reaching out beyond the limited understanding of his fellows, but then repeatedly drawing horizons around him with his images of the high command and the imperial court, and his bold assertions of general 'truths'. Such are the uses of history in *Beim Bau der Chinesischen Mauer*, and Kafka's delicate ironies suggest both the value and the frailty of its structures of meaning.

NOTES

[1] Francisque Sarcey, *Le Siège de Paris: impressions et souvenirs* (Paris, 1871), p. 2.

[2] *Benjamin über Kafka: Texte, Briefe, Aufzeichnungen*, ed. Hermann Schweppenhauser (Frankfurt/M., 1981), p. 142.

[3] Theodor W. Adorno, *Prismen: Kulturkritik und Gesellschaft* (Munich, 1963), p. 268.

[4] Christian Goodden, '*The Great Wall of China*: The Elaboration of an Intellectual Dilemma', in *On Kafka: Semi-Centenary Perspectives*, ed. Franz Kuna (London, 1976), pp. 128–45, explores this idea of containment, relating it both to the wall and to the intellectual quest in which the narrator is involved, but does not stress the historical dimension of that enquiry or the containing effect of its questionable conclusions.

[5] Frank Kafka, *Shorter Works Volume I*, edited and translated by Malcolm Pasley (London, 1973), pp. 74–75. All the following quotations are from these pages.

[6] Pasley, p. 75. The square brackets enclosing the last paragraph indicate that Kafka deleted these lines in his manuscript.

[7] Nietzsche, *Werke*, ed. Karl Schlechta (Munich, 1960), I, 214.

J. L. Hibberd

'CET AUTEUR RÉALISTE': ROBBE-GRILLET'S READING OF KAFKA

'Cet auteur réaliste' is Franz Kafka as described by Alain Robbe-Grillet, the leading practitioner and apologist of the French 'new novel', in an essay written in 1955 and published in the volume *Pour un nouveau roman*[1] in 1963. His response to Kafka's work is an important one. It is a sign of Kafka's influence beyond the German-speaking world on a prominent avant-garde author of our time. It is also part of a major recent development in the theory of fiction. For though Robbe-Grillet's reading of Kafka is, like his use of the word 'realist' or 'realistic', provocative, it is by no means totally idiosyncratic and isolated. Here, however, I am concerned not with its historical significance but with its adequacy as an interpretation. Does it enhance our understanding of Kafka? Should it replace other and more traditional approaches to his work? Robbe-Grillet's observations certainly provoke counter state-ments. By stressing the similarity of his own work to Kafka's he invites a more detailed comparison of their novels, but one which reveals dimensions in Kafka's writing which the Frenchman refuses to acknow-ledge. But first let us look at what he says about Kafka. Even here some reference to Robbe-Grillet's practice as novelist will be necessary, for his critical remarks are primarily an attempt to justify that practice.

Robbe-Grillet's starting point is his dismissal of allegorical readings of Kafka. For him they are simply inappropriate because they are irrelevant to the task of the contemporary novelist. It is that task that concerns him, not the problems of Kafka scholars nor what Kafka himself may have intended. So he maintains that Kafka's 'onirisme métaphysique' (PNR 15), the aspect of his work which, he says, links him with Surrealism and has attracted most attention, is of no interest except in so far as many novelists have been misled by it. In emulating the supposedly allegorical and metaphysical Kafka they have been blind to his real achievement; they have betrayed 'le réalisme du maître' (PNR 180). He concentrates on Kafka as novelist and calls him a realist in order to claim him, together with Flaubert, Dostoyevski, Proust, James, Faulkner and Beckett (PNR 146) as a precursor of the 'nouveau roman'.

But what does he mean by realism? What is this all-important, forward-pointing quality of Kafka's work? Here Robbe-Grillet's thinking is rather fluid. His theoretical stance changes.[2] In the 1955 essay in which Kafka figures most prominently, he advocates the description of things as phenomena independent of man. A few years later he concentrates on things as objects of subjective perception. Later still he stresses the free ludic activity of the writer. But these are shifts in emphasis or angle of vision rather than of principle. The three stages overlap and it is not possible to keep them altogether separate one from another when considering his interpretation of Kafka. Whatever Robbe-Grillet's emphasis, it is clear that for him realism involves description, yet has nothing to do with naturalism, 'vérisme' or objectivity. Rather it is connected with a striving for 'une subjectivité totale' (PNR 15, 177, 148). It is not literary realism in the accepted sense, not social or nineteenth-century realism. Robbe-Grillet believes that such realism is quite unrealistic, for he denies that reality is an intelligible system whose sense can be revealed by an omniscient narrator for the comfort of the grateful reader. In 1955 he holds that the human mind is necessarily separate from the unconscious world of things, it cannot force that world into a pattern of meaning (or of absurdity). The world simply *is*. In it things are seen to exist, to be present, and their presence defies all attempts to domesticate and humanize them within a satisfying system. It is, he asserts, Kafka's great strength that he presents this real world:

Ce dont une lecture non prévenue nous convainc . . . c'est de la réalité absolue des choses que décrit Kafka. Le monde visible de ses romans est bien, pour lui, le monde réel, et ce qu'il y a derrière (s'il y a quelque chose) paraît sans valeur, face à l'évidence des objets, gestes, paroles, etc. . . . . Peut-être les escaliers de Kafka mènent-ils ailleurs, mais eux sont là, et on les regarde, marche par marche, en suivant le détail des barreaux et de la rampe . . . Même ce dont le héros est en quête disparaît, devant l'obstination qu'il met dans la poursuite, ses trajets et ses mouvements, seuls rendus visibles, seuls vrais. Dans toute l'œuvre, les rapports de l'homme avec le monde, loin d'avoir un caractère symbolique, sont constamment directs et immédiats. (PNR 179 f.)

Robbe-Grillet is paying tribute to the vividness of Kafka's writing. It seldom goes unnoticed, and he is not the first to wonder at it. It impressed André Gide, who also called it realism.[3] Yet this quality deserves to be stressed, particularly because it may be forgotten in a search for hidden meanings. Robbe-Grillet exaggerates that danger. If, he argues, we concentrate on the 'something else' that the things described are imagined to represent, we destroy their tangible reality. In his view reality and meaning are mutually exclusive; meaning is a fiction, reality is not 'récupérable'. Kafka's world he says, is an obviously fictional, constructed world — like that of the 'nouveau roman'. It is a work of the imagination which does not aim or claim to reproduce or to explain reality. Yet he believes that honest fiction can teach us how to view reality (PNR 182): it reveals the unintelligibility of existence and the creativeness of the imagination; it stresses the unbridgeable gulf between things and consciousness, reality and meaning. That is the only message he allows in Kafka, and he claims that it does not go beyond what is stated in Kafka's texts and does not transcend human experience and knowledge; it is neither allegorical nor metaphysical. The realism he finds in Kafka is his own realism which owes much to existentialism and phenomenology. It is the realism that Robbe-Grillet aims to impart through his own novels.

The allegory that Robbe-Grillet rejects can be defined as a literary technique of allusion which proclaims supposed objective meaning in terms of concepts which he believes to be unreal. His later theoretical pronouncements allow for metaphorical or symbolic writing, indeed he himself uses symbols in his novels, but symbols whose function may be limited to the mentality of the hero or narrator. The famous centipede of *La Jalousie* is such a symbol. He acknowledges the vital role of figural perspective in Kafka and in modern fiction, and greets it — when it is not an invitation to seek the false security of a psychological system — as a means to true realism, to a text which offers total subjectivity, 'expérience vécue,' not 'schémas rassurants' (PNR 149 f).

Others have recognized the importance of narrative perspective in Kafka. But if they have worried long and hard at a technique whose function Robbe-Grillet takes to be self-evident, it is because they have not found it easy to accept that Kafka's narratives do not point beyond the mentality of his heroes and beyond their own fictional bounds. Kafka himself, after all, linked his writing with his 'traumhaftes, inneres Leben' ('dreamlike inner life'), and beyond that with historical reality, with the predicament of Western Jewry, and with his time in general. Reference to such self-interpretation, and the implied equation of intention with achievement, will not, however, satisfy those who insist that the work of art must be interpreted as an autonomous entity. Robbe-Grillet writes of the text, not of what Kafka meant it to be or thought it was. But when he says that the object for which Kafka's hero searches is unimportant and should not concern us, he is belittling that — the court or the castle — without which there would be no novel, as well as that which seems to claim to be objective or transcendental. He even comes close to denying its existence because it does not fit his definition of things as objects whose only significance is that they may be used as tools (PNR 65). Yet the court and the castle are not simply things, but systems of authority with human representatives and servants. They provoke questions about the intelligibility of reality, but also about power and moral justification. Robbe-Grillet, for whom all materialist and idealist systems are equally metaphysical and unrealistic, is remarkedly silent on the moral issue. 'Je suis, moi, très allergique au concept de vérité', he says,[4] and he is unwilling to admit the seriousness and centrality of Kafka's concern with the absolute values of truth and justice and with the enigma they represented for him.

Robbe-Grillet's reading of Kafka is biased. He is anxious to claim him as a forebear and thereby give status to his own work. But is it even partially correct? What about his remarks on Kafka's descriptions, 'la réalité absolue des choses que décrit Kafka', the main thrust of his contemptuous dismissal of those who find allegory and metaphysics in Kafka?

Robbe-Grillet refers to staircases ('on les regarde, marche par marche, en suivant le détail des barreaux et de la rampe'). Here, as in general, he ascribes to Kafka something more readily found in his own work. It is in *Les Gommes*, not in Kafka, that we find a description of a staircase with its treads, risers, banister and rail. Thanks to Roland Barthes, Robbe-Grillet is known for his 'chosisme', his extended, obsessively minute descriptions of objects. In them, for instance the repeated delineations of a lamp-post in *Dans le labyrinthe*, he concentrates on scientific precision in the rendering of the visible world. He deliberately avoids anthropomorphism, that being in his view the source of metaphysics and error. His attempts at comprehensive precision are almost incantatory, they conjure up the physical presence and otherness of everyday ordinary things. Yet, as he came to recognize, 'chosisme' and his own early theory do not adequately describe even his own practice. Thus he later turned to the notions of total subjectivity and of writing as play. The stairs in *Les Gommes* do lead 'elsewhere', to a playful allusion to the Tarot cards and the theme of fate in that novel. The variations in the picture of the lamp-post in *Dans le labyrinthe* produce confusion rather than clarity, they reflect the mind of the perceiver as well as the solidity of the object. 'Chosisme' is still less appropriate as a key to the descriptions in *Der Prozeß* and *Das Schloß*. Kafka is much more concerned with interhuman relationships than with relations between man and inanimate things,[5] except notably when things reveal the despotism of technology and bureaucracy, when tools are the masters of man. When he describes things, he does not typically attempt comprehensive precision, but selects apparently significant, striking detail. Over many lines of print, Robbe-Grillet conveys the idea that objects say nothing. With a few words, Kafka gives expression to the expectation that they have vital information to impart. The particular seems to promise insight into the general, the visible world to point to the invisible. Robbe-Grillet consistently, in all stages of his theory and practice, aims to rule out transcendence. Kafka allows for it as a possibility and a psychological necessity. His worries about the limitations of language and literature presuppose a reality beyond sensuous perception and beyond expression: 'Die Sprache kann für alles außerhalb der sinnlichen Welt nur andeutungsweise . . . gebraucht werden' ('For everything outside the world of tangible phenomena, language can only be used allusively'; H 34). Such 'allusion' is indeed central to Kafka's writing, but Robbe-Grillet would have us dismiss it as the perverse product of fantasy.

In order to show how Kafka's descriptions differ from what Robbe-Grillet would have us see in them, I turn to a brief passage in *Der Prozeß*:

K. trat vor die Kanzel und untersuchte sie von allen Seiten, die Bearbeitung des Steines war überaus sorgfältig, das tiefe Dunkel zwischen dem Laubwerk und hinter ihm schien wie eingefangen und festgehalten, K. legte seine Hand in eine solche Lücke und tastete den Stein vorsichtig ab . . . (P 247)

K. walked up to the pulpit and examined it from all sides; the carving of the stone was extremely careful; the deep shadows among the foliage, and behind it, seemed as if imprisoned and held fast; K. put his hand in one such hole and cautiously felt the stone . . .

This description of the stone carving on the pulpit in the cathedral certainly emphasizes the physical presence of an inanimate object. But it highlights one feature to the exclusion of others. That feature is not the object itself, but a space in and behind it. Nevertheless we may, taking the part of Robbe-Grillet, comment that the dark hole is mere emptiness, serving only to invite the hero to establish the impassive three-dimensional solidity of the carving; that any symbolic, anthopomorphic significance of the darkness is of the hero's making ('wie eingefangen und festgehalten'); that its fascination for Josef K. is symptomatic of his obsession with the invisible whose only true function is to circumscribe the knowable. We may, furthermore, assert that the word 'Laubwerk' is a cunning substitute for the synonymous 'Blätter' and announce that these carefully wrought leaves stand for the pages of the novel, behind which lurks no meaning but the absence of meaning. Such a commentary is not totally implausible and obviously false, even if it leaves aside the personality of Kafka, paying no attention to his hope that he might find and express some objective truth through his writing. But does it do full justice to the text itself, to the suggested link between the dark space and confinement and arrest ('wie eingefangen und festgehalten'!)? This connexion with the trial *may* indeed be purely subjective. Yet equally importantly it is rather complicated, for it suggests two different analogies, both tentative, both probably inexact, and together forming a tantalizingly blurred symbol. For the dark emptiness may refer to the hero or to the court. Just as the space is enclosed by the stone, so Josef K. is apparently trapped and kept in the darkness of ignorance by the court which like the inside of the stonework can be felt but not seen. But the court itself is a dark mystery hidden behind an elaborately contrived exterior. Are these analogies significant? Does the darkness stand for the hero, or the court, or both, or for neither and nothing at all? The space behind the stone is filled with mystery. It is not clear that it is empty of meaning. Like so many details in the novel it appears to be a sign whose significance is obscure. That which may lie behind or beyond visible and tangible reality does not recede 'face à l'évidence des objets' and appear 'sans valeur'; Josef K.'s examination of the object leads him to it.

Empty spaces, says Robbe-Grillet, attract metaphysics as a chimney draws in smoke (PNR 180). Kafka's castle and his court are not complete voids, but they function in that way, and that is why Robbe-Grillet would have us ignore them. Kafka does not attempt to reduce even real emptiness to absence of meaning. He allows and encourages the reader to fill it with possible meanings, uncertain and apparently contradictory meanings which he himself suggests or hints at and which correspond to the enigmatic interrelation of hero and court or castle, perhaps also of mind and matter, fiction and reality, where insufficient is known about either to throw light on the other. Unlike Robbe-Grillet, Kafka is not convinced that it is better to assume that absence or silence conceals nothing. In *Pour un nouveau roman* Robbe-Grillet sketches a monodrama in order to illustrate a situation the modern novelist should avoid. It concerns a person who believes that the silence which answers his call is no true silence and proof that no one is there, but a refusal to answer, and therefore a cause for despair and anguish. That person's attitude, Robbe-Grillet implies, is unrealistic. Here again, however, his practice does not conform with his own theory. There are in his novels many disturbing gaps or absences which suggest the severe limits of rational understanding and the space for imaginative creation.[6] Certainly the situation he describes in the theoretical essay is typically Kafkaesque.[7] In *Das Schweigen der Sirenen* (*The Silence of the Sirens*) a pretended silence or simulated absence is the most cunning of all fatal traps. In *Eine kaiserliche Botschaft* (*An Imperial Message*) the failure of any message to arrive is no certain proof that there is no messenger and no message. Kafka does not share the 'realism' of Robbe-Grillet, the pragmatism of one who does not yearn for what he cannot be given and for whom the distinction between reality and imagination is clear cut. Above all he worries that all meanings are dubious, whereas Robbe-Grillet shuts out such worry as futile. Kafka's power to convince the reader of the reality of the universe he describes cannot be explained so simply as Robbe-Grillet explains it.

Does, then, the Frenchman totally misunderstand Kafka? Let Kafka remind us: 'Richtiges Auffassen einer Sache und Mißverstehen der gleichen Sache schließen einander nicht vollständig aus' ('The correct perception of a matter and misunderstanding of the same matter do not entirely exclude one another'; P 259). Robbe-Grillet is right to accept that there is no authoritative voice in Kafka's work and to note that he had an eye for 'le faux', for things that are incompatible with expectations of accustomed pattern. He hits the mark when he says that things and episodes in Kafka resist and survive attempts to explain them. As another critic writes, Kafka's world 'cannot be apprehended as a transparency for an underlying essence'.[8] That is what Robbe-Grillet means when he rejects the supposedly allegorical Kafka. Allusions to something that is not specifiable are not allegory. But like so many interpretations of Kafka, Robbe-Grillet's is too narrow, too simple and too confident in negating what others have too confidently affirmed. In his defence it must be said that he does not hide his partiality, and that he does not claim to be objective or to attempt what now seems the ultimate task of Kafka criticism, to explore the various possible meanings of his work and to show how together they are like the sections of his Great Wall of China, presumed to be part of one design and yet obviously lacking in connection. Robbe-Grillet recognizes disconnection in Kafka but misconstrues its significance. He does not understand that Kafka hopes that oneness and truth beyond subjectivity are conceivable and that for him they are worth worrying about.

Robbe-Grillet is in a position to recognize opaqueness in Kafka, for opacity is his own speciality as a novelist. He too describes uncertainty, incomprehension, obsession, alienation, helplessness, and provides the reader with no sure answers, teasing him with apparently significant allusions and frustrating his expectation of a story that reflects an intelligible or purposeful universe. He too does not keep reality and imagination separate in his work (he justifies their merger as an authentic rendering of the experience of conscious man). Yet he describes a different world and creates a different opacity.

The difference between Robbe-Grillet and Kafka is like the contrast between Nietzsche and Kafka, of whom it has been said that the one 'derives wisdom from his ignorance and claims to know', the other 'stays with his ignorance and waits'.[9] But the difference must be further shown and defined if we wish to delimit the justness of Robbe-Grillet's reading of Kafka. I therefore turn now to a technique characteristic of the Frenchman's work and of the 'nouveau roman' in general, one designed to produce opacity, and ask how far it is foreshadowed in Kafka. I confine my enquiry to *Der Prozeß* and *Dans le labyrinthe* of 1959,[10] the book that stands midway in Robbe-Grillet's career as a

10

novelist and closest to Kafka (or at least to Kafka as Robbe-Grillet sees him).

The device is the 'mise en abyme', that reduced and partly distorted mirror-image of the novel within the novel, whose function in the 'nouveau roman' is to undermine the assumption that fiction reflects reality and its meaningful patterns. In *Dans le labyrinthe* each 'mise en abyme' reproduces in miniature the world of that novel as experienced by the soldier and described by the narrator or narrators. For example, we read that the meaning of the picture which has an important place in the text is 'très incertaine' (25); that it is impossible to decide what is represented on the patterned wallpaper — 'il est difficile de l'interpréter' (20); and that in the snow-covered streets 'il n'y a qu'un entrecroisement de lignes sans signification' (15). When the soldier uncharacteristically speaks at some length, we are told, not what he says, but that 'he goes on talking, getting lost in a plethora of ever-increasingly confused precision, realizing this, stopping at almost every step in order to start again on a fresh tack, persuaded now, but it is too late, that he has gone wrong from the very outset and seeing no way of extricating himself' (151). This description of his speech sums up the structure of the narrative as a whole. In the novel, as in his speech, 'ever more detailed explanations' are attempted, only to be withdrawn, so that there remains 'a series of disconnected phrases . . . that is phrases without apparent connection, mostly unfinished, and in any case very obscure' (150). Another 'mise en abyme' uses apparent self-contradiction instead of disconnectedness, but it too underlines the impossibility of comprehension and explanation. This time it is a crack in the ceiling that is described, and, by implied analogy, the novel:

the crack, hair-thin, scarcely sinuous, whose form . . . has something at once precise and complicated, so that one would need to follow it assiduously from bend to bend, with its curves, tremblings, slight reverse movements, but one would need more time, a little time, minutes, seconds, and it is already too late now. (211)

This passage echoes two earlier descriptions of cracks with almost identical characteristics. Is it the same crack, the same ceiling, the same room each time? Probably not. Robbe-Grillet is questioning our habit of systematizing reality, of equating like with like and expecting the same object to appear the same at all times no matter who looks at it. The mirrorings within his novel touch on questions of chance and design in the world. But his prime point of reference is the novel itself and the creative process it embodies. If the three cracks are similar, and several rooms are almost identical, it is because each description of an object or a place is a development of or variation on the first description.

In *Der Prozeß* the parable of the doorkeeper has first claim to be considered as a 'mise en abyme'. But it is not the only candidate. I have mentioned another already: the dark space behind the tracery on the pulpit. Others include the warder's outfit whose function is not ascertainable (9); the indecipherable significant look the warder Franz gives the hero (14); the clearly audible yet incomprehensible words of the 'Auskunftgeber' and the girl in the court offices (91); and the characterization of the legal process as 'ein sinnloses und meistens . . . ergebnisloses Verfahren' ('a senseless and for the most part inconclusive process'; 61) in which progress can seldom be observed (213) and where 'immer wieder viele Dinge zur Sprache kommen, für die der Verstand nicht ausreicht' ('time and again many things come up for discussion that are simply beyond comprehension'; 209). Dress, gesture, speech, and parable are like the trial and like the novel; they are naturally assumed to have a meaning that is not apparent. In particular it may be obscured — as in the case of the trial it is explicitly said to be — by the multiplicity of opinions about it ('die verschiedenen Ansichten häufen sich um das Verfahren bis zur Undurchdringlichkeit' — 'around the proceedings the differing views pile up to the point of impenetrability'; 236). That is not quite the situation mentioned by Robbe-Grillet as the avoidable consequence of unnecessary speculation, where the phenomenal world is hidden even by any one interpretation. Kafka's world is perhaps so real, not because it suffers no meaning, but because it permits too many.

In *Dans le labyrinthe* one 'mise en abyme', the pattern in the snow, is explicitly said to have no significance whatsoever. Another, the crack, would not normally be seen as a challenge to the observer's intelligence. The comparable features in *Der Prozeß* are such as are regularly expected to convey meaning. That is especially true of the parable which is ostensibly told in order to enlighten the hero. The chaplain announces that it concerns something ('Täuschung', 'deception') which it doesn't name — in other words that is allegorical or symbolic. But this tale of wasted life and ignominious death is no normal allegory, for its point of reference cannot be determined. It may illustrate the deception of the 'Mann vom Lande', or of the doorkeeper, of both, or of neither. The chaplain may be wrong to assert that it concerns deception at all. The real deception may be the story's claim to meaning. Its authoritative status is doubly dubious, deriving at best from the dubious Law, to which it may, however, be an apocryphal addition (it belongs to the 'Vorschriften zum Gesetz', 'Writings which preface the Law'; 255). Robbe-Grillet, too, introduces puzzles of this kind. He lists several conceivable but doubtful interpretations of the pattern on the wallpaper. It could represent a flower, a clove, a flame, a dagger, or an electric torch (19 f.).

10*

The dagger shape seems potentially significant as a leitmotif in his novel. But the meaning (if it has one) of the dagger (if it is one) relates only to a formal pattern in that novel. Any other object could serve the same function within an abstract design. The whole business of interpretation is unnecessary. What is represented on the wallpaper does not matter. In contrast *Vor dem Gesetz* (*Before the Law*) claims import even without reference to its context in *Der Prozeß* which simply underscores this claim and its enigmatic character. Even in isolation the parable asks to be made sense of by reference to concepts of truth, error, justice and guilt. The value of those concepts is not so easily confined to an aesthetic function. The argument that the significance of a work of art derives not from what is arranged, but solely from the arrangement itself, does not, when applied to Kafka's stories, carry total conviction.

Vor dem Gesetz clarifies nothing except the impossibility of understanding. It is not an exact mirror image of *Der Prozeß*: the situations and deaths of the 'Mann vom Lande' and Josef K. are not identical. It is, like the 'mise en abyme' characteristic of the 'nouveau roman', confused and confusing, obscure and obscuring. It may be contrasted with a duplication in miniature which throws light on the overall meaning of the work it reflects. Such a more traditional, revelatory mirroring presupposes a structure discoverable in reality and discovered in the novel.[11] When, for instance, Novalis's Heinrich von Ofterdingen finds in a book in the hermit's cave illustrations of his past and future life he encounters a mystery and a sign of predestined purpose, a promise of revelation and fulfilment. The exact correspondence between the book and his life is more than a subjective hypothesis, it encourages or confirms a heartening faith in purposefulness. Kafka's 'mises en abyme', and Robbe-Grillet's, frustrate the expectation of revelation. Novalis conveys the thrill of anticipated discovery; Kafka the hopelessness of the search for enlightenment. But — and here the parallel with Robbe-Grillet breaks down — although Kafka's mystery will never be solved, he gives an overwhelming impression of the need to solve it. The puzzles of *Dans le labyrinthe* (what is in the soldier's box and why, who is he and whom does he seek?) turn out to be of little importance except in so far as the novelist uses them to tease the reader. More important ultimately is the riddle of the narrative perspective. That is a puzzle of a rather different sort; it is not one that concerns the hero. Robbe-Grillet's 'mises en abyme' scarcely operate as a challenge to him; in so far as they can be related to the hero they seem to be the product of his confusion, not its cause. The focus is on the reader's predicament. In Kafka, as in Novalis, the 'mise en abyme' is clearly relevant to the hero and related to the meaning of the novel. That meaning, whether it concerns the task of the poet, a social structure, the workings of the conscience, or the hidden purpose of existence, Robbe-Grillet would call metaphysical. The history of Kafka studies shows that most of his readers are led to believe that the puzzle of his work might be decipherable and is worth deciphering. The majority of Robbe-Grillet's readers are unlikely to retain such hopes, for he does everything to discourage them. For him there is no ultimate meaning or goal, whereas Kafka notes that there is a goal but no path to it (H 61). He sees life (or at least his life) as an attempt to reach an unattainable goal, writing as an attempt to intimate the inexpressible, to find or build a path. We might call that path a stairway and recognize that, taken figuratively, Robbe-Grillet's observation about Kafka's staircases contains a half-truth. It recognizes that his literary constructions lead nowhere; but not that they are built in the frail, almost non-existent hope of leading somewhere.

Kafka has not broken with traditional novel form or with belief in the meaningfulness of existence as decisively as Robbe-Grillet. Robbe-Grillet abandons the integration of description and narrative that we find in Kafka. Thus, Kafka's work has not so often provoked the complaint or abuse directed against the 'nouveau roman' — that it is unreadable and a trap for idiots ('un piège à cons').[12] Significantly Kafka is not mentioned in that part of *Pour un nouveau roman* which looks at the abandonment of traditional plot structure in the modern novel. Though episodes in *Der Prozeß* are repetitions in a pattern of frustration they do follow in a time sequence, they imply a progression dependent on some principle of cause and effect. They move towards an end, they are part of the linear plot, that feature of traditional fiction which Robbe-Grillet is anxious to eradicate from his novel since it presupposes pattern in reality. In *Dans le labyrinthe* it is always now, past and present are irretrievably confused in the eternal present of the narrative tense.

Robbe-Grillet's novel does, of course, have an ending — of sorts. It leaves all important questions unanswered and is in that significant respect comparable with the ending of *Der Prozeß*. But, unlike the last pages of *Dans le labyrinthe*, Kafka's last chapter, in bringing the plot to a conclusion, implies that final judgements and deductions should now be made. The hero himself is conscious of the call to draw a moral. The final phrase — 'es war, als sollte die Scham ihn überleben', 'it was as if the shame would outlive him' — invites the reader to dwell on the implications of this humiliation. If the hero is aware of resonances which, however vaguely apprehended, may transcend his experience and knowledge, the reader, sharing his perspective, must also consider them. In contrast Robbe-Grillet's plot is so elusive or non-existent that conclusions seem out of the question. His text ends with the partial symmetry of a return to the descriptions that open the novel. Its finality is marked by the last six words which indicate that the unidentifiable narrator now turns his back on the maze: 'et toute la ville derrière moi' (221). The novel echoes itself and fades away. Rather than an invitation to explore its meaning, the last paragraph brings disheartening mentions of the line on the ceiling and the wallpaper pattern, things that defeat accurate description and interpretation. There are distinctly discouraging phrases: vision becomes blurred in the effort of acute observation, the objects fade from sight. The opportunity to make conclusive observations has been lost — though there probably never was such an opportunity. The novel has told of the confusion and death of a soldier, and the reader has been required to feel his anguish. But the text also more consistently demands to be seen as a game of creation. That game is over. It has been a game of the imagination and the intellect in which the author cannot lose, for he is the arbiter of his fiction. Kafka, too, teases the reader. But in his game the narrator identifies with the loser throughout the hopeless struggle in which life and comprehension are at stake. Kafka is not obviously, like Robbe-Grillet, self-consciously in control. For Kafka's reader emotional involvement in the plot and the intellectual challenge posed by the text are inseparable, and the impact of each is greater because of that unity.

This is not the place to pursue these contrasts further. Investigation of the role of description and of the 'mise en abyme' in *Der Prozeß* and *Dans le labyrinthe* has indicated a fundamental difference between two novels which both frustrate confident interpretation. Both give expression to a conviction that some things cannot be known, above all that man cannot know whether there is a correspondence between the mental and physical worlds or between them and a higher spiritual reality or divine law. Yet *Der Prozeß* assumes the possibility, even the likelihood, of such correspondences. It persuades us that such uncertainties matter, that we must, from psychological or existential need, seek for necessary relations, we must ask whether there is a higher essence and what is its nature, sublime or base. Kafka, like many of his contemporaries in their dissatisfaction with science and rationalism, rejects as inadequate what can be known for certain. Robbe-Grillet, in contrast, scorns as metaphysical any science that claims certain knowledge. He recognizes only the validity of fiction whose claims are less, not more, than those of traditional science. *Dans le labyrinthe* would teach us to live with ignorance and have us recognize that the desire to grasp the uncertain causes of all things distracts man from the real conditions of existence. It would persuade us to avoid useless speculation and to concentrate on what might be known, namely the workings of our own minds. So Robbe-Grillet focuses on mental activity and its process of inventing arbitrary patterns based on association and partial analogy, a process seen in the activities of the writer and reader of his kind of fiction. He would have us accept that to live as a conscious being is to invent and to indulge in a play of the imagination which may have no ultimate purpose, but which is necessary and even pleasurable. So he can assert that the novel teaches man 'to invent the world' and 'to learn to invent his own life' (PNR 169). Thus Robbe-Grillet justifies his fiction. Kafka, we know, could not justify his writing to his satisfaction in that or any other way. *Der Prozeß* allows for the inventiveness of the human mind, for its production of illusion, but it portrays life not as the invention of meaning, but as a search for it. That search is frustrated, not because there is no apparent meaning, but because there are too many possible and mutually incompatible meanings. In Kafka's novel that which the individual chooses to believe or to imagine is not sufficient; man requires confirmation of truth from higher authority.

Robbe-Grillet reads Kafka with the insight of an intelligent fellow writer of fiction. He rightly warns that an author's experience or a fact becomes something quite different when transformed into fiction, so that any connection between imagination and reality must be treated very warily. He recognizes that to regard Kafka's work as an allegory to which one must find the key is to do violence to that work. He sees that Kafka does not establish an underlying unity in the world. But he fails to acknowledge that Kafka's stories do not treat incomprehension as an acceptable condition, that in Kafka's world the question, 'Do things make sense?', is not to be sidestepped. Robbe-Grillet happily assumes that reality and Kafka have no meaning. Kafka despairingly admits that he has found none. In pretending that the partial likeness of Kafka's work with his own provides a basis for sufficient understanding, Robbe-Grillet indulges in conscious oversimplification. In equating lack of clear meaning with denial of meaning he misrepresents Kafka. His reading of Kafka cannot, therefore, replace all other interpretations. But it deserves an honourable place in the history of Kafka criticism alongside interpretations which it contradicts but with which it has this in common: it does not encompass the whole truth. It may serve to remind us that there is, in reading Kafka, a risk that understanding and misunderstanding are not necessarily mutually exclusive.

NOTES

[1] A. Robbe-Grillet, *Pour un nouveau roman* (Paris, 1963), p. 178. Further references in the text below are to this edition (PNR).

[2] See Stephen Heath, *The Nouveau Roman* (London, 1972), pp. 67 ff.

[3] A. Gide, *Journal 1939–1949, Souvenirs* (Paris, 1954); entry of 28 August 1940.

[4] *Robbe-Grillet: Analyse, Théorie (Colloque de Cérisy*, Paris, 1976), I, 47.

5 See J. Alter, 'Perspectives romanesques et tension sociale: Le Château et le Labyrinthe', *Actes du VIe Congrès de l'Association Internationale de Littérature Comparée* (Bordeaux, 1970), p. 169.

6 See Olga Bernal, *Alain Robbe-Grillet: le roman de l'absence* (Paris, 1964).

7 See Dorrit Cohn, 'Castles and Anti-Castles, or Kafka and Robbe-Grillet', *Novel*, 5 (1971/72), 29.

8 Maja J. Goth, 'Existentialism and Franz Kafka', *Franz Kafka. His Place in World Literature*, ed. W. T. Zyla (Lubbock, Texas, 1971), p. 86.

9 Goth, p. 91.

10 Further references in the text below to this edition, Paris, 1959.

11 See J. Ricardou, *Le nouveau roman* (Paris, 1973), pp. 50 ff.

12 P. de Boisdeffre, cited Heath, p. 33.

J. P. Stern

FRANZ KAFKA ON MICE AND MEN

Dedicated to René Wellek on the occasion
of his eightieth birthday, 22 August 1983

Not many days in the year pass without reminding us — and I think we
need such reminders — that ours is an age in which peace, the threat of
war and war itself are contiguous. This of course has always been the
case. Yet for a number of historical reasons our generations — from
René Wellek's to that of our youngest students — have experienced and
continue to experience this ordinary state of affairs as something special.
It is in this double awareness, and also in order to throw some light on it,
that this paper was written; this awareness is relevant both to our story,
Josefine, die Sängerin oder das Volk der Mäuse, and to the city and country
in which Franz Kafka, René Wellek, and incidentally myself, were born.
Reading and re-reading this story with its setting and ours equally in
mind, I became aware that certain remarks which Kafka made in his
diary (25 December 1911; T 151–53) about the function of literature in
the life of a small nation, though they were occasioned by his experience
of the Yiddish actors who were then visiting Prague, apply in all their
details much more directly to the Czech literature he knew than to the
Yiddish literature he was only just becoming acquainted with; and these
remarks contain the first and almost the only intimations he has left us of
the story he wrote twelve years later. The nation into whose midst the
narrator takes us is a beleaguered nation; obviously this warlike setting
and its consequences are of far-reaching importance for an understanding of the story; but I was also struck by the obverse, noting how
important the story is for an understanding of a people — any people —
in such a predicament. At the same time it became clear to me that there
was an important difference. The nation about whom this story is told is
not only beleaguered and threatened, but it is aware, constantly and
almost unremittingly aware, of the threats to its existence and survival,
and ready to meet these threats, whereas the nation from which René
Wellek and I come was not; and this, more than anything else (I believe,
and I think he may agree) was the major cause of its undoing. Yet to say
all this is to say no more than that this is a story about a special yet very

ordinary human situation; that it tells us something special about the relationship between 'das Übliche' and 'das Außerordentliche'. The purpose of this paper is to show what this may be.

A literary work of art is what it is for many reasons and by virtue of many causes, and among these reasons is a given public's readiness to treat it as such to the extent, at all events, of wanting to confront and consider it in a special way.

And this — the designation of the nature and status of a literary work of art, in certain special conditions (such as 'there's a war on'), or rather in *any* conditions to the extent that any conditions *are* special — is one of the themes the story before us brings to our attention. It is about more than that, of course, because every consideration of an aesthetic or literary matter, fictional or otherwise, that is worth attending to is always more than itself; but the story is also about the nature and status of a work of art.

Written down after 17 March 1924[1] in Prague, Kafka's last story was conceived during the previous eighteen months, the only really happy months of his later life. He had finally made his escape from Prague and was living in Berlin with Dora Dymant, a Polish Jewish girl who worked as a nurse in a Jewish children's home; he was learning Hebrew; for reasons I do not understand (and no biographer of his has ever explained) he was also very poor and occasionally hungry, miserably cold; on and off he was unwell, too, yet he was happy and free. He published the story first in *Die Prager Presse* on Easter Sunday 1924.[2] By the time he was correcting the proofs for publication in bookform, he was in a hospital outside Vienna, in the last stages of tuberculosis of the larynx, unable to speak. It is said that he cried a little when he read the proofs. He died there in June 1924.

This is his most serene — indeed his only serene — story, and it is also his subtlest; it does not fit the 'dark side of the moon' interpretations of his work — perhaps this is the reason why so many critics have ignored it.[3] It is concerned with the relationship between Josephine and her public, the mouse nation; her public and her people are one and the same thing. It may be that this is the sort of relationship Kafka himself desired; certainly it is the opposite of what he achieved in his lifetime.

The story begins as inconspicuously as may be, with a mere naming; 'Unserere Sängerin heißt Josefine' ('Our singer is called Josephine'). In what follows there are very few events, or very little action, or whatever you choose to call that of which there is relatively little in German narrative prose. Instead, we are taken by the narrator, who is a member of Josephine's nation–public, on a conducted tour of the various hills and dales of the landscape of this relationship. Around the twentieth paragraph this panoramic survey comes to rest on one aspect of the relationship, Josephine's request for special status and recognition — a request that turns into a little bureaucratic scuffle; and then — the story has thirty-four paragraphs — her partial or total disappearance concludes the story. Her disappearence is neither caused by nor yet independent of the perpetual defeat she has suffered in her fight for special status and recognition. It is, as you can see, a mere nothing of a story.

Josephine is a singer, *the* singer of her nation–public. She undoubtedly regards and projects herself as a prima donna. About the quality of her singing there are many doubts — the narrator himself, in conveying the doubts of her public, adds some of his own. The narrative and the strategy of its arguments serve the purpose of illuminating every corner of that landscape through which we are conducted, the landscape of a relationship. In the course of these reflective arguments, quality (the quality of her singing) turns into a question of status, of ontology, into the question: Is it song, is it music at all that Josephine presents in front of, and thus to, her nation–public? But while there is this objective doubt about the quality and status — the *kind* — of her performance, no word of subjective doubt is uttered. Josephine has, as we shall see, a hard time of it, her life is a burden to her (or so at least she says), but self-doubt is not part of the trial she so bravely undergoes. The story asserts a value. And (to anticipate) a part of that value will be found in Josephine's subjective self-assurance and its consequences, in her adamant will.

There are three narrative areas to consider: (i) the nature and status of her singing, (ii) the character of the nation-public, including the character of the narrator-reporter, and (iii) the character of Josephine. In each case something over and above the named thing is implied, not on the whole by way of allegory or symbol, as by way of metonymy (so much for some recent generalizations in the wake of Roman Jakobson about modernist prose).[4] The three areas I have singled out — song, public, performer; or: music, nation, creative individual; or again: expression, reception, leader; or again: art, life, mediator — these three areas are closely inter-connected, it is difficult to discuss them separately; there is a tightness in this story's interlocking structure, of the kind we associate not so much with narrative prose as with poetry.

(i)   Early on, § 4, we are given the narrator's description of what Josephine's performance is like. He uses a metaphor which, like most metaphors in this story, strikes a note of humility, modesty and good humour. The operative word is 'Pfeifen', which has often been mistranslated as 'squeaking'; the paragraph begins: 'Es ist aber eben doch nicht nur Pfeifen, was sie produziert' — 'you see, what she produces is not just whistling' ('Pfeifen' is unambiguously the word, both here and in a letter in which Kafka complains of being kept awake by 'the whistling of mice').[5]

Kafka's humour here is unlike that of any of his Central European contemporaries. It is neither satirical (as in Karl Kraus) nor ribald and self-defensive (as in Jaroslav Hašek); it is not socially or historically determined humour of the kind that accompanies the nostalgic view of an extinct society (as in Hofmannsthal or Joseph Roth), or the nostalgic view of speech patterns deviating from accepted linguistic norms (as in Josef Weinheber). It is in a sense purer than any of these. The humour — 'ein leises Lachen' — is grounded in the special yet ordinary situation which the story explores, and it has an undertone of melancholy — the melancholy we feel in the presence of weakness and transience; or again, it is the humour that issues from the dialectical relationship between what things are and what we take them to be, *and* how what things are in the world is partly determined by what we take them to be. Here then is the metaphor that is to characterize Josephine's art. We note the way it is explored and applied, and the humour generated by its ordinariness *and* its movement away from 'das Übliche':

Es ist aber eben doch nicht nur Pfeifen, was sie produziert. Stellt man sich recht weit von ihr hin und horcht, oder noch besser, läßt man sich in dieser Hinsicht prüfen, singt also Josefine etwa unter andern Stimmen und setzt man sich die Aufgabe, ihre Stimme zu erkennen, dann wird man unweigerlich nichts anderes heraushören als ein gewöhnliches, höchstens durch Zartheit oder Schwäche ein wenig auffallendes Pfeifen. Aber steht man vor ihr, ist es doch nicht nur ein Pfeifen; es ist zum Verständnis ihrer Kunst notwendig, sie nicht nur zu hören, sondern auch zu sehn. Selbst wenn es nur unser tagtägliches Pfeifen wäre, so besteht hier doch schon zunächst die Sonderbarkeit, daß jemand sich feierlich hinstellt, um nichts anderes als das Übliche zu tun. Eine Nuß aufknacken ist wahrhaftig keine Kunst, deshalb wird es auch niemand wagen, ein Publikum zusammenzurufen und vor ihm, um es zu unterhalten, Nüsse zu knacken. Tut er es dennoch und gelingt seine Absicht, dann kann es sich eben doch nicht nur um bloßes Nüsseknacken handeln. Oder es handelt sich um Nüsseknacken, aber es stellt sich heraus, daß wir über diese Kunst hinweggesehen haben, weil wir sie glatt beherrschten und daß uns dieser neue Nußknacker erst ihr eigentliches Wesen zeigt, wobei es dann für die Wirkung sogar nützlich sein könnte, wenn er etwas weniger tüchtig im Nüsseknacken ist als die Mehrzahl von uns.

You see, what she produces is not just whistling. If you stand a long way away from her and listen, or even better, if you put yourself to the test on this point and, with Josephine singing, say, together with other voices, set yourself the task of picking out her voice, you will invariably identify no more than a commonplace whistling, which if it stands out at all does so by its delicacy and weakness. But when you are standing in front of her it is not just a whistling; to understand her art it is necessary not only to hear her but also to see her. Even if it were only our everyday whistling, there is anyway something special about a person who solemnly stands up in order to do merely what is usual. To crack a nut is certainly not an art, therefore no-one would dare to call together an audience and crack nuts in front of them by way of entertainment. But if someone nevertheless does so, and succeeds in his intention, then it cannot be a mere matter of nutcracking. Or rather, it *is* a mere matter of cracking nuts, but it turns out that we have been overlooking this art because it was well within our powers, and that it has taken this new cracker of nuts to show us the real nature of this art; and the effect might even be enhanced if he were just a little less competent at cracking nuts than the majority of us.

Other things are said about Josephine's performance. What we may call its moral and practical functions are ambiguous and self-cancelling, for while the singing gives comfort to the nation–public in moments of danger and war, it also lulls them into a false security and carelessness which results in many deaths. Again and again its relative ordinariness is emphasized. It is not, or only in very few moments, great and profound *music*; or, we might say, it is not an art with many metaphysical or religious connotations, as the nation's art of old — their ancient songs — is said to have been in the distant, immemorial past. And finally, the source of the greatest effect on the more experienced among its listeners is not the music itself; it is the silence to which it gives rise, the moments when it *isn't*:

Ist es ihr Gesang, der uns entzückt oder nicht vielmehr die feierliche Stille, von der das schwache Stimmchen umgeben ist?

Is it her song that charms us, or is it not rather the solemn silence that envelops that feeble little voice?

And now, invited to complete the metonymy, we realize with something of a shock that that is how things are always: silence envelops music, music is music-and-silence.

Why is so much of what is said about this music so negative, designating all the things it isn't? But then, we may reflect, is this negativity not an attribute of metaphysical and religious language generally, so much of which is couched in negations like *in*finite, *ab*solute, *im*mortal, *un*conditioned, or even *trans*cendent, *meta*physical?

Moreover, these negatives call out for interpretation: the nutcracking metaphor (for instance) in its maddening humility seems directly to point to such a humble story, a story about next to nothing such as this one, and by extension (for we are still within the realm of metonymy) to Kafka's art as a whole. And when, in §28, the narrator reports that Josephine is proposing to punish her public by shortening the coloratura and claims that she has in fact been doing so although he, the narrator, must confess to having failed to notice this because he hasn't the faintest idea what a coloratura is, we are again bidden to read this as an indication of the vast excess, in works of art, of effort and wrought artefact over the effect noticed and understood, let alone appreciated, by the public at large; we are reminded of the famous Flaubertian disequilibrium, the excess of cost over assigned value, reflected on at length by Nietzsche in the third of his *Unzeitgemäße Betrachtungen* (*Untimely Meditations*).

But even this is not the full extent of the metonymous meaning, for surely what all those humble and negative qualities and the emphasis on ordinariness point to is language itself. Our attention is drawn to the fact that the most extraordinary and precious — the most poetic — collocations of language are compounded of the most ordinary and humdrum words; and only within special contexts, framed in a special way and informed with the aesthetic intention of 'let this be a performance, a special public display' — only within such a total context do these very ordinary words cease to be ordinary and become something special. The story itself provides an illustration. Its language is lack-lustre, relaxed, colloquial and full of informal qualifications — it is a composition in the most 'ordinary' language we can think of (and perhaps the contradiction submerged in the phrase '*most* ordinary' helps us to make the point at issue). But then, all words, *when you come to think of it*, are capable of turning into something special. They follow what I shall call the 'Transformation Principle'.

And the silence? It accompanies us from the first paragraph of the story, where we read that 'the silence of peace is our favourite music'; and this 'solemn silence' which forms a framework around Josephine's weak little voice is the real reason why the older and more experienced members of her public find comfort in her performance, for in that silence they can dream their dreams of safety and peace. Again we recall that this extraordinary state of affairs is really nothing of the kind, that it arises from an emphasis on something perfectly ordinary. Not only music but words too would lose their distinctness and thus their meanings were it not for the silence between them, so that the silence or absence of words becomes as it were the metaphysics of words; becomes that which is both beyond them and at the same time one of the things that gives them their meaning. And right at the end of the story, when Josephine 'disappears entirely', it is as if she were completing that silence with her own existence, completing that metaphysical meaning which the ordinary silence between ordinary words had merely intimated in and through her performance. Perhaps a life, too, like a word or a note of music, is given part of its significance by the silence that follows it. A precarious balance is struck between the life-enhancing and death-bearing qualities of Josephine's performance, and when it is said that the silences are what she, now apparently entirely gone, will be remembered by, this immortality of 'a mere memory' — the memory of mere nothings, 'dieses Nichts an Stimme, dieses Nichts an Leistung' — does not resolve the balance between life and death as the message of her art, but leaves it finally open.

Thinking about the quality and kind of Josephine's performance, are we to conclude that in the narrator's or perhaps even in Kafka's view the nature of art (and of literature) is adequately represented by the nutcracker metaphor and, by inference, through the story as a whole? Or is the meaning we are to take more restricted and, like the metaphor itself, more modest? Is Kafka talking merely about his own art, at most about the art of his own time? Every fictional narrative imposes a restrictive context, yet every metaphor used to illustrate the context invites a generalization. What is given here is not a 'definition of art', and yet it *is* a general statement. What is perhaps surprising about it, in the face of all the usual solemn talk about 'the artist's role in society', is the emphasis on display and performance, which is also the source of the story's gentle humour: and this emphasis is determined by the personal and historical context, by Kafka's unsolemn, ironical understanding of his own work and of the literary tradition in which the work is precariously situated. This exclusive emphasis on display may be inappropriate in other contexts (for other writers, at other times). Yet the substance of what is being emphasized here — and neglected or ignored in most other literary treatments of the theme of art — seems irrefutable: it is the importance of what Bertolt Brecht called 'Zeigen', 'showing', in which he saw the essence of dramatic art. Similarly, what this story tells us is that there is no art without the intention of 'Let there be not talk but performance, not communication but display', *and* without this intention being acknowledged by those who, whether the performance was intended for them or not, assemble to watch it; or, more briefly: there is no art without the aesthetic intention on the one hand, and those intended on the other. But the organ of every intention is the will, and, for once in Kafka's writing, the will that is acclaimed here is not evil.

(ii)   Many things might be said about Josephine's nation–public — the narrator mentions their childishness, toughness, and resilience, their readiness to protect her *and* to be sustained by the comfort they take from her. Their lack of a musical gift and lack of history-mindedness are stressed more than once, and so is the hard life they have to lead, their absolute refusal to accede to Josephine's pleas for exemption from the ordinary chores and duties of a nation perpetually at war, or at least perpetually wary and endangered. Among the particular triumphs of the story is the finesse with which the interrelationship between the nation–public and our heroine is worked out,[6] whereby she is shown to be a creature of their need; but then again the opposite is equally true, that they are there for her protection and, in their capacity as a public, they are hardly more than an adjunct — uncomprehending and inferior at that — of her art.

As all music is music-and-silence, as all discourse is (in the worldly view of it) words separated by silence or (in another, the metaphysical view) silence disrupted by words; so, too, all solitude, including Josephine's solitude, is encompassed by society, or (not to mince words, as Kafka's narrator does not mince them) by 'die Volksgemeinschaft'. Any word (the thought should not be lost on us) may be bettered by its context. There is good reason why this is (as I believe) the only story of Kafka's in which those taboo words, 'Volksgemeinschaft' and 'Volksgenosse', occur, for this is the only story of his where community is the bearer of a value; the other aspect of that value is represented by Josephine's self-assurance and capacity for self-sacrifice.

And with this value-giving — this validation of Josephine through her close contact with her nation–public — we take leave of that long and somewhat mournful sequence of self-reflecting literary themes which punctuate German literature, from *Torquato Tasso* to *Tonio Kröger* and beyond (not to mention such frights as *Die Verwirrungen des Zöglings Törless*), where self-pity and solipsism are fashioned into an accusation against society and its philistine misunderstanding of the artist. In this as in so many other respects our story offers a marvellous liberation. Of course the people misunderstand Josephine's art: after all, they are said to be totally unmusical; and she is sustained by this, since the more they misunderstand her, the more assured in her achievement she feels and the higher her art soars. However, the point is not, or not only, that *she* needs them, but that her *art* needs them; that, whatever is the true value of her art, that value and the art itself is as nothing without its reception. Not for the psychological reason that an *artist* cannot live without his public, but for the aesthetic reason that there is no *art* without its public, that 'music' or 'art' or 'literature' are concepts which belong to, and derive the major part of their meaning from, the cultural and thus social aspect of our experience and vocabulary. This is not, let me emphasize, the egregious Marxist notion of a given public of consumers 'producing' art by their demand, but both public and creative individual are equally involved in, equally necessary for, the process. Nor is this the old tag about 'beauty' (or for that matter *art*) being 'in the eye of the beholder', but in the will of the performer, where the will is taken to be nothing without its object:[7] and the true object of the will is other people.

However deluded Josephine may be about the value and function of her art on the one hand and the perceptiveness of her listeners on the other; whatever sustainment she may derive from her delusion and from their readiness to jolly her along; however critical the narrator may be of her character and hoity-toity habits; and whatever may be the relative proportions between the two determining factors in any given case, the ontological stature of art — its compound nature as a public phe-nomenon, *a showing* — is not in doubt. This is an anti-Romantic, intensely human and (dare one say it?) democratic view, in which the ordinariness of art and its special quality are indissolubly combined.

The numerous descriptions of Josephine's and her public's mutual relationship call out to us to extend the images, to complete the metonymy and think of Josephine's nation–public as something wider, more comprehensive than . . . a nation of mice?

At this point a peculiar aspect of the text had better be mentioned. It is that the word 'Mouse' — or rather 'Mäuse' — having occurred in the title, never again occurs in the text;[8] not only that — but there is not a word of physical or indeed any other description in the story (fur, sharp teeth, short arms and necks, only Josephine's is longer) which could not be applied either to mice or to many other creatures, among them men and women. So that, once we have entered the story, we cannot forget the word in the title, yet we cannot substantiate it either. Indeed, Kafka's daring metonymous game goes so far as to describe the public as being 'mäuschenstill' (§6) — 'as quiet as a mouse' — using an adverb whose unusual literal meaning with its special bearing on the text briefly supplants its ordinary metaphorical meaning, and in the process teasingly hints at the hide-and-seek tactics of the narrative. (And the sound Josephine and the public emit is called 'pfeifen' not 'piepsen' — 'whistling' not 'squeaking' — precisely because the human connexion is to be retained throughout; though there is a point where other, funnier verbs are used.)

One recurrent aspect of Kafka's writings is, as I have said, the urgency with which, for one reason or another, they call to us for interpretation, exegesis, deciphering. Here is one such reason: we were told, in the title, that this is a story about the mouse-nation and then, for pages on end, we are left to ask, Who on earth are they really? Everything about them fits equally the notion of mice or of men. I mentioned at the outset that in the diary entry about the literature of a small and beleaguered nation Kafka seems to have had in mind the Czech literature of his time. On the other hand critics have pointed out (somewhat misleadingly) that in the whole of Kafka's 'literary' work the word 'Jew' or 'Jewish' does not occur, from which, predictably, they have inferred that everything he wrote is about Jews. (Moreover, people 'in the know' have said that

with his portrayal of Josephine, Kafka had Karl Kraus in mind;[9] seeing
that we are told, quite explicitly, that Josephine has no enemies, this
seems less than convincing.) True, many things in this story — bar one
attribute — make the 'Jewish' interpretation plausible; and indeed there
are certain poignant and almost fervent passages which seem strongly to
confirm it. I think especially of the lyrically balanced repetitions in the
long sentence about the nation's children in §17:

Wir haben keine Schulen, aber aus unserem Volke strömen in allerkürzesten
Zwischenräumen die unübersehbaren Scharen unserer Kinder, fröhlich
zischend oder piepsend, solange sie noch nicht pfeifen können, sich wälzend
oder kraft des Druckes weiterrollend, solange sie noch nicht laufen können,
täppisch durch ihre Masse alles mit sich fortreißend, solange sie noch nicht
sehen können, unsere Kinder!

We have no schools, but from the midst of our people there emerge, at the
shortest of intervals, the countless hosts of our children, merrily chirping
and squeaking, as long as they have not yet learned to whistle, rolling along
or being bowled along by the pressure behind, as long as they cannot yet
run, clumsily swarming and sweeping everything along with them, as long
as they cannot yet see — our children!

Perhaps Kafka was recalling his visits to the Jewish children's home
where his friend, Dora Dymant, was working at the time he wrote this
story. But again, with a certain well-known affirmation of Shylock's in
mind, I would insist on the metonymous status of the Jewish interpretation, and argue — on the mysterious 'Transformation Principle' — that
Jews, too, when you come to think of it, are human beings, metonyms
of the human race.

However, there is one attribute which certainly militates against such
an interpretation. We are told, not just once but on three occasions,
including the last sentence of the story, that this nation is emphatically
not history-conscious.[10] And this emphasis on a society which has
hardly any historians and a very defective historical memory seems to
foil a reading of the story as an allegory on a tribe which remembers the
destruction of its capital city and temple vividly enough to make it the
centre piece of its political consciousness and ideology 1980 odd years
after the event. Is Kafka playing a game with us, his readers, and quietly
— 'mäuschenstill' — putting us off the scent? Perhaps. Or is he
suggesting (again like Nietzsche) that a people whose past consists of
little more than a series of national disasters is ill served by its history and
is well advised to cultivate the unhistorical attitude of fruitful and
healthy oblivion? There is then good reason why we should not halt at
the partial metonymy of a Jewish interpretation but go the whole way,
from mice to men. And when we do that, the special place of this story
in Kafka's work becomes again manifest, for the central point that

emerges is this: the writer who, in the critics' view, invariably figures as the exemplar of alienation, unemphatically and almost involuntarily transports all humanity into that condition, and in doing so modifies it in such a way as to show that there too, in that state of fear and trembling, 'in [their] wretched existence amid the tumult of a hostile world', there is community and comfort, thoughtfulness and tact, wry amusement and even laughter. Patriotic sentiments make us blush with embarrassment. Perhaps only a writer like Kafka, confiding in a mode as ironical as this, can validate them for us. For here once again the special — as the object of patriotic sentiments — becomes the ordinary, the common condition of mankind.

(iii)   Is there anything to be said about Josephine that is not already contained in the descriptions of her whistling or singing or (as the narrator–critic says, §18, in some exasperation) 'whatever it is she wishes to call it'? She may have 'nothing by way of a voice, nothing by way of [artistic] achievement', we read (§15), yet when she gets going there is no doubt that a supreme artist is at work. And every aspect of what she is and what she does is considered under this double perspective of the ordinary and the special, all the way down to physical details; as when, in §30, we are told that her limping, apparently caused by an accident, completely disappears after she has concluded a particularly brilliant performance, which 'she actually leaves less tired than when she began, with a firm tread, if her mincing scuttle may be referred to in such terms'. Even the syntactic patterns of individual sentences are put at the service of this double perspective.

In her capriciousness and the scorn she has for her audience, in her conviction that they don't understand her art and if they did it wouldn't *be* art, and in countless small touches Josephine is represented as the ideal-type prima donna as well as the solemn guardian of what to her is a sacred art (but the word is not used). The one permanent source of conflict and friction, which I have mentioned already, are her unceasing and (we are explicitly told) unrealistic requests for exemption — an artist's ticket of leave — from the chores of her nation–public's daily life, including of course the defensive and warlike activities which are an inescapable part of that life. As a matter of fact she knows perfectly well how unrealistic these demands are. After all, she is and will always remain a member of that peculiar little nation, whose paramount virtue — the text here reads almost like Hobbes — must be freedom from illusion and a realistic assessment of every emergent situation. So what she really asks for is not exemption from work but recognition of status, her almost sacred status of the nation–public's singer; and her absolute demand too is adamantly and absolutely refused.

This emphasis on status derived from the conscious public display or ostension of her art is vitally important to the argument which encompasses the entire story; it subsumes and validates the metaphor of art seen as the cracking of nuts mentioned early in the story; in the performance artist and art are one. When her art is refused the recognition she demands for it, Josephine disappears 'entirely', as the text says. Her raison d'être is no more.

And right to the end, to the opening of the last paragraph, when the prospect of her departure evokes the comment, 'So possibly we shall not be missing very much', this duality of the most ordinary thing in the world being transformed into the most precious and rarest of things is maintained. The full validation of this curious *positive* metamorphosis I have called the 'Transformation Principle'. One way of explaining it is to extend the central metonymy by connecting the perpetual war the mouse-nation is fighting with the wars we know; the wars whose memory is our traumatic heritage. To do this is not to trivialize that memory. It is to take this story seriously in all its poignancy, humanity and humour.

One of the finest novels of the Great War, Frederic Manning's *Her Privates We* (1926), ends with the death in battle of its hero, Corporal Bourne. Throughout the story Bourne has been a loyal member of his battalion, yet he was never entirely at home among his fellow soldiers. He applied for a commission, which has come to nothing, he had vague literary plans which have come to nothing, he seems to be more reflective than the others, part of the whole yet also a bit isolated. When his corpse is brought into the dug-out, the Sergeant ruminates briefly about him:

He was sorry about Bourne, he thought, more sorry than he could say. He was a queer chap, [the Sergeant] said to himself, as he felt for the dug-out steps. There was a bit of a mystery about him; but then, when you come to think of it, there is a bit of a mystery about all of us.

That is all. It is both the living and the aesthetic principle according to which our story is constructed, and I see it as a profound philosophical and literary insight—a crowning insight, to be found nowhere else in Kafka's work, but validating the claim the work has to a profound humanity; a humanity not separate from or opposed to a spiritual value (a separation and opposition which are so often thematic in Kafka's work), but setting up a continuation and a coherence between 'das Übliche' and 'das Außerordentliche': between the worldly, the ordinary, the grey-in-grey, and the spiritual, the metaphysical and the religious.

Perhaps we can formulate this principle by saying that the grace which we are capable of bestowing on each other is the grace which elevates the ordinary into the special; and that this grace is not in the substance but in the 'when you come to think of it', in the luminous point of view from which the substance is seen. Whether the same principle applies to another kind of grace altogether, we cannot tell with equal assurance; we certainly cannot *imagine* a dispensation that would be radically different.

The story began as inconspicuously as possible, simply because it had to begin somehow; and it ends almost as inconspicuously, in ripples and echoes. For some reason that is never fully disclosed but which is connected with her failure to have her status recognized, her uniqueness accepted, Josephine has gone into hiding; at least, 'she has disappeared, she doesn't want to sing, she doesn't even want to be asked to sing, this time she has left us entirely' ('sie hat uns diesmal völlig verlassen'). Which is it to be: 'diesmal' or 'völlig'? Does she merely calculate on a triumphant return? She is the prima donna to the end. Has she miscalculated? Or has she spent herself, given her life for the power of her song? Did she really speak the truth when, pleading to be granted the privileges she felt were due to her art, she claimed she was the victim of exhaustion, of self-sacrifice? She has gone away. Died, perhaps? The tone of the story is gentle throughout, yet here, right at the end, Kafka is intent on giving it an added strength. One thinks of the words he himself used at the end of his life, when, afraid that his friends were leaving him alone, he called out to them to stay. 'I am not going away', one of his friends said. 'But I', he said, and we read that he said it in a strong voice, 'But I am going away!'[11]

But then the past tense switches to the future, Josephine is only about to 'go away'. Soon she will 'joyfully lose herself amid the countless hosts of our heroes' of old. And since this is a nation that has hardly any historical consciousness, her liberation or redemption will be redoubled and heightened — 'eine gesteigerte Erlösung': it will be a redemption from the burden of her own life as well as from the perpetuation of that life in the memory of her race.[10] She is no more than 'a little episode in the history of our nation', there are hardly any historians to record that episode: the consolations of artistic immortality are viewed as ironically as is her singing. Perhaps there is a point in the life of an artist where the hope of being read, or listened to, by future generations appears as no more than a last vanity to be conquered. But at that point, too, art comes to an end. Fame, Rilke observed, is no more than a wreath of misunderstandings; posterity, Proust wrote, fashions the artist in its own image. If what Josephine will be remembered by are the silences in which her song and voice were enveloped — the silences which enabled her public to dream their dreams of peace — is that not tantamount to being remembered for a mere nothing, not to be remembered at all?

Her life (she tells anyone who cares to listen) has been little more than a burden to her, yet she takes this to be a sure sign of her election; and though he is critical of most of her claims, the narrator agrees: she is one of the elect. Whatever may be the ultimate truth about the *value* of her performance, he tells us (and we may add that there is nobody in the story to assess that), the cost of it to her in strenuous effort is absolute: 'Sie greift nach dem höchsten Kranz, nicht, weil er im Augenblick gerade ein wenig tiefer hängt, sondern weil es der höchste Kranz ist; wäre es in ihrer Macht, sie würde ihn noch höher hängen' (§26; 'She reaches for the highest garland, not because at that moment it happens to hang a little lower, but because it is the highest; were it in her power to do so, she would hang the garland higher still'). And this final confirmation of the relative value inherent in Josephine's pursuit of an unknown, silent absolute is a move we are familiar with from almost all of Kafka's writings. At this point, where the subjective, relative value of strenuousness is gently yet unambiguously invoked and elevated into something like an absolute, the story I have presented as an exception joins his other stories and meditations, and becomes as one with them. Here too the usual and the extraordinary are one.

NOTES

[1] For biographical details see, e.g. Chris Bezzel, *Kafka-Chronik* (Munich, Vienna, 1975), pp. 192–94. Kafka speaks with distaste of the prospect of being a hard-currency traveller in a Germany suffering from hyper-inflation (see his letter to Max Brod from Planá, 12 July 1922); in mid-January 1924, to Max Brod, he reports that he will have to quit his lodgings because he cannot pay the rent, although at that time the Czech Crown was a hard currency and the most modest remittance from Prague would have provided abundant succour. By January 1924 Kafka was mortally ill.

[2] *Die Prager Presse*, Sonntagsbeilage, 20 April 1924, pp. iv–vii; publication details in Joachim Unseld, *Franz Kafka: ein Schriftstellerleben* (Munich, Vienna, 1982), passim. The first book edition in *Ein Hungerkünstler: vier Geschichten* (Berlin, *Die Schmiede*, [15 August] 1924), which includes *Erstes Leid*, *Eine kleine Frau*, *Ein Hungerkünstler* and *Josefine . . .* For my quotations I have used the newspaper publication, which is the better text; I am grateful to Gerhard Neumann for putting a copy of it at my disposal.

[3] Some exceptions: Heinz Politzer, *Franz Kafka: Parable and Paradox* (Ithaca, N.Y., 1962), pp. 308–12, similarly in *Franz Kafka der Künstler* (Gütersloh, 1965), pp. 437–51; C. R. Wodding, 'Josephine the Singer', in *Franz Kafka Today* (Madison, 1958), pp. 72 ff.; Wilhelm Emrich, *Franz Kafka* (Bonn, 1970), pp. 167–72; see also below, notes 8 and 12.

[4] I mean the notion expressed by a number of recent critics that metaphor rather than metonymy is the characteristic trope of modern prose; see David Lodge, 'The Language of Modernist Fiction: Metaphor and Metonymy', in *Modernism 1890–1930*, ed. Malcolm Bradbury and James McFarlane (Harmondsworth, 1976), pp. 481–96.

[5] See Kafka's letter to Felix Weltsch, Zürau, mid-November 1917: '. . . eine Mäusenacht, ein schreckliches Erlebnis . . . Was für ein schreckliches stummes lärmendes Volk das ist . . . Auf die Kohlenkiste hinauf, von der Kohlenkiste

hinunter, die Diagonale des Zimmers abgelaufen, Kreise gezogen, am Holz genagt, im Ruhen leise gepfiffen und immer das Gefühl der Stille'.

6 On one of the 'conversation papers' which Kafka used in order to communicate with his friends when speaking became too painful, he writes to Max Brod, 11 or 12 May 1924: 'Die Geschichte bekommt einen neuen Titel / Josefine die Sängerin / oder / Das Volk der Mäuse / Solche oder-Titel sind zwar nicht sehr hübsch, aber hier hat es vielleicht besonderen Sinn, es hat etwas von einer Waage' (quoted from Unseld, see note 2 above). See also Max Brod, *Franz Kafka, eine Biographie* (New York, 1937), p. 348: 'Einordnung des Einzelnen in das Schicksal eines Volkes'.

7 See Immanuel Kant, *Grundlegung zur Metaphysik der Sitten*, §2, in *Gesammelte Schriften* (Berlin, 1903), IV, 417.

8 See Benno von Wiese, 'Franz Kafka: ein Hungerkünstler', in *Die deutsche Novelle von Goethe bis Kafka* (Düsseldorf, 1956), II, 333.

9 The origin of this attribution may be Kafka's hilarious letter about Karl Kraus to Max Brod, Matljary, June 1921. For the 'Jewish' interpretation see Brod's biography (note 6 above), pp. 234–36.

10 In his diary entry of 25 December 1911 (T 151–53) Kafka writes: 'Dieses Tagebuchführen einer Nation [i.e. the current literary production of a small nation], das ist etwas ganz anderes als Geschichtsschreibung'.

11 Kafka to Robert Klopstock: 'Gehen Sie nicht fort'. Klopstock: 'Ich gehe ja nicht fort.' Kafka: 'Aber ich gehe fort.' Quoted from Bezzel (see note 1 above), p. 198.

12 Will she really be 'personally forgotten but immortal in her contribution to the survival of her folk', as Roy Pascal wrote in the last, unfinished chapter of his last book (*Kafka's Narrators*, A Study of his Stories and Sketches (Cambridge, 1982), p. 231)? Even that, I think, goes beyond the limits of meaning imposed on us by the text: she will be part of our history, certainly, *but* we have no historians, 'da wir keine Geschichte treiben' . . .

INDEX

SOME RECENT AND FORTHC   G
VOLUMES IN THE SER!
PUBLICATIONS OF THE INSTITUTE OF GERMANIC STUDIES

30   *Goethe Revisited; essays for the 150th anniversary of his death,* ed. by
     E. M. Wilkinson (in collaboration with John Calder (Publishers) Ltd,
     London)
     ISBN 0 85457 110 8   192 pp.   1984   £5.95

31   *Minnesang in Österreich,* hrsg. von Adrian Stevens und Fred Wagner
     (in collaboration with Verlag Karl M. Halosar, Vienna)
     ISBN 0 85457 111 6   iv, 244 pp.   1984   £12.95

32   *London German Studies II,* ed. by J. P. Stern
     ISBN 0 85457 112 4   viii, 198 pp.   1983   £7.90

Forthcoming

Adalbert Stifter heute: Londoner Symposium 1983 hrsg. von J. Lachinger,
A. Stillmark und M. W. Swales (in collaboration with the
Adalbert-Stifter–Institut, Linz)
ISBN 0 85457 119 1

Geschichtsbewußtsein im Mittelalter — Heiligkreuztaler Colloquium 1983,
hrsg. von Christoph Gerhardt, Nigel Palmer und Burghart
Wachinger (in collaboration with Max Niemeyer Verlag, Tübingen)
ISBN 0 85457 123 X

Modern Swiss Literature. Unity and diversity, ed. by John L. Flood (in
collaboration with Oswald Wolff (Publishers) Ltd)
ISBN 0 85457 125 6

BITHELL SERIES OF DISSERTATIONS

BSD 6   *The banal object: theme and thematics in Proust, Rilke, Hofmannsthal,
        and Sartre,* by Naomi Segal
        ISBN 0 85457 099 3   x, 147 pp.   1981   £9.00

BSD 7   *Spinoza in Germany from 1670 to the Age of Goethe,* by David Bell
        ISBN 0 85457 117 5   xiv, 192 pp.   1984   £9.00

BSD 8   *History and poetry in Novalis and in the tradition of the German Enlighten-
        ment,* by Nicholas Saul
        ISBN 0 85457 121 3   x, 206 pp.   1984   £9.00

BSD 9   *Contemporary German Autobiography. Literary Approaches to the Problem
        of Identity,* by Barbara Saunders
        ISBN 0 85457 127 2   *at press*

Prices, which are for UK only, include postage. They are liable to adjustment without notice.
For overseas orders, add 20% to the price quoted.

All publications are obtainable direct from the Institute of Germanic Studies, 29 Russell
Square, London WC1B 5DP.

Customers in North America may place their orders through Humanities Press Inc, Atlantic
Highlands, NJ 07716.